Teaching the Pronunciation of a Lingua Franca

Also published in
Oxford Handbooks for Language Teachers

Teaching the Pronunciation of English as a Lingua Franca

ROBIN WALKER

OXFORD
UNIVERSITY PRESS

OXFORD
UNIVERSITY PRESS

Great Clarendon Street, Oxford OX2 6DP

Oxford University Press is a department of the University of Oxford.
It furthers the University's objective of excellence in research, scholarship,
and education by publishing worldwide in

Oxford New York

Auckland Cape Town Dar es Salaam Hong Kong Karachi
Kuala Lumpur Madrid Melbourne Mexico City Nairobi
New Delhi Shanghai Taipei Toronto

With offices in

Argentina Austria Brazil Chile Czech Republic France Greece
Guatemala Hungary Italy Japan Poland Portugal Singapore
South Korea Switzerland Thailand Turkey Ukraine Vietnam

OXFORD and OXFORD ENGLISH are registered trade mark of
Oxford University Press in the UK and in certain other countries

BOOK ISBN: 978 0 19 442198 0
CD ISBN: 978 0 19 442199 7
PACK ISBN: 978 0 19 442200 0

Printed in China

This book is printed on paper from well-managed and certified sources.

CONTENTS

ACKNOWLEDGEMENTS

First and foremost, I want to thank the three people who were fundamental in making this book happen: Barbara Seidlhofer, Henry Widdowson, and Jennifer Jenkins. My thanks also to Jennifer Jenkins for providing such invaluable feedback on my first draft, and to Julia Sallabank, Grzegorz Śpiewak, David Deterding, and Ronnie Lendrum for their constructive criticism of individual chapters. Thank you also, to Julia Bell at OUP for her vital support and guidance in the later stages of writing, and to Ann Hunter for her excellent editing.

My sincere thanks to the contributors to Chapter 5 for their willingness to participate. I am especially indebted to David Deterding for his generosity with his expertise and patience. I am equally indebted to the real people behind the anonymous ELF voices on the CD. Without their contagious enthusiasm, my job would have been a great deal less enjoyable. The one speaker I can name is Petra Kuchtová, who very kindly lent her Czech ELF voice to the title and track numbers on the CD.

Last, but far from least, I would like to thank Isabel, who instantly saw the importance of this book, who supported me unstintingly during the writing of it, and who helped me to see that an expanding circle offers an infinite horizon.

Robin Walker

The author and publisher are grateful to those who have given permission to reproduce the following extracts and adaptations of copyright material:

David Crystal and Cambridge University Press for permission to reproduce one figure from *English as a Global Language* (2nd edn.) by David Crystal, 2003, Cambridge University Press.

Mark Hancock and Cambridge University Press for permission to reproduce one figure from *Pronunciation Games*, by Mark Hancock, 1995, Cambridge University Press.

Mark Hancock and IATEFL for permission to reproduce an exercise from *Speak Out!*: 36.

Jennifer Jenkins and TESOL-SPAIN for permission to reproduce minimal-pair exercises from TESOL-SPAIN Newsletter 27, Spring 2003.

Oxford University Press for permission to reproduce adaptations of Table 1 from 'A Sociolinguistically Based, Empirically Researched Pronunciation Syllabus for English as an International Language, *Applied Linguistics* 23/1: 83–103 (Jennifer Jenkins: 2002); of Figure 7.2 from *The Phonology of English as a Lingua Franca* (Jennifer Jenkins: 2000); and for permission to reproduce an exercise from *Tourism 1: Provision* (Walker and Harding 2006).

LIST OF ACRONYMS

EFL   English as a Foreign Language

ELF   English as a Lingua Franca

ELT   English Language Teaching

ENL   English as a Native Language

ESL   English as a Second Language

GA   General American

L1   First language

L2   Second language

LFC   Lingua Franca Core

NS   Native speaker

NNS   Non-native speaker

RP   Received Pronunciation

INTRODUCTION

How this book came into being

At the 1995 IATEFL Conference in York, I went to a talk on priorities for pronunciation. As her starting point, the speaker took something called 'English as an International Language'. It was the only talk in the whole conference on this surprising subject, and though the tiny room was full, there were no more than 30 people there. In April 2009 I went to a conference in Southampton. The organizer was the speaker from York, and the whole event was about English as an International Language, or English as a Lingua Franca, as it is known today. The conference occupied a complete faculty, and there were hundreds of participants. In only fourteen years, ELF had become a fully-fledged area of research in Applied Linguistics.

Research in Applied Linguistics, as with most research, studies what is happening in the 'real world'. Sometimes, however, research can seem a little distant to those of us who live and work in that world. It is true that the exponential rise in the study of ELF can only be matched by its equally rapid growth among English language users. But as teachers and teacher educators, rather than researchers, we can be forgiven for asking 'What has this to do with us?' As the Hungarian speaker puts it so succinctly on Track 18 of the CD that comes with this book, 'that is research, but what are the objectives?'

I have been asked this question many times over the last ten years with respect to ELF research and to the teaching of pronunciation, and the main aim of this book is to try to provide an answer. To do this, Chapter 1 looks at the roles English plays in the world today, and at the way that its latest role, that of lingua franca, requires us to re-think our goals for teaching English pronunciation. In Chapter 2 I look briefly at priorities in pronunciation teaching over the past 40 years. I then take a detailed look at the Lingua Franca Core, a set of pronunciation features that research has found to be central to intelligibility in ELF.

New roles, new goals. New ideas, new techniques. Change in a constantly changing world. This is something that some of us no longer relish. I remember my feelings vividly after the talk in 1995. I was rather disconcerted. And

I was discouraged. I had just spent considerable time working out priorities for my students in the school of tourism where I worked. But if the speaker was right, a number of these were irrelevant to their future needs.

Over the past ten years 'many practising teachers have voiced their doubts to me about an ELF approach to pronunciation. In the talks and seminars that I have given on this topic, their enthusiasm has normally been tempered by well judged concerns. Chapter 3 addresses these concerns, and then explores the important benefits that can be gained by adopting an ELF approach to pronunciation.

Research – hypothesize, observe, analyse, conclude. The cycle is almost self-perpetuating. From the conclusions spring fresh hypotheses. These require fresh data, and so round we go again. But unless the object of study changes, the data collected will be the same. It is not enough, then, to observe and to describe ELF pronunciation. From the conclusions drawn, we need actions that will generate change. In other words, if ELF pronunciation is to become more than a body for academic dissection, if it is ever to help the users of English out there in the real world, we as teachers need to implement an ELF approach in our classrooms. But how?

The practicalities of an ELF approach are the subject-matter of the last three chapters of this handbook. Chapter 4 offers what its title suggests – 'Techniques and materials for teaching ELF pronunciation'. Some of them are old, but are re-appraised in the light of new goals. Others are new and specific to ELF. Next, Chapter 5 looks at how we can make use of what all learners bring into the classroom wherever they are in the world – their mother tongue. Finally, Chapter 6 discusses two aspects of teaching pronunciation that are all too often forgotten – planning and assessment.

Some time ago, Professor Barbara Seidlhofer of the University of Vienna, called for teacher education that would enable teachers:

> to judge the implications of the ELF phenomenon for their own teaching contexts and to adapt their teaching to the particular requirements of their learners. Such teacher education would foster an understanding of the processes of language variation and change, the relationship between language and identity, the importance of social–psychological factors in intercultural communication and the suspect nature of any supposedly universal solutions to pedagogic problems.

(Seidlhofer, B. 2004: 'Research perspectives on teaching English as a lingua franca'. *Annual Review of Applied Linguistics* 24: 209–239)

Teaching the Pronunciation of English as a Lingua Franca attempts to provide the pronunciation side to this education.

Why an audio CD?

No book describing pronunciation would be considered complete today without an audio CD. So far, however, the CDs accompanying pronunciation courses have used native speakers with standard accents, predominantly Received Pronunciation or General American. As I explain in Chapter 4, with certain precautions, there is nothing wrong with teachers continuing to use these standard accents in class until commercial courses are available that employ ELF accents.

However, regardless of the model, teachers following an ELF approach to pronunciation will need to expose their learners to as wide a range of non-native speaker accents as possible, and the first purpose of the audio CD is to provide samples of some of the more common accents. In total, there are 20 different accents on the CD, representing 15 different L1 backgrounds. All of the speakers are from Expanding Circle countries (see Chapter 1), with the exception of Speakers A and T, who are from Malaysia and Brunei respectively. English is Speaker A's first language. For all the other speakers, it is their second or third. Only two of the speakers (Speaker I and Speaker L) had any real knowledge of ELF prior to the recording sessions. One or two were able to make educated guesses. Most knew nothing at all.

Most of the recording work for the CD was done in a studio in the city of Oviedo, in the north of Spain. The majority of the speakers either lived in the area or were on an extended visit in university undergraduate or postgraduate programmes. Their ages ranged from 21–55, but most of them were aged between 21–30 at the time of the recordings.

Using the audio CD

The first 20 recordings are unscripted conversations about a range of topics that fall roughly into one of three topic areas:

1 English, ELF, and language learning (Tracks 1–8)
2 Cultures – differences and misconceptions (Tracks 9–15)
3 Work and studies (Tracks 16–20).

I refer to these recordings regularly throughout the early chapters of this book, either to illustrate some specific aspect of ELF pronunciation, or to illustrate some of the arguments for and against an ELF approach. You can do the same in class with your students. However, before asking them to study a specific feature of ELF pronunciation, it is essential that they be given time to become familiar with the content of what is said in a recording. First and foremost, Tracks 1–20 are examples of people communicating with each other.

The last 10 recordings are speakers from each of the languages covered in Chapter 5 'reading' a set text. To make the recording feel more natural, the speakers were asked to imagine that they were leaving a voice message for a friend called Zoe. The purpose of these tracks is to allow you and your students to compare the way that speakers from different L1s deal with different aspects of the pronunciation of ELF.

The awareness of variation that this produces should help them to accommodate more easily to different accents in unscripted texts, recorded or live. In addition, if your learners have problems with a particular sound, or with certain consonant clusters, you can ask them to listen to speakers from different L1s dealing with the same problem feature(s). By listening to others, learners may come across a speaker whose way of dealing with the problem feature they can imitate easily, and therefore solve their problem.

Whether you use the CD to practise listening, or to identify and practise specific features of different ELF accents, I strongly recommend that prior to listening, you give your students some background information about the speakers. Point out, for example, that although they vary in levels of proficiency, all of the speakers on the CD are regular, successful users of ELF. By offering further information from the speaker profiles below, your students may go on to discover that they share other things in common with the speakers, such as their experience in learning English, the languages they speak, any experience of living in an English-speaking country, or the use(s) they make of their English. This identification with the speakers often increases their validity as models in the eyes of your learners.

The speakers

Speaker A (Tracks 1, 4, and 15)

Born in Malaysia, Speaker A acquired English naturally as a child. It is her first language and Malay her second. She also speaks basic Mandarin, Hokkien, Hungarian, and Spanish. Speaker A has lived in the USA and the UK. She knows almost nothing about ELF.

Speaker B (Tracks 1, 4, 15, and 23)

Speaker B was born in Germany. English is her second language. She learned it initially at school and has spoken it for over 10 years. She also speaks Spanish, basic Arabic, and Polish. She lived in the USA for one year, and now uses English for academic study, communication with friends of all nationalities (including German), on the Internet, and for watching English-language films. She knows nothing about ELF.

Speaker C (Tracks 2, 9, 13, and 18)

Speaker C was born in Hungary. She learned English at school and has spoken it for over 10 years. It is her second language, and she also speaks Spanish. Speaker C has never lived in an English-speaking country. She uses English for her work in Hungary, and was writing her PhD in English at the time of the recording. She also reads and watches films in English. She knows almost nothing about ELF.

Speaker D (Tracks 2 and 13)

Speaker D was born in Poland. He learned English both naturally and through study, and has spoken it for over 20 years. It is his second language. He also speaks French, Spanish, and German. He has never lived in an English-speaking country. He uses English to communicate with family and relations in the UK and Israel, and teaches English in a private language school. He reads and watches films in English, and knows very little about ELF.

Speaker E (Tracks 3, 16, and 29)

Speaker E was born in Russia. He learned English at school and has spoken it for 9 years. It is his third language, with Spanish as his second. He has never lived in an English-speaking country, but he did spend one year in Holland. He uses English for international communication, and knows nothing about ELF.

Speaker F (Tracks 3, 16, and 30)

Speaker F was born in Argentina, where she learned English at school. It is her second language, and she has spoken it for over 20 years, but has never lived in an English-speaking country. She has a degree in English and runs a private language school. She knows nothing about ELF.

Speaker G (Tracks 5, 14, and 22)

Speaker G was born in China. He learned English through study and has spoken it for 12 years. It is his third language, with Spanish as his second. He also speaks Korean. He has never lived in an English-speaking country, and uses English for work, for watching films in English, and for getting to know other cultures. He knows nothing about ELF.

(This speaker expressed concern before the recording session that he had forgotten a lot of English because he was living and working in Spain.)

Speaker H (Track 5)

Speaker H was born in Germany. English is her second language. She learned English through study and has spoken it for over 13 years. She also speaks French and Spanish. She lived in Australia for one year, and is studying for a degree in English. She uses it for communication with friends all over the world, and knows very little about ELF.

(Despite having a native-speaker accent, this speaker expressed a strong desire not to be named in association with the recordings because of her accent, which she felt was not good enough.)

Speaker I (Tracks 6 and 21)

Speaker I was born in the United Arab Emirates. English is her second language. She learned it through study and has spoken it for over 20 years. She uses English for academic purposes. At the time of the recording she was living in the UK, where she was researching the impact of an ELF approach to teaching pronunciation in secondary schools in the UAE.

Speaker J (Track 6)

Speaker J was born in Taiwan, with Taiwanese Mandarin her first language. She also speaks other Taiwanese dialects. English is her second language. She learned it through study and has spoken it for over 13 years. She was doing a Master's degree in the UK at the time of the recording, and uses English for international communication, as well as for academic purposes. She knows almost nothing about ELF.

Speaker K (Tracks 7, 20, and 25)

Speaker K was born in Japan but has lived in Spain for over 30 years. Spanish is her second language. She has been studying English for 12 years and has never lived in an English-speaking country. She also speaks French and Italian. Speaker K lectures in Art History and uses English for academic purposes, communicating principally with British, Dutch, and American art experts. She knows almost nothing about ELF.

Speaker L (Track 8)

Speaker L was born in Morocco but has lived in Spain for many years. He lived in the UK for some years and now teaches English at a Spanish university. His mother tongue is Arabic, but he is a completely fluent speaker of both English and Spanish. He knows about ELF, and has written and spoken about the non-native speaker of English.

Speaker M (Tracks 9, 13, and 18)

Speaker M was born in Romania. English is her second language, but she also speaks Spanish. She has never lived in an English-speaking country. She has been studying English for 17 years, and uses it for academic purposes, and to communicate with colleagues on her European Master's programme. She knows almost nothing about ELF.

Speaker N (Tracks 10, 19, and 28)

Speaker N was born in Brazil. English is her second language, but she also speaks Spanish. She has never lived in an English-speaking country. She has been studying English for 10 years, and uses it for academic purposes, and to read scientific articles as a hobby. She knows almost nothing about ELF.

Speaker O (Tracks 10 and 11)

Speaker O was born in Portugal. English is her second language, but she also speaks Spanish, French, and basic German. She has been studying English for 11 years, and lived in the UK for one year. She uses English for communication with friends, for reading, and for watching films. She knows a little about ELF.

Speaker P (Tracks 11 and 19)

Speaker P was born in Turkey. English is her second language, but she also speaks Spanish. She has been learning English for 12 years through study and naturally, but has never lived in an English-speaking country. She uses English for academic purposes, and for communication with friends. She knows nothing about ELF.

Speaker Q (Tracks 12, 17, and 24)

Speaker Q was born in Greece. He learned English through study and has spoken it for 8 years. He also speaks German and Spanish. He has never lived in an English-speaking country, and uses English for publishing scientific work, for watching films in English, and for communication with European friends. He knows nothing about ELF.

Speaker R (Track 14)

Speaker R was born in Spain. English and French are her second languages, but she also speaks German. She has been learning English for over 20 years through study and short stays in the UK. She lived in Holland for one year. She uses English mainly for academic purposes and travel, but will lecture in English in the future. She knows very little about ELF.

Speaker S (Tracks 18 and 27)

Speaker S was born in Poland. English is her second language, but she also speaks basic Spanish and German. She has been learning English for 16 years through study, but has never lived in an English-speaking country. She uses English for academic purposes, for reading, and for communication with friends. She knows almost nothing about ELF.

Speaker T (Track 26)

Speaker T was born in Brunei. His first language is Malay, and English is his second. He has been learning English through study since he was in primary school, and lived in the UK for one year as a child. He uses English every day at work, and knows nothing about ELF.

1 ENGLISH: CHANGING ROLES, CHANGING GOALS

Introduction

When the first expeditions set out from the British Isles to settle America in 1600, approximately six million people spoke English. Two hundred years later, not long after the first expedition had sailed from Britain to Australia, that number had risen to 20–40 million. At the beginning of the 20th century, the number of speakers of English was 116–123 million, and now, as we advance into the 21st century, estimates range from 1,000–1,500 million speakers.

Although the reasons for the phenomenal growth in the use of English are well detailed elsewhere (Crystal 2003; Svartvik and Leech 2006), in this chapter I will briefly review the history of the spread of English, before going on to look at what happens to languages when they are in use. This will lead to a consideration of what pronunciation goals might be appropriate for learners of English in different contexts around the world today.

English today

The growth of English

When the early settlers left the British Isles in the 17th and 18th centuries looking for new lives in America and Australia, they left a country where English was the mother tongue, and founded countries where, over three hundred years later, English continues to be the mother tongue of the majority of the inhabitants. The process was repeated elsewhere around the globe, and today it is quite common in ELT and Applied Linguistics to see the UK, Ireland, the USA, and Australia grouped together with Canada, New Zealand, the Caribbean, and South Africa in what is now referred to as the Inner Circle.

The term was introduced by the linguist Braj Kachru (1985), in his model of the sociolinguistic profile of English (see Figure 1.1). The Inner Circle brings together countries where the inhabitants learn English as their first language (L1), or mother tongue. In all of these countries it is an official language, and in some cases it is the only official language. Of course, in the majority of Inner Circle countries, it is not the only language spoken. A significant proportion of US citizens speak Spanish, for example, and both Welsh and Gaelic can be heard if you travel to certain parts of the British Isles. A more extreme case is South Africa, where English is calculated to be the first language of less than ten per cent of the population (Crystal 2003).

Nevertheless, the greatest concentrations of those who have English as their first language can be found in the Inner Circle countries. These people are frequently referred to as its native speakers, although exactly what we mean by the term is an area of much discussion. However, a conservative estimate made by Professor David Crystal (2003: 67) suggests that there are currently some 400 million people for whom English acts as a native language (**ENL**). In other words, it is the language they learned in their infancy, and is the main language for communication between the inhabitants of the country they live in. In addition, it is the language used for communication with the inhabitants of other countries in the Inner Circle.

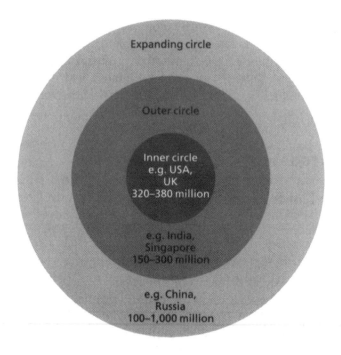

Figure 1.1 Kachru's three circles model of English worldwide (From Crystal 2003: 61)

The Outer Circle of Kachru's model refers to those countries where English serves as a second language. Unlike the Inner Circle, where the language spread as a result of the migration of native speakers from the British Isles, the presence of English in Outer Circle countries is related to their status as former colonies of the British Empire – India, Pakistan, Malaysia, or Singapore in Asia, or Kenya, Tanzania, and Nigeria in Africa. On the accompanying CD (Track 4) Speaker A talks about the past and present status of English in Malaysia, for example.

During the presence of the British as a colonizing force, English was used as the language of administration in Outer Circle countries. In this respect, its spread throughout these countries arose 'from the needs of the British Empire to teach local people sufficient English to allow the administration of large areas of the world with a relatively small number of British civil servants and troops.' (Graddol 2006: 84) The Empire builders also believed the English language and its canon of literature to be a civilizing force, and slowly introduced both language and literature studies into schooling throughout the Empire.

As result of these policies, English now has a special status in the Outer Circle. It is used extensively as an official language for administration, and it is also present to an important degree in education and the media. Interestingly, despite the fact that it was imposed upon them by a colonizing power, on gaining their independence many Outer Circle countries deliberately chose to use English as an official language. In some cases this was because the diversity of other languages spoken around the country made English a useful tool for internal communication. This is the case with India or Malaysia, **multilingual** environments where English is used in a significant amount of internal communication, even though it is not the first language of the majority of the respective populations (Rajadurai 2004).

A second reason for countries retaining English on becoming independent was that they no longer regarded it as a 'foreign' tongue. Over time local varieties had arisen. Influenced in terms of grammar, vocabulary, and pronunciation by the languages native to each country or region, these new varieties were felt to belong as much to the local populations as to the original colonizing force. As a result of these processes, we now have Indian English, Nigerian English, Singapore English, and so on. That is to say, we now have fully-fledged varieties of English that collectively are known today as the 'New Englishes'.

The task of calculating the number of Outer Circle speakers of English is a difficult one. This is not just because of certain logistical problems when trying to obtain appropriate data, but also because we need to decide at what level a speaker of English as a second language ceases to be a 'learner', and attains the status of 'competent user'. If we are calculating the number of speakers of English in an Outer Circle country, do we include only those who have achieved native-speaker, or near native-speaker competence, or do we also include speakers with only a smattering of phrases, such as a waiter or a taxi driver in a popular holiday resort?

If we limit our calculations to 'native-speaker competence', do we mean competence with respect to an Inner Circle **variety** of English, or are we referring to competence in a local variety? Nobody questions the idea that American, Australian, or British English are legitimate varieties of English, with their own grammatical, lexical, and phonological norms. However, the same holds true for Indian English, Nigerian English or Singapore English and a speaker can be a native-speaker of Indian English, for example, without being fully competent in British or American English.

Taking these and other related issues into account, Crystal estimates that there are some 430 million users of English as a Second Language (ESL) in the world today (2003: 60–67). This figure is higher than the total number of first language speakers of English. Moreover, while the number of speakers of English as a Native Language (ENL) is relatively stable, the number of ESL speakers will rise in line with the current increase in the populations of the Outer Circle countries. Another interesting point of comparison between ENL and ESL users is that the latter, by definition, are bilingual as a minimum, and are often **plurilingual**. A person born in Kenya, for example, will typically be fluent in at least three languages – their mother tongue (an African language according to their ethnic background), and the country's two official languages, English and Swahili. In contrast, a significant proportion of ENL speakers are monolingual, and may at best have some basic knowledge of the foreign language they were taught at school.

The last of the three circles in Kachru's model, the Expanding Circle, is composed of those countries where English is neither a first language, a second language, nor an official language. As the name suggests, the numbers of speakers of English in the Expanding Circle is constantly growing and, for this reason alone, it is not easy to determine their number with any precision. In addition, just as with the numbers of ESL users, there is a problem about when speakers of English from the Expanding Circle can be considered to be competent users. On a daily basis millions of people from the Expanding Circle successfully communicate with each other through English. These competent users are not learners, but their English is not native-like with respect to any Inner Circle variety of the language.

Crystal takes 'a medium level of conversational competence in handling domestic subject matter' (2003: 68) as his criterion, and estimates a total of approximately 750 million speakers of English in the Expanding Circle. This is far higher than the number of Inner Circle speakers and, as I have just suggested, the figure is growing rapidly. In other words, for the first time ever, we have a situation where the number of native speakers of a language is greatly outnumbered by the number of non-native speakers. Crystal's calculations give a ratio of 1:3, and as more and more people in the Outer and Expanding Circle countries learn English, this ratio will shift further still in favour of the non-native speakers.

This trend has a number of important implications for English language teaching. The one that is central to the purpose of this book is the way in which speakers from the Expanding Circle countries are actually changing English, and in particular its pronunciation. What is more important still is the fact that these non-native speaker developments in English do not correspond to standard native-speaker norms. To understand how this situation has come about, we need to look at the role English is now playing in the Expanding Circle.

A new role for English

Until now, English has been taught as a foreign language (EFL). That is to say, English teaching has assumed that all learners are seeking competence in English in order to communicate with its native speakers in one or other Inner Circle country. With this role in mind, the goal in pronunciation teaching has been for learners to achieve a native-speaker **accent**. The two dominant models used to this end have been the standard British accent, **RP (Received Pronunciation)**, and the standard US accent, **GA (General American)**.

Increasingly, however, speakers from the Expanding Circle use English to communicate with speakers from other Expanding or Outer Circle countries. This new role for English is well illustrated by the analysis of present-day international travel movements, which shows that 'three-quarters of all travel is between non-English speaking countries' (Graddol, 2006: 30). Additionally, in the case of countries like China, where there are inhabitants from over 50 different L1 backgrounds, English 'is used extensively in the domains of science and technology, the media, business and tourism and international connections with its greatest presence in the educational system, both formal and informal' (Gil 2005: 282). That is to say, English in China not only performs a role as a tool for international communication: in some domains it is used for internal communication between Chinese people who do not share the same mother tongue. In these domains, in fact, it is beginning to take over from Pŭtōnghuà, the preferred means of internal communication in China until now. In this respect, this new role of English in China parallels the role it plays in Outer Circle nations such as India or Malaysia.

More and more today, English is used by Japanese professionals on business in Brazil, by Polish hotel staff welcoming tourists from around the world, or by Indian migrant workers who have taken up jobs in the Gulf States. When the role of a language is to be a tool for communication between non-native speakers, we cannot rationally call it a 'foreign' language. Who is the foreigner, for example, when a speaker from Chile interacts with a colleague from Kazakhstan, using English? In a situation like this, the concept of 'foreigner' and of 'foreign language' is not applicable. Instead, we have a situation where English is acting as a **lingua franca**. That is to say, it is acting as the common language for speakers whose mother tongues are different.

English as a Lingua Franca

The term 'lingua franca' was first used to denote the **pidgin** that was employed for commerce in the ports of the eastern Mediterranean during the Middle Ages. Based on Italian, this medieval lingua franca also contained elements of Arabic, French, Greek, Spanish, and Turkish. Before that, Latin had acted as a lingua franca throughout the Roman Empire, and it continued to do so even when the Empire had collapsed. In East Africa, Swahili has been a lingua franca for traders and commerce for over 200 years now. English, then, is by no means the world's first lingua franca, but it is the first language to be used for global communication, and its rapid spread means that it is the first time that a language is being used by far greater numbers of non-native speakers than native speakers.

One outcome of the way English has so quickly taken on this new role is that various names are currently being used to refer to what is effectively the same phenomenon. English as a Lingua Franca, English as an International Language, English as a Global Language, or Global English: all of these names have been used up to now in order to refer to the new role of English. Throughout this book I will use the term 'English as a Lingua Franca' (**ELF**), in preference to others. Moreover, when I use the term ELF, I am referring fundamentally to interaction between non-native speakers. This does not mean that ELF interaction, by definition, excludes native speakers. Statistically, however, the possibility of ELF interactions occurring in the absence of native speakers is far higher than that of them occurring in their presence.

Does the presence of native speakers in ELF interactions alter these interactions in any way, or are they identical to ELF interactions entirely between non-native speakers? If you have used English in ELF contexts, your own experience may already have provided you with the answer to this question. It is quite common to hear ELF users refer to moments when the arrival of a native speaker to a group of non-native speakers has had a negative impact on the interaction. Speaker A on the CD (Track 1), for example, explains that during her stay in Budapest, where she used English as a lingua franca continually, 'nobody could understand the British'. The laughter that follows suggests that this has been Speaker B's experience, too, but it is not an experience that is limited to ELF among university students. It is also true of the use of English in large international organizations such as the EU or the UN.

In organizations where English has become the corporate language, meetings sometimes go more smoothly when no native speakers are present. Globally, the same kind of thing may be happening on a larger scale.

> This is not just because non-native speakers are intimidated by the presence of a native speaker. Increasingly, the problem may be that few native speakers belong to the community of practice which is developing amongst lingua franca users. (Graddol 2006: 115)

Summing up, ELF represents a community of users of English. The members of this community are predominantly non-native speakers. Native speakers are not excluded, but if they wish to join the ELF community, they can only do this by respecting ELF norms. What native speakers cannot do in ELF contexts is to impose their particular set of native-speaker norms. Nor can they expect the members of the ELF community to adjust to these norms.

Describing English as a Lingua Franca

As with all languages, the norms of use for ELF are determined by its users. As teacher trainers, trainee teachers, practising teachers, or as learners, we need to know what these norms are so as to be able to make use of them. Work leading towards a description of ELF is being carried out in various parts of the world, though notably in Europe and South East Asia. In one study, David Deterding and Andy Kirkpatrick (2006) analysed recordings of conversations of groups of ELT teachers on a training course in Singapore. The speakers were from the countries of the Association of South-East Asian Nations (ASEAN). Because of this, the study included people from both the Outer Circle (Brunei, Malaysia, the Philippines, Singapore) and the Expanding Circle (Cambodia, Indonesia, Laos, Myanmar, Thailand, Vietnam), for whom English was acting as a lingua franca during their time in Singapore. The authors found that despite the significant differences in the Englishes each speaker brought to the conversations there were 'very few instances where speakers fail to understand each other. These examples of ASEAN lingua franca English are characterised by mutual understanding, cooperation and tolerance' (Kirkpatrick 2007: 163).

On a much larger scale, the Vienna-Oxford International Corpus of English (VOICE: http://www.univie.ac.at/voice/), is gathering 'a sizeable and feasible corpus dedicated to capturing the use of ELF from a variety of first language backgrounds and a range of domains' (Seidlhofer 2004: 219). The VOICE project concentrates on spoken ELF in Europe, although the subjects come from more than 50 different first language backgrounds. The overall purpose of the project is to provide fellow ELF researchers with a database that they can use for their own investigations. One of the main research interests of the VOICE team itself is to determine which grammatical and lexical features are common to ELF use irrespective of the speaker's first language background.

Although the project is still at an early stage, it has been found that ELF users regularly:

- do not use the third-person singular present tense *–s* marking but use the same form for all persons (*I like, she like*)
- use the relative pronouns *who* and *which* interchangeably instead of *who* for humans and *which* for non-humans (as in *things who* and *people which*)
- omit definite and indefinite articles where they are obligatory in Standard English, or insert them where they do not occur in Standard English (e.g. *they have a respect for all, he is very good person*)
- pluralize nouns that do not have plural forms in Standard English (*informations, knowledges, advices*)
- use the demonstrative *this* with both singular and plural nouns (*this country, this countries*)
- extend the uses of certain 'general' verbs to cover more meanings than in Standard English, especially *make*, but also *do, have, put, take (make sport, make a discussion, put attention)*

(Seidlhofer, 2007: 92)

Previously such departures from Standard English have been interpreted as errors. However, the VOICE project is beginning to reveal that the grammar and lexis of ELF displays certain patterns of use that are not standard in native-speaker terms, but which are completely regular in ELF interactions, and which are not an obstacle to successful communication. In the future, knowledge of such ELF patterns could allow teachers to re-define their objectives in English language teaching.

Undoubtedly, the most significant research to date into the description of ELF in terms of implications for classroom practice focused on pronunciation. By carefully examining spoken interactions between speakers from different L1 backgrounds, Professor Jennifer Jenkins was able to identify a relatively small number of pronunciation points that were central to intelligibility in ELF (2000). We will be looking at Jenkins' work in detail in Chapter 2, but the four areas she identified in her Lingua Franca Core (LFC) can be summarized as:

- an approximation to most RP/GA consonants
- the appropriate treatment of consonant clusters
- length differences between vowels
- the placement of nuclear (sentence) stress.

Even from this simple summary, you will probably have already spotted that the LFC does not coincide with more traditional lists of priorities for pronunciation teaching. A number of 'favourites' such as **schwa, weak forms, rhythm,** and **tones** are notably absent from the LFC. It follows that the workload in achieving competence in the items of the LFC is going to be lighter than that needed to successfully complete a native-speaker oriented pronunciation programme.

There are other advantages to an ELF approach to pronunciation. We will look at these briefly at the end of this chapter, and in more detail in Chapter 3, whilst in Chapter 4 I will explain the practicalities of applying an ELF approach to teaching pronunciation. However, before doing that, I want to examine the concepts of variation, accent, and intelligibility. It is essential to understand all three in order to fully appreciate the validity of an ELF approach to teaching the pronunciation of English.

Language in use

Variation

Variation refers to the way that speakers of the same language do not use the language in the same way. It is an entirely natural phenomenon, and a basic fact of language life. This is so much the case that it is easy to forget that without variation there would be no such thing as British, American, or Australian Englishes. Nor would we now have Indian or Nigerian Englishes, nor indeed any of the world's New Englishes. Indeed, without variation languages would be unable to serve speakers' needs: 'Heterogeneity is ... necessary to satisfy the linguistic demands of everyday life' (Labov 1982: 17).

Language variation is particularly marked with spoken language as opposed to written language since 'any widely-spoken language is likely to vary not just from region to region but also across socioeconomic, ethnic and sexual boundaries, as well as different communicative situations' (Cruz-Ferreira and Abraham 2006: 32). Variation comes about in different ways: through geographical distance and isolation, through social contact, through creativity, or through deliberate self-renewal as languages evolve in order to meet the needs of generations of speakers. Language variation also comes about because of the contact between different languages in situations of bi- or multilingualism, which is a situation that concerns ELF pronunciation directly.

Variation due to geographical distance or isolation can be found in languages in the form of changes in grammar, vocabulary, pronunciation, pragmatics, in short, the entire linguistic system. These changes give rise to different regional varieties of a language, and each of these varieties is commonly referred to as a **dialect**. The English spoken on the East Coast of the United States, for example, is quite different from that spoken in the South, which is different again from that spoken in California. This same type of variation works at a national level, too, and so New Zealand English is different from Australian English, and Canadian English from American English. Similarly, in the Outer Circle, Malaysian English, Maltese English, or Indian English are all dialects of the same language.

Variation due to social contact gives rise to varieties of a language that are known as **sociolects**. This type of variation is equally evident in both Inner and Outer Circle Englishes. Within Inner Circle countries, for example, it has been traditional to distinguish working-class, middle-class, and upper-class varieties of English. 'Cockney', the variety of English heard in East London, is one example of a working-class variety of English. 'Scouse', the variety spoken in Liverpool, is another. In the USA, the sociolinguist William Labov made a study of the pronunciation of the letter 'r' in the words 'fourth' and 'floor', where it comes after a vowel sound (Labov, 1966). He had observed that some speakers in New York pronounced this 'r', whereas others did not. Labov felt that this was not a random phenomenon, and that the pronunciation or not of **post-vocalic** /r/ depended on social factors such as the speaker's socio-economic status or their work-place environment. To test his theory, he recorded the speech of the employees in three different department stores in Manhattan. One of these was considered an expensive, upper-middle class store, the second was a middle-class store, and the third was a working-class store. In each store, Labov asked the employees a question that he knew would prompt them to use the words 'fourth floor'. The results of his study showed that the pronunciation of post-vocalic /r/ was most frequent in the upper-middle class store, and least frequent in the working-class store.

Labov's pioneering study highlighted language variation related to two factors: the speaker's social class and the speaker's workplace. Other parameters such as education, occupation, age, sex, and ethnic background also give rise to social variation. In Australia, for example, there is a difference between how men speak and how women speak. In general, it is unusual to find women speaking with a broad Australian accent, or men speaking with a cultivated one. In the USA, African Americans and Jewish Americans use quite different social varieties of English because of their different ethnic backgrounds, and if you think about the way that young children speak their first language in your country and the way that your grandparents' generation speak it, you will see that age is another factor responsible for social variation in language.

These social varieties of the language are naturally also present in Outer Circle Countries. Here, language contact is a major reason for change:

> … in many Outer Circle countries, bilingual speakers of English are using the language on a daily basis alongside one or more others and frequently their use of English is influenced by these other languages. Hence they are developing new lexical items, new grammatical standards, and their pronunciation is also being influenced by their other languages.
> (McKay 2002: 49)

In Singapore, for example, contact between English and other local languages, particularly certain dialects of Malay and Chinese, has brought about a situation in which three varieties of English co-exist in the country. The way these varieties exist depends upon the social circumstances in which speakers find themselves. That is to say, that their choice of variety depends on the function the language is required to perform.

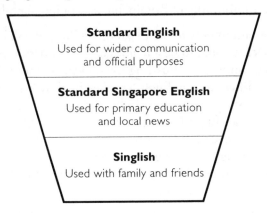

Figure 1.2 English language hierarchy for Singapore (McKay 2002: 56)

'Singlish', the colloquial variety of English at the base of the hierarchy, is used for communication with family and friends, and is the least intelligible beyond this context. Standard Singapore English is found in education and local news, whilst Standard English would be used for official purposes and for wider communication and, needless to say, would be intelligible to the greatest number of interlocutors from outside Singapore itself.

Concerned with the lack of wider intelligibility of Singlish, in 2000 the Singapore government launched the Speak Good English Movement. The broad aim of the movement is 'to encourage Singaporeans to speak grammatically correct English that is universally understood' (Speak Good English Movement). Given the extent to which Singapore depends on trade with the rest of the world, it is only natural that the government should want its citizens to be intelligible to non-Singaporeans. However, in launching the Speak Good English Movement, the Singapore government appears to have:

- ignored the fact that there is no such thing as intrinsically 'good English': 'good' here is a subjective assessment
- equated 'good English' with standard British English as opposed to the English spoken by educated Singaporeans
- assumed that 'good English' is perfect for all contexts, thus failing to understand that different varieties are appropriate to different contexts.

There is, then, an almost inverse relationship between what is socially acceptable at local level and what is intelligible at a wider level, national or international. This conflict between social acceptability and wider intelligibility is not restricted to Outer Circle varieties of English. Whilst a speaker of Scouse would have no problems being accepted and understood in working-class districts of Liverpool, he or she would struggle to be understood outside this local environment. The inverse is also true: a speaker of a very conservative RP variety of English would have problems not only of social acceptability in working-class communities of Britain, but also of intelligibility.

Turning our attention now to the Expanding Circle, it will be apparent that language contact is going to be a major factor in variation here, just as it is in Outer Circle countries. Thus English spoken by those with Russian as their L1 will be different from English spoken by those whose L1 is Chinese, Portuguese, or Spanish. Linguistically, however, Brazilian-, Chinese-, Spanish-, or Russian Englishes are equivalent to the different Englishes of the Outer Circle, whose validity is no longer questioned. By extension, the validity of Expanding Circle Englishes for ELF communication should not be questioned either, provided that these emerging Englishes successfully fulfil their primary role, and remain mutually intelligible.

Expanding Circle varieties of English might encounter difficulties in terms of acceptability when employed with interlocutors from the Inner Circle. On noticing a difference from their own English, native speakers might reject the Expanding Circle variety as a poorly-learned, or incorrectly-spoken version of Inner Circle English. If the encounter were to take place inside an Inner Circle country, with English being used as a foreign language, the native speaker could justify using NS norms to judge the other speaker's performance. If, on the other hand, the native speaker and the non-native speaker were using English in an international setting such as a conference or a trade fair, then we would be contemplating an ELF interaction. Here the non-native speaker's variety of English is just as valid as any Outer or Inner Circle variety.

Accent

Dialects are variations of a language that differ from each other in terms of the whole language system – grammar, vocabulary, pronunciation, and so on. When the variation between two groups of users is restricted to pronunciation, however, we say that they have different accents. It is possible for speakers from the same dialect to have different accents: educated speakers from England and Wales might both use the same British English dialect, but they would normally have markedly different accents.

In spoken language, accent is the most immediately tangible characteristic of a particular variety. Moreover, everybody has an accent, wherever they come from. However, where one particular accent is markedly more prestigious than others, such as Received Pronunciation (RP) in the UK, or General

American (GA) in the USA, users of this particular phonological variety often see themselves as not having an accent. The fallacy of this idea is immediately apparent when members of either group find themselves speaking to members of the other. I certainly had never seen myself as having an especially strong accent until 1976 and my first visit to the USA. On a number of occasions my 'accentless' English was the object of both curiosity and amusement, and I was asked more than once to 'say something' so that that people could hear my 'Bridish' accent. Of course, what was curious for me was the way my American friends pronounced 'British' with a [d]-like consonant in the middle, although they themselves insisted that they had no accent.

One problem with prestige accents is that they are usually perceived as being standard and correct, whilst other accents of the same language are seen as non-standard and less correct in comparison. Linguistically, however, there is no connection between a standard language and a particular accent. With respect to Standard English, for example, the sociolinguist Peter Trudgill insists that:

> Standard English has nothing to do with pronunciation. From a British
> perspective, we have to acknowledge that there is in Britain a high status and
> widely described accent known as Received Pronunciation (RP) … It is widely
> agreed, though, that while all RP speakers also speak Standard English, the
> reverse is not the case.
> (Trudgill 199: 118)

Whatever accent we have, native-speaker or non-native speaker, standard or regional, it is a part of our identity, and for some people losing their accent is the same as losing part of their identity. Forcing a new accent onto someone through classroom teaching can be perceived as obliging them to take up a new persona. 'Meddle with my accent', explained Anne Pakir in her plenary address at the 1998 TESOL Convention, 'and you meddle with my identity'.

Accents identify us not just as individuals, but also as members of a particular group. Because of this, consciously or otherwise, many people are reluctant to give up their accent, and will respond poorly to attempts to make them do so. As a language teacher you will be only too aware just how unwilling adolescents can be to give up their mother-tongue accent and 'sound English'. There can be few things more frustrating than trying to get a 15-year-old to imitate a native-speaker accent in front of his or her peers. In this respect, it is important to remember 'that the maintaining of a foreign accent saves an adolescent from being taken for the (English) teacher's pet' (Daniels 1995: 6). Adolescents often need their L1 accent in order to re-affirm their membership of their peer group. This may have been the case with Speaker L, for example, (CD Track 8), who describes a 'clash' between 'two conflicting tendencies' as a boy growing up in Morocco. Though he wanted to learn English to understand the lyrics of popular songs, he rejected the target-language culture.

Adults, too, often only get a limited distance along the road to that 'ultimate goal' of a native-speaker accent, perhaps through fear of a loss of identity. This is what Henry Daniels has in mind when he likens accent to the umbilical cord that once tied us to our mothers, and that 'to speak an L2 like a native is to take a drastic step into the unknown, accompanied by the unconscious fear of no return.' (ibid.). This is a rather extreme view of the relationship between accent and identity, but for some learners acquiring of a native-like accent in their second language can bring with it the risk of disapproval from their peer group, and consequently create an issue of a conflict of identities.

Elizabeth Gatbonton and her colleagues (2005) report on this sort of conflict for immigrant Chinese learners of English in Montreal:

> Language learners are typically subject to social forces arising from both the target- and home-language groups, pressuring them to constantly renegotiate their identities as members of both groups. In doing so, learners may either enhance or suppress one of their two identities by manipulating their language, in particular, their pronunciation of both languages.
> (Gatbonton 2005: 492)

That is to say, if learners feel that it is more important to be identified with their mother-tongue group, their pronunciation will tend to retain features of the L1 phonology, even at the cost of being perceived as having a 'heavy' accent by the target group. In contrast, if learners wish to identify with the target group, they will strive to achieve an accent that is as close as possible to that of the target group.

This conflict of interests in terms of group membership is not limited to immigrants in Inner Circle countries such as Canada. In some Outer Circle countries, speakers who have acquired an Inner Circle accent are regarded with suspicion, and are seen as 'not-one-of-us'. Thus some varieties of English have special terms for those who have been to England and acquired British Received Pronunciation (BRP) such as 'been-to-boys' (Ghana) and 'England-returned' (India) (McKay 2002: 59). Joanne Rajadurai makes a similar observation:

> [I]t is interesting to note that the tables are turned in some countries of the Outer Circle. Research has shown that in these countries, it is locals speaking English with a native-like accent who are mocked as sounding foreign and affected, and derided for putting on a false accent. In contrast, it is the local accent which is seen as 'accentless'.
> (Rajadurai 2007: 91)

These issues of the social acceptability of native-speaker accents in ESL also apply to ELF settings. As with their Inner and Outer Circle counterparts,

ELF speakers may wish to affirm their L1 identity through their L2 accent, and may not want to take on a new identity through the acquisition of a native-speaker accent. A business person from Germany, for instance, may not wish to sound British when closing a deal with a Taiwan business partner. Similarly, a Greek-born guide might not want to be thought to be American whilst showing foreign tourists around the ruins of the Parthenon.

The relationship between accent and identity is complex. On the accompanying CD, for example, Speaker C says that she would be 'very pleased' if somebody thought she was English because of her accent. She then goes on to declare that she is proud to be Hungarian, and that if asked where she was from because of her non-native speaker accent, she would say so without any problem (CD Track 2). Similarly, Speakers E and F (Track 3) both initially indicate that they would like to be taken for British because of their accents. They then reconsider the issue and conclude that neither would like to lose their respective Argentinean and Russian accents in English since they are 'something really of the identity of the person'.

The automatic assumption until now that success in pronunciation is the achievement of a native-speaker accent has a lot to do with the conflict some learners feel between their accent in English and their identity. In general, however, if speakers from the Inner and Outer Circles are free to operate in English with accents that reflect their origins, speakers from the Expanding Circle should be free to do so as well. With traditional approaches to English pronunciation this freedom has not been available. With an ELF approach it is.

Intelligibility

Accents, as we have just seen, are a natural, inevitable, and significant outcome of language variation. However, although ELF encourages accent variation in order to allow speakers to express their identity, this cannot be at the expense of intelligibility. If it were, English would cease to function successfully as a lingua franca. Intelligibility, then, is paramount to ELF communication, although as we will now see, intelligibility and accent are not the same thing.

'Geordie', the working-class variety of English spoken in Newcastle-upon-Tyne, is generally regarded as being of only limited intelligibility to anybody outside the north-east of England. The same is true for other local varieties of American or British English. Of course, the limited intelligibility of non-standard accents is something we take for granted, and is one of the reasons why most teachers would not think of employing them as goals for their learners. These goals have always been standard native-speaker accents, since it is widely assumed that such accents will be intelligible to everyone.

Two issues need clarifying here. The first is the confusion of accent with dialect. When people say that a regional accent like Geordie is unintelligible, they are almost always referring to a regional dialect, with variations not just in pronunciation, but also in grammar and vocabulary. Standard English spoken with a regional accent, however, is a different matter, and in this respect, it would be perfectly feasible to teach English pronunciation using an accent other than RP or GA. Professor David Crystal, for example, in a discussion of RP as a model for teaching pronunciation, suggests that '[m]ost people would find a Scots accent ... much easier to pick up' (1995: 365).

The second point that needs clarifying is that standard, native-speaker accents are not, in fact, inherently intelligible. For example, the following letter to the UK newspaper, *The Guardian*, responds to an article the paper had published the week before supporting British dialects/accents:

> Dialects and accents greatly enrich our linguistic culture but intelligibility must be paramount. I attended a multinational European seminar which conducted its business in English, the language common to all participants. The services of an interpreter were only needed at a meeting where a group of Oxford dons [professors] presented papers. None of the continental Europeans could make out what the academics were saying. The dialect was impenetrable to them.
> (Moore 1999)

By 'dialect', it is fairly safe to assume that Professor Moore (who is not a linguist) was referring to accent. It is equally safe to assume that the Oxford dons in questions spoke English with a standard British accent, and yet despite this, that is to say despite their using a standard native-speaker accent, they were not intelligible to their interlocutors.

This isolated incident is merely anecdotal, of course, but it coincides with the results of research carried out some time ago to determine if the spread of English might bring about problems of intelligibility between speakers with markedly different L1 backgrounds. To examine this possibility, Larry Smith studied nine 'national varieties' of English in – China, India, Indonesia, Japan, Papua New Guinea, the Philippines, Taiwan, the UK, and the USA. Samples of these varieties were recorded on tape by graduate-level speakers at the University of Hawaii. Tests of intelligibility were then administered to educated native and non-native speaker listeners. Smith concluded that there was no evidence of a breakdown in the functioning of English for international communication, but that, interestingly:

> [n]ative speakers (from Britain and the US) were not found to be the most easily understood, nor were they, as subjects, found to be the best able to understand the different varieties of English. Being a native speaker does not seem to be as important as being fluent in English and familiar with several different national varieties.
> (Smith 1992: 88)

Intelligibility, then, is not an inherent characteristic of native-speaker speech, even when this involves standard accents. Speaker K (Track 7), for example, indicates a preference for British English over American English, but then goes on to state that she cannot follow BBC English, the accent that is most frequently regarded as the standard British accent.

This lack of a direct relationship between accent and intelligibility obliges us to ask ourselves what we mean as teachers if we refer to intelligibility when we talk to students about goals for pronunciation. Sadly, there is still no single interpretation of the term. Smith and Nelson (1985) differentiate between 'intelligibility', the basic recognition of words and utterances in the speech flow, 'comprehensibility', the meaning of these words and utterances in their context, and thirdly, 'interpretability', the understanding of the speaker's intention. For example, if a speaker says 'It's very hot in here' this will be intelligible if the listener understands 'hot' and not 'hut' or 'hard', 'very' as opposed to 'berry', and so on. The utterance will have been comprehensible if the listener understands that the speaker was making a statement about the temperature in the room being high. But the utterance will not have been correctly interpreted if the listener does not open the window, or at least offer to do something to bring the temperature down. In this book I will use the term 'intelligibility' in the same way that Smith did in his 1992 study.

Rajadurai (2007) adds an additional component to that of intelligibility when she discusses 'accentedness'. This refers to the degree of 'foreign' accent as perceived by the listener. Many studies have attempted to measure the degree of foreign accent in non-native speaker English. However, in view of what we have seen so far in this chapter, what relevance do studies of 'accentedness' have to understanding intelligibility in ELF?

Reviewing intelligibility studies to date, Rajadurai points out that:

1 Almost all of the research into the intelligibility of different second-language accents has been based on judgments made by native speakers from the Inner Circle. However, in ELF contexts, where native speakers are generally absent, judgements like these are not appropriate. In ELF contexts the judges of intelligibility will be other non-native speakers.
2 The listener's attitude towards a given accent can alter their judgement as to that accent's intelligibility. In particular, when first-language listeners are asked to judge the intelligibility of second-language speakers, they tend to label what they hear as 'non-standard', 'foreign' or '(heavily) accented'. This suggests that these judgements are more subjective attitudes coloured by their knowledge that the speaker is not a native speaker, than objective measurements of intelligibility.
3 Accentedness and intelligibility have often been confused. For Canadian researchers Tracy Derwing and Murray Munro, however, they are completely different features of speech (1995, 1997). They define 'accentedness'

as the amount a particular accent differs from the local variety. Listeners will notice a high degree of accentedness in my English when I am in the USA, for example, but not when I am in England, which is where I was born. Intelligibility, on the other hand, they define as the degree of actual comprehension, that is to say the extent to which the listener has correctly understood the message. In their research they assess intelligibility through dictation-type activities, True/False questions, comprehension questions, and so on. Derwing and Munro's studies led them to believe that not only are accent and intelligibility different, but that there is no direct correlation between them: 'One very robust finding in our work is that accent and intelligibility are not the same thing. A speaker can have a very strong accent, yet be perfectly understood' (Derwing and Munro 2008: 1).

4 To a large extent, intelligibility up to now has been seen as 'a one-way process in which non-native speakers are striving to make themselves understood by native speakers whose prerogative it was to decide what was intelligible and what was not' (Bamgbose 1998: 10). The problem here is that this view of intelligibility places the burden of being understood on the speaker, without taking the listener into account at all. However, the responsibility for being intelligible does not rest solely with the speaker, since 'intelligibility is not speaker- or listener-centred, but is interactional between speaker and listener' (Smith and Nelson 1985: 333). Listening, we now know, is not a 'receptive' skill where the listener waits passively for the message to arrive and be understood. Rather it is an active process where the listener uses different strategies in order to understand the speaker, or in order to clarify understanding and jointly construct understanding together with the speaker. That is to say, successful listeners actively interrupt, seek clarification, and generally negotiate meaning with the help of the speaker.

In her review of the concept of intelligibility, Jenkins (2000) concurs with much of the above. She, too, highlights the importance of the process of **negotiation of meaning** in establishing and maintaining intelligibility, but places a special emphasis on accommodation, which is the way speakers adjust their output according to who they are talking to, what the topic is, where they are, and so on (Giles and Coupland 1991). These adjustments can involve changes in general style of speech, changes in accent, or, for example, changes in specific linguistic usage. Jenkins claims that in ELF interactions accommodation mainly involves changes in a speaker's pronunciation. Speakers make these changes, often quite consciously, in order to make themselves intelligible to their interlocutors, who, because of the very nature of ELF interactions, all have different accents.

Whereas Jenkins largely agrees with Smith and Nelson as to the interactional nature of intelligibility, she does differ from them, and indeed from much recent investigation into successful spoken communication, in one important way. Smith and Nelson claim that 'intelligibility' is less important for adequate communication than the other two aspects of the process, 'comprehensibility' and 'interpretability'. That is to say that although individual words or sounds may not actually be very intelligible, they claim that listeners are capable of using contextual clues, on the one hand, and common background knowledge on the other, in order to process the speech flow, and hence 'repair' any gaps in their understanding at the level of intelligibility.

Other researchers support this idea, notably Brown (1995), but Jenkins believes that for ELF interlocutors this is not the case. Precisely because speakers in ELF interaction come from different cultural backgrounds, their shared background knowledge is often severely limited. In addition, ELF interlocutors appear to be less efficient in the use of contextual clues. The outcome of this is that they rely far more on the words and sounds that they think they have heard than native or bilingual speakers of English, and they are only able to gain limited help from the context of what is said. I will return to this point in detail in Chapter 2.

Intelligibility, then, whilst paramount to successful spoken communication, is not a simple matter. It is not resident in any particular accent, standard or non-standard, native speaker or non-native speaker. It can only really be judged by the interlocutor since it is the result of the interaction between speaker and listener. Finally, in ELF settings, it is the result of successful processing of the **acoustic signal** – the continuum of sound that the listener hears. Unfortunately, many ELF listeners rely heavily on the correct recognition of words and utterances in the speech flow through a bottom-up process and often construct their understanding of the message on the basis of individual sounds that they may or may not have heard correctly.

Pronunciation goals for ELF

English is now a global language. This situation is not going to change in the immediate future, and so the primary goal of teaching pronunciation must now be to make learners intelligible to the greatest number of people possible, and not just to the native speakers of the language. Learners will come from different first language backgrounds, and will speak English with a wide range of different accents. This creates a potential problem with respect to the principal function of a language, which is communication. The situation is further complicated when we look at another function of language, which is that of identity. In the future, many users from Expanding Circle may want to retain their local accent as a mark of their identity. This tendency could well increase as ELF users gain confidence in their right to speak English with their individual accents.

Traditionally, these two functions of English have been seen as standing in opposition. Andy Kirkpatrick, for example, describes an 'identity–communication continuum' (2007:11), with the identity and communication functions representing the two extremes of the continuum. Ideally, the approach that we choose for teaching English pronunciation will bring these opposing forces together as much as possible. In order to do this, our approach will have two basic goals:

Goal 1 – Mutual intelligibility. This must be ensured as far as possible, regardless of the speakers' first-language backgrounds.

Goal 2 – Identity. If learners wish to, they should be able to retain their identities through their accents.

A third goal for any approach to teaching pronunciation is that of teachability. Christiane Dalton and Barbara Seidlhofer refer to this concept when they explain that:

> [s]ome things, say the distinction between **fortis** and lenis **consonants**, are fairly easy to describe and generalize – they are teachable. Other aspects, notably the attitudinal function of intonation, are extremely dependent on individual circumstances, and therefore nearly impossible to isolate out for direct teaching … In other words, some aspects might be better left for learning without teacher intervention.
> (Dalton and Seidlhofer 1994: 72–73)

As far as possible, the approach we take to teaching pronunciation should be built around contents that are teachable, and that respond well to the types of exercises and activities that we can do in the classroom.

Approach 1 – Use a standard native-speaker accent

If we were able to get learners from all over the world to speak with the same accent, they would be fully intelligible to each other. However, even if we could leave aside the difficult issue as to which accent this should be (RP, GA, General Australian, Standard Scottish English, etc.), learners cannot achieve the goal of identity through a single accent. Even if they were to achieve full competence in a particular native-speaker accent, this would be at the expense of their right to express their identity through their accent, and at the risk of being seen as 'been-to-boys' or 'England-returned'.

Of course, if a learner wants to sound like a native speaker, an important issue that I will return to in Chapter 3, then the second of the three goals is irrelevant. What is not irrelevant, however, is the goal of teachability. The attitudinal function of intonation that Dalton and Seidlhofer refer to is a case in point. Native speakers convey attitude through tone, which is the movement of the pitch of the voice. Tone, however, is generally considered to be resistant to classroom practice. Peter Roach, for example, suggests that '[t]he attitudinal use of intonation is best acquired by talking with and listening to English speakers' (Roach 1991: 169). Jenkins makes a similar point (1997). Nor is tone the only problem of a native-speaker approach in terms of teachability. Word stress and rhythm are also problematic, whilst the **dental fricatives**, the 'th' sounds in *think* and *this*, are notoriously difficult to teach.

In short, a native-speaker accent approach to pronunciation only fully satisfies the first of our three goals, and it will only do this if language teachers around the world agree to teach the same accent. This will never happen.

Approach 2 – Use a single world standard for pronunciation

David Crystal tentatively puts forward this approach when he discusses **World Standard Spoken English** (2003). For Crystal, the advantage of a WSSE approach is that its speakers 'have a dialect in which they can continue to express their national identity; and they have a dialect which can guarantee international intelligibility, when they need it' (2003: 188). A WSSE approach, then, fulfils Goal 1 and seems to satisfy Goal 2. However, Crystal also points out that 'US English does seem likely to be the most influential in the development of WSSE' (ibid.). This native-speaker base, however, runs counter to our requirement that local norms should be central to pronunciation if speakers are to retain their identity through their accent. More importantly, since WSSE has not yet been described, it fails to satisfy the teachability criterion of Goal 3.

Approach 3 – An ELF approach based on the LFC

Because the LFC is the result of the empirical study of successful spoken interaction between non-native speakers, an ELF approach responds well to Goal 1. In addition, this approach also meets the demands of the second and third goals. As we will see in Chapter 2:

- The four areas of pronunciation that make up the LFC leave a great deal of space for speakers to retain their local accents, and hence express their individual identities.
- High levels of competence in most of the areas that make up the LFC can be achieved through classroom teaching. That is to say, they are teachable.

There are other favourable outcomes to adopting an ELF approach to pronunciation teaching. For example, as we will see in Chapter 3, non-native speaker teachers can make excellent instructors for teaching the pronunciation of English. In addition, the learner's L1 pronunciation can be used as a resource for achieving competence in the LFC. Finally, the LFC gives learners a foundation that will allow them to go on to high levels of phonological competence for a wide range of possible communication settings.

Summary

This chapter has explained how English has spread around the world over the last 400 years, and how this spread has accelerated massively over the last 40 years, until English has become a global language. In addition to the traditional roles of native language (ENL), second language (ESL), and foreign language (EFL), the spread of English has given rise to a new role. With the number of non-native speakers now far greater than the number of native speakers, English now functions as a lingua franca (ELF) for the majority of its users.

As a result of this spread, English has undergone and continues to undergo variation. Language contact is a major force in forming second-language accents, and the influence of different first-language phonologies means that in ELF settings we must expect significantly different accents of English. These different accents constitute part of their respective speakers' identities, and should not be modified against the speakers' wishes. However, speakers will all obviously seek to be intelligible to each other. Whichever approach we take to teaching pronunciation, it has to make these two conflicting goals of intelligibility and identity compatible. Only an ELF approach to teaching English pronunciation is able to do this. In addition, an ELF approach provides the best response to the issue of teachability.

Further reading

On the spread of English

Crystal, D. 2003. *English as a Global Language* (2nd edn.). Cambridge: Cambridge University Press.

Jenkins, J. 2009. *World Englishes. A Resource Book for Students* (2nd edn.) Abingdon: Routledge.

Kirkpatrick, A. 2007. *World Englishes. Implications for International Communication and English Language Teaching*. Cambridge: Cambridge University Press.

Svartvik, J. and **G. Leech.** 2006. *English – One Tongue, Many Voices.* Basingstoke: Palgrave Macmillan.

On descriptions of ELF

Kirkpatrick, A. 2007. *World Englishes. Implications for International Communication and English Language Teaching*. Cambridge: Cambridge University Press.

VOICE (Vienna-Oxford International Corpus of English) Available at http://www.univie.ac.at/voice/

On variation, intelligibility, and accommodation

Giles, H. and **N. Coupland.** 1991. *Language: Contexts and Consequences.* Milton Keynes: Open University.

Jenkins, J. 2000. *The Phonology of English as an International Language.* Oxford: Oxford University Press.

2 THE LINGUA FRANCA CORE

Introduction

In Chapter 1 we saw how English is now used predominantly as a lingua franca. We explored a number of problems that this new role can produce in terms of pronunciation and, in response to these problems, we examined three different teaching approaches for ELF. I suggested that the best of the three was based on the Lingua Franca Core (LFC).

In this chapter, I will briefly describe the research that led to the notion of the Lingua Franca Core, which I will then describe in detail. I will further go on to show how the LFC is open to 'fine-tuning' by the inclusion of new empirical data. Finally, I will explain how the LFC is a starting-point, rather than an end-point, in terms of pronunciation teaching and learner goals.

Searching for priorities

In Chapter 1 I explained how until now intelligibility in spoken English has been described almost exclusively in terms of native-speaker listeners, with English operating as a foreign language. As a result, any attempts to prioritize pronunciation work for learners have been strongly influenced by contemporary beliefs about how native speakers make themselves understood to other native speakers. Thus, prior to the 1980s, the priority in pronunciation in ELT was competence in the individual sounds. Vowels and consonants were the object of most classroom activities, and it was generally accepted that until learners had attained sufficient competence in the perception and production of these sounds, it would not be advisable to progress to higher levels. Experts felt that stress, rhythm, intonation, and certain characteristics of connected speech were only appropriate for advanced learners.

The arrival of Communicative Language Teaching in the early 1980s brought about an almost complete reversal of these priorities. The argument put forward to justify this change was that 'in the absence of complete mutilation of the **phonemes** by the non-native speaker, the **suprasegmentals** will carry the day because they bear the meaning of the message' (Stevens 1989: 183). Analysis of how native speakers used stress, rhythm, and intonation to construct their spoken messages led to the conclusion that learners needed to focus their attention on these features, rather than on individual sounds.

Since the dramatic swing to suprasegmentals in the 1980s, work on individual sounds has slowly made its way back into ELT coursebooks at all levels. However, what has not changed is the focus on the native speaker as the interlocutor. As a result, pronunciation work in almost all currently available materials assumes that learners are preparing themselves for interactions with native speakers. In the light of what I said in Chapter 1, it should be clear that this assumption does not correspond to the principal use of English today.

A number of ELT experts and applied linguists were aware of this mismatch, including Jennifer Jenkins. She realized that there was virtually no empirical information as to how English operates at a phonological level when it is used as a lingua franca. In order to remedy this, she gathered empirical data about intelligibility in spoken English between non-native speakers. To get her data, Jenkins recorded interactions between learners working in pairs and groups in communicative tasks in the classroom. She also collected field data over a period of three years in both classroom and social settings (Jenkins 2000). The subjects of all of her studies were learning English in the UK, and were 'of upper-intermediate to low advanced level as recognized by the University of Cambridge Local Examinations Syndicate (UCLES)' (2000: 87).

One aim of Jenkins' research was to determine to what extent breakdowns in communication in ELF settings were due to problems at a phonological level, and to what extent they were due to problems in vocabulary, grammar, general knowledge, and so on. The analysis of her data produced some surprising results. For example, in one study Jenkins noted a total of 40 instances of communication breakdown, of which 27 were attributable to pronunciation, eight to lexis, two to grammar, and three to other causes.

Two things stand out from this data. The first is the almost negligible role of incorrect grammar as a cause of miscommunication in ELF. This is in marked contrast with the importance most coursebooks give to grammar, and the amount of classroom time most of us as teachers dedicate to this area. The second point is of direct relevance to this book, and it is the fact that pronunciation was found to be the most important cause of breakdowns in ELF communication.

Jenkins' work also led her to question current understanding of the relative importance of individual sounds as opposed to the suprasegmental features of English pronunciation. As we have just seen, Communicative Language Teaching placed attention heavily on suprasegmentals at the cost of work on individual sounds. However, Jenkins' research into NNS–NNS interactions does not support this emphasis. In her study, all of the breakdowns in communication that could be attributed to pronunciation 'were caused by the transfer of L1 sounds.' (Jenkins 2000: 88).

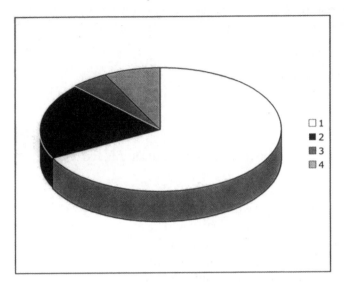

Key: 1 = pronunciation; 2 = vocabulary; 3 = grammar; 4 = other causes
Figure 2.1   The causes of communication breakdown in ELF (Jenkins 2000)

These results raised the question as to why individual sounds were involved in breakdowns to such an extent. The answer, in Jenkins' opinion, lay in the difference between what happens in native-speaker interactions, and what was happening in interactions between the non-bilingual, non-native speakers that she was studying. Native speakers, she suggested, together with non-native speakers with very high levels of proficiency, use **top-down processing** to access meaning, and to re-interpret what they think they have heard when the perceived meaning does not make sense. That is to say, they use information that may not actually be in the words they hear in order to understand the intended message. In contrast, speakers at lower levels of proficiency employ essentially **bottom-up processing** when listening. This means that they are heavily dependent on the acoustic signal – the actual sounds that they hear. This dependence can be so great that they become completely thrown by deviations in individual sounds, even when there are clear linguistic or extra-linguistic clues that contradict the sense of what they think they heard.

In one example from Jenkins' data, a Japanese student describes a picture to her Swiss-German partner. Both students can see a set of six pictures. The task was for the Swiss-German student to listen and identify which picture the Japanese speaker was describing. He had problems completing the task, however, because the Japanese student talked about 'three [led] cars'. This made him think about cars for hire (car rental). In other words he had understood 'let' cars. There was nothing in any of the pictures, however, that suggested car hire. More importantly, only one of the six pictures contained cars at all, and these were all red. The confusion was only resolved when the Japanese speaker corrected her pronunciation of the 'r' in 'red'.

A I don't understand the 'let' cars.

B Let [let] cars? Three [red] cars (very slowly)

A Ah, red

B Red.

A Now I understand. I understood car to hire, to let. Ah, red, yeah, I see.

(Jenkins 2000: 81)

In a top-down approach, listeners with a high level of proficiency would have been able to use the contextual clues. They would have immediately focused on the picture with the cars, and would have used the fact that they were all red to re-interpret the acoustic signal. In the study, the Swiss-German listener relied too heavily on what he had heard, and using a bottom-up process, was unable to make use of the contextual clues. In general, Jenkins concluded that 'given speakers' frequent inability to "say what (they) mean" pronunciation-wise, which is compounded by listeners' seemingly ubiquitous use of bottom-up strategies, pronunciation is possibly the greatest single barrier to successful communication in ELF communication' (ibid. 2000: 83).

The analysis of her empirical data enabled Jenkins to identify the features of English pronunciation that repeatedly caused breakdowns in ELF communication. This in turn allowed her to establish the Lingua Franca Core, a list of pronunciation items central to maintaining mutual intelligibility of ELF.

The Lingua Franca Core

The LFC identifies four areas where it is thought to be essential to eliminate error from a speaker's pronunciation if he or she wants to be intelligible in ELF communication:

1 individual consonant sounds
2 groups of consonants (clusters)
3 vowels
4 nuclear stress placement.

Consonant sounds

In general, when dealing with differences between the sound system of their own language and that of English, speakers employ a substitution strategy. That is to say, when a consonant of English does not occur in their first language, they subconsciously replace it with something from their first language that they believe is the same. This substitution strategy can cause serious confusion for both native speaker and non-native speaker listeners. The replacement of /f/ with /p/, for example, a substitution typical of Korean, Malay, Tagalog, and Thai and speakers of English, means that 'coffee' will be understood as 'copy'. Similarly, the consonant /tʃ/ is not present in most accents of Portuguese, and is replaced by the sound /ʃ/. This results in 'chair' sounding like 'share'.

Because of the impact the substitution of consonants has on ELF communication, the LFC requires speakers to be competent, both receptively and productively, in all but two of the consonant phonemes of English. The two exceptions are the **voiceless** and **voiced** 'th' sounds, /θ/ and /ð/, as in the words *think* and *then*, respectively. The LFC also gives additional guidance as to the optimum pronunciation of five more consonants: /p/, /t/, /k/, /l/, /r/. Descriptions and teaching ideas for the consonants of English are widely available in existing pronunciation manuals, and Chapter 5 offers further guidance for learners from ten specific L1 backgrounds, so I will limit my comments here to these seven sounds.

/θ/ and /ð/

These two consonants are classed as dental fricatives: with the tip of the tongue protruding between the top and bottom teeth, air from the lungs is expelled from the mouth. Although they are strongly identified with the pronunciation of English in the minds of ELT practitioners like ourselves, /θ/ and /ð/ are notably absent from many languages in the world, including some native-speaker varieties of English, such as Irish, Jamaican, or New York. This absence suggests a certain inherent difficulty in their pronunciation, a difficulty that is confirmed by the fact that they are often the last consonant sounds of English that native-speaker children learn to pronounce correctly. Some children, in fact, never learn to pronounce them; they substitute /θ/ with /f/, to produce 'fink' instead of 'think', and replace /ð/ with a 'd'-like sound that makes 'then' sound like 'den'. Travelling through London one day, I overheard a young girl playing with the words 'that thing', which she variously pronounced 'that thing', 'dat thing' and 'dat fing'. At one point in her game she asked her younger brother what he did, listened to his reply, and then declared 'I can say "that thing", but "dat fing" is easier'.

We also now know that /θ/ and /ð/ are especially resistant to classroom teaching techniques (Menyuk 1968; Eckman 1977; Pennington 1996). Despite teachers' persistent and well intentioned efforts, many learners, just like native speakers, consistently substitute these two sounds with similar sounds that they find 'easier'. Examples of these substitutions can be found on many tracks on the CD, and notably on Tracks 3, 4, 5, 7, 9, 10, 11, 13, 19, 20, 22, 25, 28, and 30. These substitutions characterize the pronunciation of non-native speakers even when they achieve very high levels of competence in all other aspects of the language. The difficulty in pronouncing /θ/ and /ð/ is so significant and so widespread, in fact, that their use is forbidden in communication between pilots and air-traffic controllers for certain key aviation terms. Non-native and native speakers alike are required to pronounce 'three' as 'tree', and 'thousand' as 'tousand', for example, in international 'airspeak'.

Absent from many of the world's languages, as well as from numerous native-speaker varieties of English, inherently difficult to pronounce, notoriously resistant to classroom teaching, and unnecessary for ELF intelligibility: it is not difficult to understand why the LFC does not include the dental fricatives of English. The LFC does not, however, stipulate that speakers should be discouraged from using them if they are part of the speaker's mother tongue pronunciation. Rebecca Dauer, for example, wrongly interpreted the LFC in this way: '…from my 30 years of teaching experience, I do not think having students replace /θ/ and /ð/ with /f/ and /v/ is very helpful' (Dauer 2005: 546). The LFC does not suggest that /θ/ and /ð/ be 'replaced'. It simply insists that they are not necessary for intelligibility in ELF.

/p/, /t/, and /k/

Six consonants of English, /p/, /b/, /t/, /d/, /k/, /g/, are collectively known as **plosives** (or stops) because of the way they are produced. They involve momentarily holding (stopping) the air in the mouth, and then suddenly ('explosively') releasing it. Three of these plosive (/p/, /t/, /k/), are frequently classed as voiceless, and three as voiced (/b/, /d/, /g/). However, in certain positions the key difference between voiced and voiceless plosives is **aspiration**, the release of a small puff of air immediately after a sound is made. The voiceless plosives /p/, /t/, /k/ are aspirated when they are on their own at the beginning of a stressed syllable as in 'pen', 'tip', 'attend' or 'because'; their voiced counterparts /b/, /d/, and /g/ are never aspirated. If speakers fail to aspirate /p/, /t/, and /k/ adequately, they will make 'pear' sound like 'bear', 'tin' sounds like 'din', 'coat' like 'goat', and so on. Correct aspiration of /p/, /t/, /k/ is therefore essential for ELF intelligibility.

/t/

In English the sound /t/ is made by placing the tip of the tongue against the **alveolar ridge**. However, when 't' comes between vowels, as in words like 'water', 'butter', or 'matter', it is pronounced slightly differently in American

English, which has a single, rapid tap of the tongue against the alveolar ridge. This variation is closer phonetically to /d/ than to /t/, and this can make 'matter' sound like 'madder'. The LFC proposes that learners use the British English /t/ in preference to the American English alternative.

/l/

In native-speaker English, the pronunciation of <l> in words like 'lip' or 'below' is not the same as in words like 'doll' or 'milk'. In 'lip' and 'below', the <l> comes before a stressed vowel, and is pronounced in a way that is known as 'clear' /l/, with the tip of the tongue raised to the alveolar ridge in the front of the mouth. In contrast, in 'doll' and 'milk' the <l> comes after a stressed vowel, and a variant known as 'dark' /l/ is used. Here, the back of the tongue is also slightly raised. Dark /l/ is typical of certain native speaker accents such as RP and GA, but it is not necessary for intelligibility in ELF communication.

For speakers of some L1 backgrounds, it easier to substitute dark /l/ with an [ʊ]-like vowel rather than use clear /l/. This makes 'milk' sound like 'miuk' [mɪʊk] and 'doll' like [dɒʊ]. The LFC includes [ʊ] as a valid alternative to dark /l/. An example of this can be heard on Track 15 on the CD where Speaker B pronounces 'school' as [skuːʊ], and again on Track 11, where 'film' is pronounced as [fɪʊm]. Interestingly, this same substitution was stigmatized in the past among RP speakers, probably because of its association with the working-class London Cockney accent. Today, however, the use of [ʊ] is increasingly common among young, educated speakers in London and South East England, and may become the standard pronunciation for /l/ in this position for this group.

/r/

The situation with /r/ is similar to that of the dental fricatives /θ/ and /ð/, both in terms of inherent difficulty and in terms of variation. Some native speakers never learn to pronounce /r/ in the way that is considered standard for the English they speak. In addition, the type of /r/ used changes from one group of native speakers to another. The /r/ of Scottish English is quite different to that of RP or GA, for example. The LFC does not describe exactly how /r/ should be pronounced, but as with /θ/ and /ð/, the learner's mother tongue will be a deciding factor. The most common variant of /r/ in native-speaker Englishes is [ɹ], a sound that is made by holding the tip of the tongue just behind the alveolar ridge, but without any contact being made. This variant, which is known as a post-alveolar approximant, is notoriously difficult for learners of English who have a different variant in their mother tongue.

Another common variant of /r/ is the trill [r], where the tip of the tongue repeatedly touches the alveolar ridge. This variant is a feature of some native-speaker Englishes such as Scottish English, and is typical of the pronunciation of many other languages including Arabic, Polish, northern dialects of German, Russian, and Spanish. The Spanish speaker on Track 14 uses a trilled /r/ with the words 'other' and 'your', for example. Spanish also uses a third variant of /r/, a /d/-like flap, [ɾ]. We met this variant in the section on /t/. A fourth variant, the **uvular** [ʁ], is the made in the throat and is characteristic of French and southern German accents of English. This variant is not as widespread as any of the others, so is not likely to be as intelligible in ELF communication. Finally, the /r/ of the German speaker in Tracks 1, 5, 15, and 23 is mainly the result of the speaker rounding her lips, such that in some places it sounds more like /w/.

In addition to differences in articulation, native-speaker varieties of English can be put into one of two groups with respect to when they pronounce an 'r' in the spelling of a word. In one group 'r' is always pronounced regardless of whether it comes before or after vowels. These varieties are known as **rhotic**, and include GA, Canadian English, Scottish English, Irish English, and many Caribbean Englishes. In contrast, non-rhotic varieties such as RP, Australian English, and most varieties of New Zealand English, do not pronounce an 'r' when it comes after a vowel or before a consonant as in words like 'car' or 'card'. For the LFC, Jenkins opted for the GA rhotic variety of /r/. She chose this option 'mainly because 'r' is indicated orthographically in situations (i.e. post-vocalic) where it does not feature in RP pronunciation when a word is spoken in isolation (for example, 'four') or is followed by another consonant (for example, 'four books') rather than a vowel (for example, 'four eggs') (2000: 139). That is to say that because rhotic varieties reflect the 'r' in spelling more closely, they should be easier for ELF users, and should increase ELF intelligibility.

Consonant clusters

Clusters are groups of two or more consonants. These are found at the beginning of individual words, as in '<u>cl</u>uster', or '<u>gr</u>oup', in the middle of words, as in 'clu<u>st</u>er' or 'co<u>ns</u>onants', and at the end of words, as in 'consona<u>nts</u>'. English allows up to three consonants in any position in a word. The word '<u>str</u>engths', for example, has initial and final three-consonant clusters. In word-final position, four-consonant clusters are possible, such as in 'texts' [teksts]. Clusters can also occur across word boundaries. A cluster of four consonants is formed, for example, across the word boundary in 'consona<u>nt cl</u>uster'.

Clusters are not common to all languages, and even when they are, not all languages allow the same combinations of consonants. The outcome of this is that many learners find the pronunciation of English consonant clusters difficult. Faced with this difficulty, they employ two broad strategies:

- deletion of one of the consonants in the cluster
- insertion of a short [ɪ]- or [e]-like vowel between two of the consonants.

Of these two strategies, deletion affects intelligibility considerably. The deletion of the 's' in 'strain', for example, produces 'train', and taking the 'train' is not the same as taking the 'strain'! If deletions occur in several places in an utterance, intelligibility can be seriously threatened. Many listeners, for example, would have problems understanding [ju wɒ jɔ ˈbɜde ˈpeze] ('You want your birthday present?'). On Track 5 of the CD Speaker G pronounces 'English' as [ɪŋgɪʃ], deleting the /l/. On Track 22 the same speaker deletes the /l/ on 'blog', whilst the Malay speaker on Track 26 deletes the /r/ in 'problem'. Deletions like these can threaten intelligibility.

The second strategy learners use, addition of a vowel, is found to cause fewer problems in ELF. The insertion of a short /e/, for example, is typical of Spanish L1 accented English whenever a word begins 's+consonant'. Thus, 'Spain', with an initial cluster that is not found in Spanish, is pronounced [eˈspeɪn]. If the speaker deletes either of these consonants, the outcome will be either 'pain' or 'sane'. To say you are 'in pain' or 'insane' is certainly not the same as being 'in Spain'.

Jenkins gives a graphic example of the impacts of addition and deletion when she explains how 'a Japanese learner's rendering (in context) of the word 'product' as [pəˈrɒdʌkʊtɔ] was perfectly intelligible to her ... receivers, whereas the Taiwanese learner's version [ˈpɒdʌk] was not' (Jenkins 2000: 142). The speakers on Tracks 6, 19, 21, and 22 all employ this strategy. As a general rule, then, simplification of consonant clusters by addition of a short vowel is an acceptable strategy and will help to retain intelligibility in ELF communication. Deletion, on the other hand, is likely to have the opposite effect, and should be avoided.

Although deletion is not an acceptable strategy in word-initial clusters, it can be used with certain clusters that occur in the middle or at the end of words in English. Native speakers commonly pronounce words like 'postman', 'aspects', or 'next week' as [ˈpəʊsmən], [ˈæspeks]. and [neksˈwiːk]. In all three examples the /t/ in the middle of the respective cluster has been deleted. This deletion of sounds is known as **elision**, and is characteristic of native-speaker English in all contexts except those of slow, careful speech. The elision of /t/ or /d/ when either is the central consonant of three in a cluster does not seem to affect intelligibility in ELF. In addition, eliminating one of the three consonants in a cluster has clear benefits for many learners because it makes the resulting two-consonant cluster easier to pronounce. Almost without exception the speakers in Tracks 21–30 elide the /t/ or /d/ in clusters. There are many other examples of the correct elision of /t/ or /d/ on the other tracks, particularly Tracks 3 and 4.

Vowel sounds

There is far more variation in the vowels of English than in the consonants. The vowel in the word 'bat', for example, is pronounced in more or less the same way in American, Australian, and British English, but very differently in New Zealand English, where it sounds more like 'bet'; standard North American English uses the same vowel in 'hot' and 'heart', but these are different vowels in British English; Australians pronounce 'day' in a way that makes it sound like 'die' to non-Australian ears.

Differences in vowel qualities are also marked as you travel around Inner Circle countries, especially the UK. In England, for example, the word 'bus' is pronounced /bʌs/ in the south, but /bʊs/ in many parts of the north. Similarly, words like 'grass' or 'bath' are pronounced /græs/ and /bæθ/ in some areas, and /grɑːs/ and /bɑːθ/ in others.

In an attempt to make sense of the huge variation in native-speaker accents the phonetician Bryan Jenner examined what they all have in common (1989). The outcome of his research was a graded list of pronunciation priorities called the 'Common Core' (1989). This differentiated between two characteristics of English vowels, their quantity (length) and their quality, and placed much greater importance on length:

> Native accents show such enormous differences in vowel quality that it cannot be claimed that these are vital for mutual intelligibility. Nor can it be claimed that there is a minimum set of vowel shapes that must be acquired by the foreign learner, since different native varieties do not make all the oppositions found in SBE [Standard British English] or any other 'standard' variety.
> (Jenner 1989: 3)

The LFC takes a similar position and requires teachers and learners to focus their attention on the long–short differences between vowels[1] rather than achieving any exact, native-speaker quality. In addition, the empirical evidence that the LFC is based on revealed a significant number of occasions where communication broke down when the long vowel of 'bird' or 'her' (/ɜː/) was mispronounced. Because of this, the LFC includes the need for a good approximation to the native-speaker quality of the central vowel /ɜː/. On Track 7, for example, the Japanese L1 speaker pronounces the word 'term' as [tɑːm], which proves almost impossible to understand.

The LFC focus on vowel length applies to diphthongs as well as pure vowels. English diphthongs have approximately the same length as the long English pure vowels. ELF users whose first language has no diphthongs will tend to shorten English diphthongs in a way that makes them sound like pure vowels. Words like 'note' and 'not' will sound the same, for example. The answer to this problem for ELF intelligibility lies in achieving sufficient length in the diphthong rather than in trying to attain an exact, native-speaker quality.

Problems with the length of English vowels are marked not only in speakers' attempts to distinguish between **minimal pairs** that constitute long–short pairs such as 'beat' and 'bit', which have different vowels, but also between pairs that share the same vowel. With pairs like 'mate–made' or 'ice–eyes', where both words have the same vowel quality, the difference that listeners perceive is purely one of length. This happens because in English the length of a vowel varies according to its context. Broadly speaking, a vowel in English can be found in one of three environments:

- in an open syllable, as in words like 'bee', 'zoo', or 'throw'
- in a syllable closed by a voiced (lenis) consonant, as in words like 'made', 'eyes', 'bag', 'leave', 'peas', etc.
- in a syllable closed by a voiceless (fortis) consonant, as in 'mate', 'ice', 'back', 'leaf', 'peace', etc.

Vowels in open syllables have been shown to have approximately the same length as vowels in syllables closed by a voiced (lenis) consonant. However, when an accented syllable is closed by a voiceless (fortis) consonant (i.e. /p/, /t/, /k/, /tʃ/, /f/, /θ/, /s/, /ʃ/), this has the effect of shortening the preceding vowel. The word 'mate', for example, is perceived by listeners as being different from 'made' not because of the voiceless/voiced nature of the final /t/ or /d/, but because the vowel in 'mate' is shorter than the same vowel in 'made'. Vowel length also explains the difference between ice/eyes, back/bag, leaf/leave, or peace/peas, with the vowels in 'ice', 'back', 'leaf', and 'peace' being shorter.

Two general points are worth making before finishing this section on the LFC and vowels:

1 Of the languages covered in Chapter 5, for example, only Arabic, German, and Japanese have vowel systems where differences in vowel length can create differences in meaning. Learners from languages where vowel length is more or less constant, such as Chinese, Greek, Malay, Russian, or Spanish, usually have important problems in this area.

2 The LFC focus on length is not to say that learners are free to use any vowel in any place. If a speaker pronounces 'beat' like 'Bart' one time, for example, like 'bird' the next, and like 'board' the third time, communication will most probably break down. There is a great deal of tolerance of variation in vowel quality in ELF, but the qualities of individual speakers must be reasonably consistent. Someone who is used to listening to American English, for example, might initially be confused by the way a British English speaker pronounced words like 'caught' or 'thought'. But if the speaker in question always does this, the listener will quickly 'tune in' to this different quality. Vowel qualities for ELF pronunciation need to be consistent in this same way, and in Chapter 4 we will look at how this consistency can be achieved.

Nuclear stress placement

The last of the four major pronunciation features that make up the LFC is the area of nuclear stress. Analysis of spoken English shows that speakers divide what they say into groups of words. These often coincide with grammatical structures such as clauses or simple sentences. However, they can be as short as one word, and on average tend to be around four words. Various names have been given to these naturally occurring groups of words, including tone units, thought groups, and word groups. I will use the term 'word group' in this book.

The first benefit that comes from the use of word groups is that they break the speech flow up into manageable, meaningful blocks of information. This makes the task of the listener easier for two reasons. Firstly, it provides the information in packages that bring out the meaning more clearly than if the speaker simply pauses at random. Secondly, the small pauses between each word group allow the listener time to process what he or she has heard. Breaking speech up into word groups in this way is especially valuable in monologues, as opposed to dialogues or conversation. Typical 'monologues' include lectures at institutions of higher education, presentations in the world of business, instructions in public places such as stations or airports, or commentaries by tour guides at monuments and other tourist attractions. In these situations the listener cannot easily interrupt the speaker and request clarification, and the onus is on the speaker to make life as easy as possible for the listener. Using word groups is one way of doing this.

Not pausing adequately, in contrast, can have a serious impact on intelligibility. Firstly, it can lead to breaks in the speech flow in unexpected places, and this will reduce intelligibility. A weather forecaster saying:

1 'We can expect heavy rain in the southwest from Monday onwards. The situation will improve slowly.'

is telling us something quite different from:

2 'We can expect heavy rain in the southwest. From Monday onwards the situation will improve slowly.'

Secondly, poor pausing, or more specifically, too little pausing, reduces planning time for the speaker. This can easily lead to errors of pronunciation and/or vocabulary, which will in turn complicate the job of the listener.

In spoken English, one syllable in each word group is prominent. That is to say, it is made to stand out from the others. To do this, the chosen syllable is made louder and longer than the others. In addition, the most significant pitch movement (tone) in the word group coincides with this syllable, which is called the nucleus (or tonic). The correct placement of nuclear stress is important for intelligibility in ELF:

Nuclear stress, whether unmarked (on the last content word in the word group) or contrastive (somewhere else) is the most important key to the speaker's intended meaning. It highlights the most salient part of the message, indicating where the listener should pay particular attention. And contrastive stress is especially important in English as it does not have the morphological and syntactic resources that many other languages have to highlight contrasts: English has few inflections and the word order is relatively inflexible.
(Jenkins 1997: 18)

In a conversation between friends, the word group 'I've rented a flat' could be said in three different ways:

1 I've rented a FLAT.
2 I've RENTED a flat.
3 I'VE rented a flat.

In 1, the nuclear stress falls on the last lexical item. This is known as **unmarked stress**, and is, we could say, a 'neutral' way of saying this phrase. It tells the listener what type of accommodation the speaker has taken. In both 2 and 3, the nucleus is earlier in the word group. Both are examples of **contrastive stress**, and the placement of the nucleus on a word other than the last lexical item gives these two word groups different meanings. By choosing to make 'rented' the nucleus, for example, the speaker draws attention to the idea of not having bought a flat. In 3, the focus has been put on the fact that it was the speaker who rented the flat, and not some other person mentioned in the conversation. Both speakers on Track 5 make effective use of contrastive stress, as does Speaker B on Track 15.

Using nuclear stress inappropriately can seriously confuse listeners by drawing their attention to the wrong part of the message. In the example below (Jenkins 1997: 19), a Swiss speaker explained to her Taiwanese listener how many cigarettes she smoked a day. The Taiwanese partner responded by saying 'You smoke more than I DO.' There was no attempt at contrastive stress, which correctly done would have led to 'You smoke more than *I* do', with the nuclear stress on 'I' in order to make the contrast between the speaker's smoking habits and his partner's. Instead, the nucleus fell on the last word in the word group, and, as a result, the speaker had to repeat the utterance several times before he was understood.

In another example from her field data (ibid.: 18–19), Jenkins reports on a Hungarian speaker asking his Brazilian and Swiss-French partners for a coloured pen. To do this he asks 'Do you have a blue VUN?', placing the nuclear stress on the last word. This incorrect placement was further compounded by an error in the sound /w/, which was pronounced as [v], probably because of L1 transfer. The outcome was that neither partner understood the request and simply repeated 'Vun?' 'Vun?', the word that the misplaced nuclear stress had drawn their attention to. Had the speaker said 'Do you have a BLUE vun?', his partners would probably have understood him despite the /w/–/v/ substitution.

Non-core features

A number of features of English pronunciation that are widely considered to be central to intelligibility for English as a Foreign Language (EFL), where the listener is a native speaker, are noticeably absent from the LFC. These non-core features include:

- /θ/, /ð/, and dark /l/
- exact vowel quality
- pitch movement (tone)
- word stress
- **stress-timing**
- vowel reduction, schwa, and weak forms
- certain features of connected speech – linking, **assimilation**, **coalescence**

I explained the reasons behind the omission of /θ/, /ð/, dark /l/, and vowel quality from the Lingua Franca Core in the previous section of this chapter. In this section I will concentrate on the three remaining non-core items. Before doing this, two points need clarifying:

1 The LFC allows for variation in the non-core items. That is to say that individual speakers are free to pronounce these items differently in the knowledge that variation here will not result in any lack of ELF intelligibility.
2 In traditional approaches to pronunciation, variation in the non-core features of the LFC is perceived, at best, as a producing a 'foreign' accent. All too often, however, variation is equated to 'error'. With ELF this is not the case. For example, if two speakers pronounce 'sold' with different vowel qualities, the difference is not a question of correctness. It is simply an instance of L2 regional variation. We do not question this sort of variation between speakers from the Inner Circle, and should not question it among speakers from the Expanding Circle in ELF communication.

Non-core items with no impact on ELF intelligibility

Pitch movement (tone)

As teachers, most of us will have had our own experience of students who seem perfectly capable of imitating a tone that has been modelled for them in class, but who are unable to use the same tone appropriately when participating in communication tasks later. This inability to transfer tones from drills and other imitation activities to acts of spontaneous speech is to do with the way tone is selected. The choice of a particular tone is made at the very beginning of the sequence of neurolinguistic processes involved in human speech. These processes do not allow speakers to consciously select tone in the same way that they can consciously articulate a particular consonant. Instead, speakers subconsciously use the same tone that would be appropriate for the same message in their mother tongue.

In addition to this neurolinguistic obstacle of subconscious L1 phonological transfer, some pronunciation experts now feel that the complex ways that tone is used in English are 'unteachable'. By this they mean that it cannot easily be generalized into rules that are simple enough to be taught effectively in the classroom.

> For pedagogical purposes, it might in fact be helpful to think about the various aspects of pronunciation along a teachability–learnability scale. Some things, say the distinction between fortis [voiceless] and lenis [voiced] consonants, are fairly easy to describe and generalise – they are teachable. Other aspects, notably the attitudinal function of intonation, are extremely dependent on individual circumstances, and therefore nearly impossible to isolate out for direct teaching. (Dalton and Seidlhofer 1994: 72–73).

A third problem with the teaching of tone is that pronunciation experts seem unable to agree as to the actual meaning of individual tones. Richard Cauldwell, for example, spent many years working at Birmingham University's English Language Research Unit, where he further developed the discourse intonation theory originally laid down by David Brazil (1997). Despite this invaluable experience, in a posting to an e-list discussion among international pronunciation experts about the meaning of different tones, Cauldwell declared that:

> after working for nearly twenty years with Discourse Intonation on examples of spontaneous speech I no longer feel that tones 'mean' anything. My view is that they are one of the ways of making your speech interestingly variable. Particular meanings already contextually present can be cued (drawn attention to) by particular realisations of a tone … but, in my view, it is a misrepresentation of reality to say that rising tones have a dominant referring meaning. Or indeed, any meaning.
> (Cauldwell 2006)

Neurolinguistically inaccessible, pedagogically unteachable, possibly meaningless – even though they are not damaging to intelligibility in ELF, the teaching of tones is not a good investment of classroom time.

Word stress

Word stress is another non-core feature where variation is unlikely to have a negative impact on ELF communication. This was clearly the case on Track 2, where Speaker C made numerous non-standard pronunciations in terms of words stress. Jenkins (2000: 150) regards word stress as 'something of a grey area', and points out that although it is reasonably important for native-speaker listeners, it rarely causes intelligibility problems among non-native speakers, except when an error in words stress occurs in combination with an error in a particular sound.

In terms of classroom practice, the full set of rules that govern word stress in English is probably unteachable because of its complexity, just as with the rules governing tone. Word stress, for example, depends on the number of syllables in a word, the origin of any suffixes, the position of a word in a phrase ('thirteen' can be stressed on either syllable depending on where it comes in an utterance), the grammatical category of a word, and so on.

However, even though our goal is ELF intelligibility, it may be worth paying some attention to word stress for two reasons:

1   The exact role of word stress in ELF is not yet fully understood, and some studies suggest that incorrect word stress could have a negative impact for both native and non-native speaker listeners (Field 2005; Rajadurai 2006).
2   Work on word stress provides us with preparatory exercises for work on nuclear stress placement. As we saw in the previous section, this is essential to ELF, and the mechanisms for perceiving and placing stress at the level of whole utterances is the same as the mechanism for perceiving and placing stress at word level.

Stress-timing

Stress-timing refers to the way that native speakers of English appear to 'squash' syllables together so that stressed syllables in the speech flow can come at more or less regular intervals. Stress-timing is a key feature of the rhythm of native-speaker English, and has come to occupy a significant place in the teaching of pronunciation. Today, in fact, it enjoys priority status in many teaching programmes, despite the fact that the division of languages into stress-timed or syllable-timed is widely questioned. Jonathan Marks, for example, points out that '[a]lthough the notion of stress-timing is often referred to in pedagogic models of English pronunciation, and forms the basis for some classroom materials for pronunciation development, there appears to be no hard evidence that it really exists' (Marks 1999: 191). Peter Roach makes the same point:

> There are many laboratory techniques for measuring time in speech, and measurement of the time intervals between stressed syllables in connected English speech has not shown the expected regularity; moreover, using the same measuring techniques on different languages, it has not been possible to show a

real difference between 'stress-timed' and 'syllable-timed' languages.
(Roach 1991: 123)

Whether it exists or not, work on stress-timing would not be a good use of classroom time for students whose target is ELF, particularly as it is not necessary for intelligibility in ELF. More importantly, the features of native-speaker pronunciation that are claimed to create the effect of stress-timing can all have a negative impact on ELF intelligibility, as we will now see in detail.

Non-core features with a negative impact on ELF intelligibility

Vowel reduction, schwa, and weak forms

In order to make stressed syllables more prominent in the speech flow, native speakers 'weaken' unstressed syllables. To do this, they replace the vowels in unstressed syllables, usually with weak vowel schwa (/ə/), although also with the short vowels /ɪ/ or /ʊ/. This process of vowel reduction is also applied to unstressed syllables within words, and this is reflected in dictionaries. The word 'chocolate', for example, can be found transcribed as both ['tʃɒk.ᵊlət] and ['tʃɒk.ᵊlɪt]. The transcription shows that the letter 'a' in the written word is pronounced either as /ə/ or /ɪ/. Similarly, the second letter 'o' in the written form is pronounced as /ə/ or, as the use of superscript indicates, is simply not pronounced at all. That is to say, it is so strongly reduced that it disappears altogether, leaving the spoken word with only two syllables.

Vowel reduction is also apparent in the unstressed pronunciations of grammatical categories such as pronouns, auxiliary verbs, articles, and prepositions. All of these words have two pronunciations in English, with a 'strong' form where the vowel is given its full value, and a 'weak' form, where the vowel is reduced. The strong form is used for citing the word, or for when it is deliberately made the nucleus of a word group for reasons of contrastive stress. Compare the vowels in the auxiliary verb 'can', in:

'I can DO it.' (unmarked stress; 'can' = weak form pronunciation = [kən])

'I CAN do it.' (contrastive stress; 'can' = strong form pronunciation = [kæn])

> Weak forms (and vowel reduction) are given considerable attention in EFL
> coursebooks and in pronunciation programmes. However, despite this
> attention the vast majority of learners, including many who become fluent
> bilinguals, use few weak forms other than 'a' and 'the'. In this sense, despite the
> fact that it is easy to formulate clear rules about weak form use, they are
> unteachable.
> (Jenkins 2000: 147).

The LFC, in its strong version, omits weak forms altogether not just because they are unteachable, but also because they are unnecessary. It is possible to stress a syllable without weakening surrounding syllables; all languages, and not just the so-called stress-timed languages, distinguish between stressed and unstressed syllables. More importantly, the use of weak forms can actually make it harder for listeners to understand what is being said since they may not perceive the weakened syllables. For this strong version of the LFC teachers, especially native-speaker teachers, should not only avoid teaching weak forms, they should avoid using them, too. In practice, this is basically a question of more careful enunciation in class, which almost automatically leads to weak forms being replaced with their strong form equivalents without affecting the correct use of nuclear stress.

A less extreme version of the LFC suggests that instead of teaching vowel reduction and weak forms, we should simply encourage learners to shorten unstressed vowels in weak forms whilst retaining their quality. At the same time, however, because many ELF users will have to deal with weak forms in the speech of native speakers that they meet in international contexts, learners should be given training in understanding speech that is characterized by weak forms and vowel reductions. That is to say, we need to differentiate between what learners are able to understand (i.e. their receptive phonological competence) and what they can do (i.e. their productive phonological competence). We will come back to this differentiation between **receptive competence** and **productive competence** in Chapter 4.

Features of connected speech

In rapid native-speaker speech, the reduction of full vowels to schwa is often accompanied by elision, assimilation, or coalescence. The outcome of these changes is that a question such as 'Where do you want to go?' can become [wedʒəwɒnəˈgəʊ]. Coalescence and a weak form and turn 'do you' into [dʒə]. Elision and a weak form convert 'want to' into [wɒnə]. These changes seldom cause problems for native speaker listeners, or for bilingual listeners. The same is not true, however, for many ELF interlocutors.

In the context of native speaker speech, 'rapid' means speeds of 350 syllables a minute or more. Three points need making here:

1. Firstly, most speakers of ELF do not reach such speeds.
2. Secondly, it has been shown that applying connected speech changes at lower speeds can make a message completely unintelligible.
3. Thirdly, what native speakers do in order to facilitate things for themselves is not automatically relevant to what users of ELF need to do in order to be intelligible to each other. In other words, even if students of ELF were to be successful in their attempts to use schwa, assimilation, or coalescence, they would not be helping their non-native listeners. Connected speech

changes, though essential for facilitating the rapid colloquial speech of native speakers, can actually decrease ELF intelligibility. Many ELF users with experience of speaking to both native and non-native speakers know this only too well.

Fine-tuning the LFC

The LFC is a description of the features that Jenkins' empirical research has shown to be essential in order to maximize intelligibility in ELF contexts. However, as she herself pointed out, there is a 'need for empirical evidence from different international groupings to confirm (or not) the detailed claims of the LFC' (Jenkins 2000: 235). Further evidence of the sort Jenkins calls for will help to fine-tune the contents in different ways.

On the one hand, further data can confirm the validity of the items in the LFC. Research into ELF in south-east Asia, for example, led David Deterding and Andy Kirkpatrick to conclude that the 'frequent use of [t] in place of /θ/ seems to be well established in the region, and it does not cause much of a problem for listeners from ASEAN countries' (2006: 395). A case study investigation into Malaysian English by Joanne Rajadurai concluded that for international intelligibility the dental plosives [t̪] and [d̪] are acceptable alternatives to the dental fricatives, /θ/ and /ð/, (2006), but that [f, v] were not as intelligible. Dental plosives are characteristic of the pronunciation of many of the speakers on the CD (see Tracks 3, 4, 9, 10, 13, 14, 19, 28, and 30), and [f] is also occasionally heard for /θ/.

Experimental research in Europe by Ruth Osimk also examined this feature of the LFC, although she found that it was the use of /s/, /z/, and not /f/, /v/ that was less intelligible than the other common substitutions of /θ/ and /ð/ (2009). On the CD, Speaker K (Japanese L1, Tracks 7 and 25) continually substitutes /θ/ and /ð/ with [s] and [z], respectively, but as she is not involved in conversation in either track, it is impossible to know if this makes her more or less intelligible. On the other hand, Speaker G (Chinese L1, Tracks 5, 14, and 22) pronounces /ð/ as [l] with no apparent impact on intelligibility.

Osimk's and Rajadurai work also investigated the importance of a number of other features of the LFC, including the aspiration of the voiceless plosives /p/, /t/, /k/, and rhoticity. Their findings confirmed the importance of aspiration for ELF intelligibility. However, with rhoticity, Rajadurai did not find any justification in the LFC's preference for rhotic accents, whilst Osimk found that her listeners 'recognised the words that contained a non-rhotic pronunciation of /r/ more often than those which contained a rhotic pronunciation of /r/' (2009: 82). This clearly differs from the LFC, although in her conclusions Osimk admits that 'it is not clear if the results point towards a higher intelligibility of non-rhotic /r/' (ibid.), and she suggests that this is an area that is worth further investigation.

Another way that further empirical data of the sort Jenkins' called for will help to fine-tune the LFC is in revealing items that need to be added to it because of specific, local pronunciation issues. In her study, for example, Rajadurai noted that Malaysian English is characterized by an excessive use of **glottal stops**. She argued that these, whilst not a threat to intelligibility in themselves, have the effect of shortening the preceding vowel, which does threaten intelligibility. Examples of this can be heard on Track 26. Comparing her findings with the LFC, Rajadurai suggests that for Malaysian speakers of English, an additional requirement will be to avoid the use of glottal stops.

In another piece of small-scale research, Ricardo da Sili Silva examined the extent to which the LFC explained miscommunication between Brazilian-Portuguese speakers of English and a range of non-native speaker listeners. The results of his study largely supported the LFC but, like Rajadurai, suggested the need to add one further feature. The English of speakers whose first language is Brazilian-Portuguese is characterized by 'the strong reduction of final syllable vowels' (da Silva 1999: 24). The result of this is that 'happen' sounds like 'happy' or 'hap', 'party' like 'part', or 'factory' like 'fact'. For Brazilian-Portuguese speakers, then, the LFC would need to be fine-tuned to take into account the need to avoid this characteristic strong vowel reduction, and to retain the full syllable values of words. There is a very clear example of this on Track 28, where 'fancy' is pronounced as [fæns].

In a third study, Simon Cole investigated the importance of vowel quality, a non-core item. He monitored interactions between non-native speakers from different first-language backgrounds in both classroom and social settings in Japan. There were limitations to Coles' research: the interactions were prompted by written questions and so were not spontaneous; the interactions were not followed up by interviews and the opportunity for the speakers to listen to what they had said; the quantity of data was very limited. Aware of these limitations, Cole nevertheless tentatively concluded that 'some learners, depending on their L1, need instruction on specific vowel sounds to raise awareness of them' (Cole 2002: 33).

The above research, and future research, provides new data that may mean that the LFC will have to be modified. A number of speakers on the CD, for example, pronounce the '-ing' at the end of words as [ŋk] instead of /ŋ/ (Tracks 6, 19, 21, 27, 28, and 30). Further data could demonstrate that this consonant substitution is acceptable in ELF, and the LFC would need to change to take this into account. This should neither surprise nor dismay us. The LFC is not a closed set of rules that is impermeable to what is happening in ELF. Rather, it is the part of an on-going empirical description of how non-native speakers achieve mutual intelligibility. This means that it will evolve as ELF evolves, and as more is learned about the nature of the pronunciation of English as a Lingua Franca.

Going beyond the Core

In terms of going beyond the LFC, Jenkins outlines a five-stage programme that will take learners from being able to communicate effectively in lingua franca settings (Stages 1 to 3), to being able to communicate effectively in a wide range of situations, and with both native and non-native speaker interlocutors (Stages 4 and 5). Jenkins' five stages are:

1 Addition of core items to the learner's productive and receptive repertoire
2 Addition of a range of L2 English accents to the learner's receptive repertoire
3 Addition of accommodation skills
4 Addition of non-core items to the learner's receptive repertoire
5 Addition of a range of L1 English accents to the learner's receptive repertoire.
   (Jenkins 2000: 209–211)

Stage 1 in Jenkins' programme will be the initial focus for any teacher starting work on the pronunciation of ELF for the first time with a new group, whilst competence at the level of Stage 2 will help learners to deal with the different accents they will come across in ELF encounters. The accents on the CD that accompanies this book will allow you to work on this second stage, and in Chapter 4 you will find activities designed to help learners in this area.

Accommodation skills will equip learners to actively adjust their pronunciation in order to help their interlocutors. Because they are important for ELF communication, we will look at them in detail in Chapter 4.

The last two stages of Jenkins' programme take into account that native speakers will sometimes be present in ELF settings. Many of these native speakers will have non-standard (regional) accents, and some may not be good at adjusting their pronunciation to the setting. Competence in Stages 4 and 5 will allow non-native speakers to accommodate more easily to the demands of native speakers who are unaware of ELF pronunciation, or who are unable to approximate to ELF norms.

An ELF approach does not respond to the needs of learners whose goal is a native-speaker accent. If learners are clear about wanting this, then it is our job to help them. However, as I have pointed out elsewhere:

> even when a learner's goal is a NS accent, nothing in the LFC is 'unnecessary' or constitutes an 'obstacle' for the learner. That is to say, nothing needs 'unlearning'.

The opposite is not true; speakers competent in a standard NS accent such as RP, need to avoid using certain features of their accent, especially certain suprasegmental features, in order to be intelligible in ELF settings. (Walker 2008: 9)

We can look at the LFC two ways. We can see it as an incomplete set of native-speaker pronunciation features, or we can see it as a complete set of features for international intelligibility. If we choose the first way, the LFC will make a very good foundation for all learners. They will be very well placed to progress to a native-speaker accent once they are competent in the LFC. On the other hand, if we see the LFC in ELF terms, we can guide our learners through Jenkins' five-stage programme. By doing this, we will steadily increase their ability to deal with the wide range of accents, both non-native speaker and native-speaker. Either way, the LFC is an excellent foundation for learners wherever they are, and whatever their long-term pronunciation goals.

Summary

In this chapter I have briefly looked at some of the early ideas on priorities for teaching English pronunciation and I have introduced the Lingua Franca Core, the only list that has intelligibility in non-native speaker interaction as its goal. I have presented the different features of the Lingua Franca Core in detail, and have then looked at the non-core features. I have shown how the non-core features allow regional variation, which can help speakers to retain their first-language identity if they wish to do so. I have also shown how some non-core items can be damaging to international intelligibility. In the last part of the chapter I have indicated that the LFC will evolve as new data on ELF communication becomes available. I have also suggested that the LFC admits small adjustments that will respond to the demands of different first-language backgrounds. In Chapter 5, I will take a closer look at the role of the learner's first language. Before that, in Chapter 3, I will discuss some of the issues that might arise if you decide to adopt the LFC in your own teaching.

Further reading

On the Lingua Franca Core

Jenkins, J. 2000. *The Phonology of English as a Lingua Franca.* Oxford: Oxford University Press.

Jenkins, J. 2003. 'Community, Currency and the Lingua Franca Core'. TESOL-SPAIN Newsletter 27 Spring: 3–6. Available on the Internet at www.tesol-spain.org/newsletter/jenkins.pdf

On nuclear stress placement and meaning

Brazil, D. 1994. *Pronunciation for Advanced Learners of English.* Cambridge: Cambridge University Press.

Celce-Murcia, M., D. M. Brinton, and **J. M. Goodwin.** 1996. *Teaching Pronunciation. A Reference for Teachers of English to Speakers of Other Languages.* Cambridge: Cambridge University Press.

Dalton, D. and **B. Seidlhofer.** 1994. *Pronunciation.* Oxford: Oxford University Press.

On the variation of length in English vowels

Gimson, A. C. and **A. Cruttenden.** 2009. *An Introduction to the Pronunciation of English* (7th edn.). London: Edward Arnold.

On weak forms, word stress, stress-timing, and connected speech

Avery, P. and **S. Ehrlich.** 1992. *Teaching American English Pronunciation.* Oxford: Oxford University Press.

Roach, P. 2009. *English Phonetics and Phonology* (4th edn.). Cambridge: Cambridge University Press.

Endnote

page 34: RP and General Australian English distinguish between long and short vowels. American English, in contrast, describes its vowels using a tense–lax system as a key feature. However, in the standard American accent (GA), the tense vowels are significantly longer than the lax vowels. In this sense, GA tense–lax differences parallel the long–short distinction in RP and General Australian.

3 ADOPTING AN ELF APPROACH

Introduction

Adopting an ELF approach to teaching pronunciation generates a number of legitimate concerns. Some of these are concerns that Directors of Studies or Heads of School might express. Others arise from doubts that teachers have. Learners, too, may have reservations about new goals. Part A of this chapter addresses these concerns and covers issues such as standards (Concerns 1–4), the need for a model (Concerns 5–6), and the ethics of choosing goals for learners (Concerns 7–8). Concern 9 looks at how teachers feel about ELF, and Concern 10 at how learners perceive both native-speaker and ELF accents as goals.

Nobody, of course, would adopt any approach to any activity in life if this did not bring clear benefits. This is also true for the LFC and ELF, and Part B of this chapter looks at six of these benefits in detail. Benefits 1 and 2 are about the workload and high achievability inherent in an ELF approach, whilst Benefits 3–5 reassess the usefulness of the learner's L1 pronunciation. Finally, Benefit 6 examines the validity of NNS teachers as instructors for the teaching of the pronunciation of ELF.

Part A – Reactions to adopting an ELF approach

Concern 1 – An ELF approach will lower standards

Concerns about standards are natural and need addressing, especially when they revolve around the idea that teaching through the LFC is the same as admitting that anything our learners pronounce is correct, that 'anything goes'. It should be clear from Chapter 2, however, that this idea is simply not true. The Lingua Franca Core is just as demanding as native-speaker models in terms of the correct pronunciation of the consonants of English, for example. Learners will also need to achieve high levels of competence in the other features of the LFC. In other words, pronunciation for ELF sets high standards, but these are not the same standards as those required of learners hoping to achieve competence in a native-speaker accent.

The situation is rather like that of the classes in a dance academy. Some students will be learning ballroom dancing, whilst others will be studying modern dance. Both dance styles share many common features, though each has certain skills and techniques that make it different from the other. But both dance styles require students to work to high standards, even though the standards for one style are not the same as those of the other.

The business of setting standards is central to all learning processes. However, the approach to standards proposed by this handbook is based on the belief that it is important to set achievable standards. Michael Swan, a leading ELT materials and coursebook writer, shares this approach:

> People sometimes feel that the best way of achieving a good standard is to aim for perfection: we will inevitably fall short of our aim, but we will at least do better than if we started out by setting our sights lower. I don't believe that this is a valid view of things. What actually happens if you aim for perfection in pronunciation work is that valuable time gets wasted on unimportant points, and that students get discouraged as they continually fail to reach the standard that was set for them.
> (Swan 1993: 8)

The setting of unrealistic standards may explain why Speaker H (CD Track 5), requested that her name should not be associated in any way with the recordings of her speaking in English. Despite sounding like a native speaker, she explained that she was ashamed of her accent, and didn't want to risk being identified by friends or teachers.

Another problem with setting a native-speaker accent as the goal for pronunciation was expressed in an interview about feelings on English as a Lingua Franca.

> … when we were taught in school, it's it's quite strict if you pronounce – you didn't pronounce, pronounce well enough or it's not British style. So we will – many people can't er dare not to talk in class because (.) because they – we were afraid that we will be laughed at if w – we have Chinese accent or we didn't imitate exactly British English…
> (Jenkins 2007: 222)

Two additional studies (Walker 1999; León Meis 2000) suggest that because of a sense of inadequacy with respect to their own accents, non-native speaker teachers lack confidence in teaching pronunciation, or worse still, simply do not teach it. Nor is the problem restricted to non-native speakers. The use of the prestige native-speaker accent as the standard for pronunciation can also create problems of confidence for native-speaker teachers with regional accents. How do you teach English pronunciation using RP as your model if you are from Scotland or Wales, for example? Similarly, a New Jersey accent differs in several respects from General American (GA). Faced with this conflict, some teachers choose their own non-standard accent as the model. This brings them into conflict with the published materials. Other teachers, however, limit any work on pronunciation to answering students' questions as they arise, and to hoping that learners will 'pick it up' by themselves. This can have a very negative impact on standards.

Summing up, standards are central to good teaching. Taking an ELF approach to pronunciation is not a lowering of standards, but a change to different, more achievable standards. Approaches based on native-speaker accents do not necessarily produce better learning, and can lead to standards being abandoned by learners who see this goal as unachievable, or by teachers who are intimidated by these standards because of the conflict they produce with their own accent.

Concern 2 – An ELF approach will make errors acceptable

Another part of the concern over falling standards arises from confusion as to what constitutes an error in pronunciation. Errors, of course, lie at the heart of language learning, and students expect teachers to correct them. However, teachers need to be sure that what they are correcting is, in fact, an error. For instance, if a learner has chosen a native-speaker accent as his goal, and pronounces the word 'string' as /e'strɪŋ/ and not /strɪŋ/, this is an error. The teacher will need to point this out, and help the learner to eliminate the inserted /e/ sound. However, as we have just seen, ELF has its own standards. By these standards, neither /e'strɪŋ/ nor /sɪ'trɪŋ/ are errors. Instead, they are examples of the successful application of a strategy designed to ensure intelligibility in ELF communication, which is the learner's goal. On the CD Speaker 1 applies this strategy on different occasions (Track 6: lines 2, 41, and 42).

The key to what constitutes an error in ELF lies in the difference in the goals of English as a foreign or second language, and English as a Lingua Franca. With the first of these, what native speakers do is correct, and variation from the chosen native-speaker accent is an error. For pronunciation in ELF, however, an error is determined by the requirements of the LFC. These are the result of what ELF users have been seen to do in order to be intelligible. If a speaker pronounces the items in the LFC correctly, then his or her pronunciation is error free, even if the accent is quite markedly different from that of a native speaker.

Another concern about standards is the belief that ELF pronunciation is just another name for 'learner English', the vast area of proficiency between being a language beginner and being bilingual. The problem with this belief is that it fails to recognize that people can reach the end of the English language learning process without necessarily sounding like native speakers. And to deny this is to condemn most students to lifelong failure. This is especially true with pronunciation, where very few second language learners ever acquire native-speaker competence. However hard they try, what they pronounce is not identical to the idealized native-speaker performance that supposedly constitutes the end of the learning process. Because of this, 'when measured against the standard of a native speaker, few EFL learners will be perfect. Within traditional EFL methodology there is an inbuilt ideological positioning of the student as outsider and failure – however proficient they become' (Graddol 2006: 83). This situation is undesirable.

Concern 3 – The LFC is a reduced version of native-speaker pronunciation

In Part B of this chapter, we will see how the Lingua Franca Core constitutes a lighter workload for learners compared to the goal of a native-speaker accent. Giving learners a lighter workload, however, is not the same as giving them a reduced version of something. Scottish English, for example, has fewer vowels than RP, the prestige accent in the UK. But it would be a mistake to draw the conclusion that Scottish English is a 'less-than-complete' version of RP. The same is true for General American English, which also has fewer vowels than RP, but which nobody would consider to be reduced, less-than-complete, or 'deficient'.

The problem here is the confusion of 'deficient' and 'different'. As the linguists Madalena Cruz-Ferreira and Sunita Anna Abraham point out, when we try to describe a language or language variety:

> saying that variety X 'lacks' a feature Y is in a sense meaningless … If you were describing humans, it would make little sense to say that human beings lack four legs. The human locomotive system consists of two legs. So, the implied comparison to locomotive systems comprising four legs (e.g. cheetahs, dogs, elephants) is irrelevant. The human locomotive system does not lack anything given its locomotive purposes.
> (Cruz-Ferreira and Abraham 2006: 39)

Cruz-Ferreira and Abraham's analogy brings out an important point; 'systems' exist or are created to fulfil purposes. The purpose of the LFC is to facilitate mutual intelligibility between speakers of English as a Lingua Franca, while allowing for the expression of L1 identity. When we view it in this way, as a system with a specific purpose, we see that it does not 'lack' anything. Nor can it, since it has been constructed by studying how mutual intelligibility is maintained between non-native speakers. By its nature, then, the LFC is a complete, on-going system, and is the right one for ELF communication.

Concern 4 – ELF means variation, but mutual intelligibility means a common standard

There is no single, common standard among native speakers of English, but when they come together, there is usually a high degree of mutual intelligibility. How does this happen, given the wide variation in their accents? How can a Canadian-born speaker of English understand a New Zealand speaker whose accent makes 'bet' sound like 'bit'? The answer lies in a number of factors, as I explained in Chapter 1, but when native speakers talk to each other they:

- start from the assumption that the interlocutor's accent is legitimate. They do not assume that the 'difference' in the speaker's accent makes him or her automatically unintelligible.
- are aided by the desire to understand each other. I have already discussed how intelligibility is not dependent solely on what the speaker does. The listener must participate, too, and must accept part of the responsibility for successful communication.
- tolerate variation. As soon as they hear the other person's accent, native speakers begin to make adjustments to allow for any differences there might be between their own and their interlocutor's accent. Obviously, the more experience they have with a particular accent, the more easily they make these adjustments. But on the occasions when they are not familiar with an accent, they actively use a range of listener strategies to collaboratively maintain intelligibility.

The same factors will hold true for ELF communication if we apply the ideas in this book to our teaching. It is true that there will be variation in ELF accents, just as with native speakers. But if these accents deal successfully with the items in the LFC, and if speakers of ELF learn to be tolerant of a range of accents, and to accommodate to each other appropriately (see Chapter 4), then mutual intelligibility will be maintained between non-native speakers, just as it is between native speakers.

Concern 5 – If you take away native-speaker accents, you leave learners without a model

Without a stable model, learners will have nothing on which to base their attempts at pronunciation. Clearly, this is an unacceptable situation. However, an ELF approach does not leave learners without a model. As we saw in Chapter 2, it simply identifies different aspects of English accents as being:

- essential for lingua franca intelligibility
- not essential, but not damaging to lingua franca intelligibility
- damaging to lingua franca intelligibility.

If they wish, teachers can use one of the standard native-speaker accents as a model for features that are essential for ELF (i.e. from group A). Similarly, they can also use the same model for any of the non-core features from group B that their learners have expressed a desire to master. However, they have to avoid the features in group C because they have a negative impact on intelligibility in ELF.

Alternatively, teachers can use competent ELF speakers as a model, although at the time of writing this book, very few pronunciation courses include ELF accents. In this respect, the more proficient speakers on the CD that accompanies this book may help teachers to remedy this situation until a wider range of ELF accents in generally available, either through coursebook CDs or the Internet. Of course, the teacher's own pronunciation can be an equally valid model. In fact, teachers who are competent users of English in lingua franca communication are perfect models for their learners. This is especially true of non-native speaker teachers, as we will see in Part B of this chapter.

Of course, a teacher who is not competent in the items of the LFC is not a good model. But then nor is a teacher with a vocabulary of only 2,000 words, or with only an elementary knowledge of English grammar. Language teaching requires its professionals to have high levels of competence in the language they teach. But teachers who are fluent users of English for lingua franca communication, who are able to understand a range of different accents, and who can accommodate their pronunciation to different listeners, are ideally situated to be models for their students.

Concern 6 – You cannot teach an accent that nobody has

And yet what do we do with RP? It has been estimated that less than three per cent of the UK population speaks English with an RP accent (Crystal 1995). Henry Daniels refers to these as the 'phantom speakers' of English (Daniels 1995: 7); you travel around the UK, he explains, but almost never come across them. To get round the problem of asking learners to imitate an accent that is seldom heard, he advocates that they 'listen to a selection of regional pronunciations, choose the one they like, and make that their target' (ibid.: 7). ELF makes a similar recommendation, although the regional accents that learners can choose from are non-native speaker accents. The only limitation to this is that the person acting as a model should be able to produce all of the features of the LFC as and when necessary in the classroom, and should know how to adjust their speech if necessary so as to avoid using the features of native-speaker accents that can make them unintelligible in ELF contexts (see Chapter 2 for details).

A second thing we need to remember is that the LFC is not a single accent. Rather, it is a set of phonological items that are central to intelligibility in ELF. It is perfectly possible to teach these items even though they do not represent an accent as such. Moreover, once we have identified which of these items are already present in a learner's first language accent, we only need to focus on the 'missing' items. This is a relatively simple task in many cases. Chapter 5 gives detailed explanations on how to do this for a range of different language backgrounds.

Concern 7 – It is wrong to impose an ELF approach on students

The idea of imposing a specific pronunciation on learners is the antithesis of good teaching, but an ELF approach to pronunciation does not attempt to impose anything on anybody.

> ELF is only being proposed where the target interaction community is an international, i.e. largely NNS community. Although ELF researchers believe that this is the most likely situation for the majority of learners in the 21st century, they are well aware that some learners will interact primarily with NSs, and accept that for them EFL is the appropriate goal. ELF researchers also believe that the choice of goal is entirely the learner's, and accept that even a learner whose target community is an ELF one may prefer a native rather than an ELF variety as their goal. All that is asked is that learners are able to make their choice in full possession of the socio-linguistic facts.
> (Jenkins 2004: 36)

It could be argued that up to now with pronunciation it has been standard native-speaker accents, especially RP and GA, that have been imposed on learners. Very few teachers systematically ask students what their goals are in pronunciation. As a result, these accents have been unwittingly 'imposed' on learners. Speaker E, for example, describes how in high school in Russia his New Zealand teachers taught him 'a really British accent' (Track 3). In this respect, the LFC, rather than an imposition, is an element of increased choice. However, in order to make their choice, learners need to understand what ELF is, to be 'in full possession of the socio-linguistic facts'. When they are, it is quite likely that some will choose to follow an ELF approach to pronunciation. But even if they choose a native-speaker accent as their goal, they will now be doing this through informed choice, which is an improvement on the situation up to now.

Concern 8 – A bad accent gives a bad impression

Some people have likened having a bad accent to wearing old clothes to an interview – you give the interviewers a bad first impression. Others have suggested that if academics, scientists, and engineers have poor pronunciation, their colleagues will assume that their professional work is also poor. In my opinion, these lines of argument are flawed.

Sometimes when we say that a speaker has a 'bad accent', it is because we find the speaker unintelligible. This is a serious problem, but it is a problem of pronunciation, not accent. As I explained in Chapter 1, accent and intelligibility are not the same thing. A speaker can be perfectly intelligible even when they have what feels like a very noticeable accent to the listener. But if a speaker is genuinely unintelligible, this is because they are not pronouncing the sounds or other features of English appropriately.

When a person uses adjectives like 'good', 'bad', 'broken', 'faint', or 'heavy' to describe an accent, this is quite a different situation. Accents are neither good nor bad, as linguists repeatedly remind us. They are simply accents. In describing a speaker's accent as 'bad' or 'heavy', the listener is consciously or otherwise expressing a personal opinion about the speaker's accent.

Communication, especially spoken communication, is a collaborative act, as we saw in Chapter 1. That is to say that both the speaker and the listener share responsibility for success in their attempts to understand each other. American linguist Rosina Lippi-Green uses the term 'communicative burden' to refer to this joint responsibility (1997). When we talk to someone, she explains, we make a series of social evaluations of that person based upon their language, their accent, and other sociolinguistic characteristics. We then pass this information through an 'ideological filter', and as a result of this subjective process we take up a position with respect to how much we are willing to share the communicative burden.

Most of the time, we agree to carry our share of the communicative burden. Sometimes, if we feel especially positive about the person we are talking to, or if the purpose of communication is especially important to us, we will accept a disproportionate amount of the burden.

Conversely, if we do not feel positive about the social status of the person we are talking to, we may reject our share of the burden, claiming that the speaker is unintelligible because of their bad accent. In other words, the 'breakdown of communication is due not so much to accent as it is to negative social evaluation of the accent in question, and a rejection of the communicative burden' (Lippi-Green 1997: 71). Of the speakers on the CD, Speaker G is generally less proficient than most of the others. This is not surprising given that English is his third language, and that he was living in Spain at the time of the recording. But as he converses with Speaker R, she clearly demonstrates her willingness to share the communicative burden (Track 14: see especially lines 35–38).

Studies by linguists in Canada on accentedness, intelligibility, and comprehensibility (Munro 2003) have reached a similar conclusion to Lippi-Green's. The rejection of the communicative burden occurs when one of the parties involved feels socially, economically, or ideologically superior to the other. In

ELF this can happen because the relationship between two Expanding Circle countries has historically been one of antagonism and distrust. However, the rejection of the communicative burden occurs more often when a speaker from the Inner Circle is making a judgement about the accent of a speaker from the Outer or Expanding Circles. There even seems to be some sort of hierarchy operating here, with speakers from Asian countries suffering rejection more than those from European countries (Jenkins 2007).

Whatever the exact circumstances, the mechanism is the same. The socially, politically, or economically dominant listener describes the speaker's accent as 'bad' and then (subconsciously) may use this subjective assessment to free themselves of their responsibility in the process of understanding the other person, despite the speaker's accent being perfectly intelligible.

Concern 9 – Most teachers prefer a native-speaker accent

Teachers' attitudes to the idea of adopting an ELF approach vary. In the UK, Ivor Timmis studied what teachers felt about accents. He did this by distributing a questionnaire to native- and non-native speaker teachers at an ELT conference in Ireland. After analysing 180 responses from teachers from 45 different countries, he found that they were fairly equally divided between two options. A small majority preferred the option of international intelligibility, whilst one-third of the teachers he surveyed showed no preference for either option. Interestingly, the native-speaker teachers favoured international intelligibility more than their non-native speaker colleagues.

In a different study, I surveyed 350 teachers in northern Spain (Walker 1999). I found that given a choice between a range of native- and non-native speaker accents for their own ideal pronunciation, three-quarters of the mostly non-native speaker teachers chose one of the native-speaker accents. However, less than ten per cent of teachers considered a 'good' (i.e. near-native) accent to be an important skill for pronunciation teaching. These two opposing responses suggest some sort of unresolved conflict around the role of native-speaker accents in the ELT classroom. It seems strange to choose this accent for themselves, yet at the same time not consider it to be an important teaching skill.

In a third study, Sara Hannam invited native-speaker teachers who lived and worked in the UK, and non-native speaker teachers who lived and worked in Greece, to rate different English accents (2006). These included various regional British accents and a Greek English accent. She found that:

> the majority of British participants were very critical of stigmatized British accents such as Liverpool and Belfast. 85% of participants said they would not use either of these particular accents in the language classroom. However, almost all Greek participants were positive about Regional British accents, with 100% saying they would use the Liverpool accent in the classroom and 75% the Belfast accent. Greek participants were much more critical of the Greek English

accent, with only 50% saying they would be happy to use this as a model. British participants were, however, 100% positive about using the Greek English accent as a model in the language classroom.
(Hannam 2006: 4–5).

In an in-depth study, Jennifer Jenkins (2007) surveyed teachers in 12 Expanding Circle countries. Of the 326 teachers who responded, the vast majority (300) were non-native speakers of English. Jenkins asked the teachers to rank 10 native- and non-native speaker accents, indicating which were the best in a whole-world context. The teachers were also asked to rate these accents in terms of correctness, pleasantness, international acceptability, and aesthetic qualities. Two questions in the survey involved labelling and commenting on accents from countries shown on a map of the world. Jenkins found that:

> NS accents, and particularly UK and US accents, are preferred in all respects by this large group of expanding circle respondents, when evaluated overtly in the rating and ranking tasks. They are also highly valued for their perceived correctness and intelligibility in the map-labelling tasks and commentaries, although not necessarily quite as much in terms of their aesthetic qualities.
> (ibid. 2007: 186)

The overall picture from these studies is that non-native speaker teachers value native-speaker accents highly. As one teacher put it in Timmis' survey, 'It is an ideal that every teacher dreams of' (2002: 243). There would seem to be two obvious explanations for this. The first of these revolves around the prestige that having a native-speaker accent can give a teacher. Just as good teachers desire to be as competent as possible in terms of grammar or vocabulary, so they wish to be equally competent in terms of pronunciation. In the current climate, this competence is seen in terms of how close a teacher comes to having a native-speaker accent. This may explain why Speaker F says that she would 'feel more confident with [her] English' if she had a native-speaker accent (Track 3: lines 9–10).

A second reason for non-native speaker teachers to value a native-speaker accent so highly is probably the natural consequence of the personal commitment needed to approximate such an accent. If a teacher has invested a lot of time and energy perfecting a native-speaker accent, it is only natural that he or she should prefer this over the currently less prestigious non-native speaker alternatives.

The situation regarding teachers and native-speaker accents may well change as ELF becomes more widely accepted. When Jennifer Jenkins interviewed non-native speaker teachers about ELF, part of the interview invited them to think about the future:

> [W]hen the interviews turned to discussion of the future, many participants were vociferous in expressing their views about both what needed to change so

that ELF would be accepted, and the positive effect its acceptance would have on their confidence as teachers.
(ibid. 2007: 226)

It could be, then, that as ELF becomes more widely accepted, the currently 'hidden' competence of non-native speaker teachers will finally be recognized (see Benefit 6). At the same time, the restricted competence of many native-speaker teachers in accommodating their pronunciation to international contexts will become more apparent. If this happens, non-native speaker teachers' confidence in the validity of their own pronunciation as a model for their students should improve.

Concern 10 – Most learners say that they want to sound like a native speaker

A number of studies suggest that students want to sound like a native speaker. In one carried out in Austria by Christiane Dalton-Puffer, Gunther Kaltenboeck, and Ute Smit (1997), advanced level students of English were asked to rate unidentified samples of native and non-native speech. They rated the RP accent highest and the Austrian-English accent lowest, even though this was the accent closest to their own. GA was rated highest by students who had travelled to the USA, perhaps because of their familiarity with the accent.

When Ivor Timmis carried out his survey of teachers, he also looked at learners. His study explored preferences for native-speaker norms not just in terms of pronunciation, but also in terms of goals for written and spoken grammar. Overall, Timmis concluded there was still some desire 'to conform to native-speaker norms, and this desire is not necessarily restricted to those who use, or anticipate using English primarily with native speakers' (Timmis 2002: 248).

In terms specifically of pronunciation goals, two thirds of Timmis' 400 respondents showed a preference for native-speaker competence. However, when students from the Outer Circle countries of India, Pakistan, and South Africa were analysed separately, these figures were reversed, with almost two thirds choosing to be internationally intelligible but retaining their mother-tongue accent. As we saw in Chapter 1, Outer Circle countries no longer look to the Inner Circle for norms as to correct or incorrect English. They now have their own norms, and few people would think of asking speakers from the Outer Circle to 'improve' their accent and learn to pronounce English with a standard British or American accent. This could account for the confidence these speakers showed in choosing the option of international intelligibility over native-speaker competence.

In a study in the USA, Julie Scales and her colleagues set out to analyse the perceptions that 37 English language learners and 10 non-native undergraduate students had of different accents. Four accents were selected: two were native speaker (GA and British RP) and two were non-native speaker (Chinese English and Mexican English). Scales found that '[w]hen asked to choose between wanting to be easily understood and having a native accent, the majority (62%) of English learners stated that their goal was to sound like a native speaker, compared with 38% who listed intelligibility as their pronunciation goal' (2006: 723). On the one hand, these results support the idea that learners prefer a native-speaker accent as their goal. On the other hand, the learners who volunteered to take part in the study were actually in the USA, either on an intensive ESOL programme, or studying at a major American university. In this respect, it can be argued that both groups were already positively oriented towards native-speaker norms, and so might not be truly representative of ELF users of English.

One of the most interesting results of this study, however, was that only 29 per cent of the respondents were able to actually identify the American accent that they had declared was their goal. And in one case a learner from Columbia commented that her Asian classmates were difficult to understand. However, in a blind listening task 'she chose the Chinese accent as the easiest to understand and the one she liked most' (ibid.: 734). Moreover, in the interviews that Scales and her colleagues carried out with 11 of the respondents, most of them were unable to explain why they had chosen a native-speaker accent as their goal. Finally, the researchers observed that the participants in the interviews were not aware of the issues behind the choice of accent in a world where English has become the lingua franca. 'Instead, the majority assumed that the native accent was a reasonable and obvious choice to strive for' (ibid.: 735).

All of these studies illustrate that it is not easy to determine learners' preferences with exactitude. An early study by Don Porter and Sue Garvin (1989) looked at how important learners thought a native-speaker accent was. The learners in question were in the UK on a course in English for Academic Purposes. Coinciding with the studies we have just looked at, three quarters of them thought that a native-speaker accent was 'fairly important' or 'very important'. However, later in the same questionnaire, 71 per cent of the learners agreed with the statement 'I need a pronunciation of English which is good enough for people to understand me. It is an unnecessary waste of time to have a pronunciation which is better than this' (1989: 14). Porter and Garvin explain this mismatch by suggesting that it reflects 'a certain pessimism in accepting that, as a luxury, native-like pronunciation, just like a Mercedes or BMW, is something they would very much like to have, but the realities of life dictate against it at present' (ibid.). In addition, the use of 'better' shows that these learners assume (not surprisingly in 1989) that a native-speaker accent is ideal for all communication in English. In Chapter 1 we saw that this is not the case.

Learners' choice of goals will also be conditioned by how they see English being used, and how they see themselves using English. Elizabeth Erling, for example, looked at what students at the Freie Universität Berlin did with their English (2006). She found that they regularly used it in a variety of international contexts, and were in regular contact with different Englishes, including many non-native Englishes. Her study revealed that a significant number of students were not interested in English as a language to connect to the USA or the UK. It is unlikely, then, that these same students will be very interested in acquiring native-speaker pronunciation.

What learners aim for in terms of pronunciation will also be strongly influenced by what their teachers offer them. In his work in Japan, Simon Coles (2002) decided to make the difference between EFL and ELF goals clear to his students. He found that his students were 'pleasantly surprised' to find that they had a choice between ELF and NS English. This coincides with my own experience with students and non-native speaker language teachers in Spain over the last few years. Overall, as learners become more and more aware of the role of English as a Lingua Franca, and of the validity of the LFC as a pronunciation goal, their preference for native-speaker accents diminishes. However, until awareness of ELF is more widespread, most learners of English will assume that the only meaningful goal is native-like pronunciation.

Part B – The benefits of taking an LFC approach

There are a number of important benefits for both teachers and students from taking an ELF approach to pronunciation. This second part of Chapter 3 looks at each of these in turn.

Benefit 1 – A lighter workload

In Chapter 1, I suggested that an ELF approach to pronunciation brings a lighter workload for both teachers and learners. Many ELT courses contemplate a total contact time of around 120 hours a year. If 10 per cent of that time is spent on pronunciation, this is only 12 hours. In reality, few teachers spend 10 per cent of classroom time on pronunciation, making even 12 hours an optimistic figure. With so little time for pronunciation in the average classroom, a lighter workload is an important benefit.

How exactly does an ELF approach lighten the workload? This is illustrated by Table 3.1 on page 62, which compares the targets of a typical pronunciation syllabus for English as a Foreign Language (EFL) with a syllabus for ELF pronunciation. The contents for the EFL syllabus represent items that are typically covered in pronunciation courses at an approximately intermediate level. The shaded areas in the ELF column on the right of the table represent the pronunciation features that are not part of the Lingua Franca Core. The lighter workload that comes from not working on these items would free time for more concentrated practice of the LFC items, and other teaching priorities.

	Traditional EFL syllabus (native speaker oriented)	ELF syllabus (oriented towards international intelligibility)
1 Consonants	All sounds	All sounds except for the dental fricatives, /θ/, /ð/, and dark /l/
	Rhotic or non-rhotic /r/ BrE or AmE intervocalic /t/ Aspiration of /p/, /t/, /k/ in word-initial position	Rhotic /r/ only BrE intervocalic /t/ Aspiration of /p/, /t/, /k/ in word-initial position
2 Clusters	Important in all positions Elision of /t/ and /d/ only for advanced learners	Important at the beginnings and in the middle of words. Elision of /t/ and /d/ for all learners
3 Vowels	Quality – all vowels and diphthongs as close as possible to the chosen native-speaker standard accent	Quality – L2 variation acceptable if consistent
	Quantity – length as a characteristic of each vowel	Quantity – 1) long-short contrasts; 2) shortening effect of voiceless consonants important
4 Schwa and vowel reduction	Essential to word stress and rhythm	Not desirable. Can reduce intelligibility
5 Word stress	Very important	Not important
6 Stress-timing	Very important	Not important
7 Weak forms	Essential for stress-timing	Not desirable. Can reduce intelligibility
8 Connected speech features	Elision, assimilation, coalescence, and linking essential for stress-timing	Not important. Can reduce intelligibility
9 Nuclear stress	Important, but mainly for upper-intermediate or advanced levels	Essential
10 Tone	Essential for indicating attitude and grammatical structure	Not important

Table 3.1 A comparison of EFL and ELF targets (Adapted from Jenkins 2002: 99)

It is important here to point out another difference between the EFL and ELF syllabuses. Because of the huge workload that traditional EFL syllabuses involve, there have been many attempts by pronunciation experts at selecting priorities for learners (Jenner 1989; Bradford 1990; Gilbert 1999). An ELF syllabus, in contrast, lightens the workload not by leaving parts of the programme for some other moment, but by focusing on those aspects that are most important for intelligibility in international contexts. The LFC is a complete programme in its own right, and the non-core areas are not missing elements from the syllabus. Rather they are areas where L1 influence is part of the internationally intelligible, regional accent that each speaker has in ELF contexts.

Benefit 2 – Increased progress and achievability

A second benefit of an ELF approach is the sense of progress it generates. For learners moving on to higher levels of pronunciation with a traditional approach, 'progress' essentially means going back to the same areas as those in Table 3.1, but at a higher level. In contrast, with an ELF approach, competence in the LFC is the gateway to new skills, such as learning to accommodate your pronunciation to your interlocutor, or learning to deal with accent variation. In this respect, the sense of progress in ELF is more tangible. (Details of how to programme learning for ELF pronunciation are given in Chapter 6.)

Part of the feeling of progress comes from the achievability of the items in the LFC. As we saw in Chapter 2, many features that are essential in a traditional EFL syllabus are largely unteachable. This was the case with tone and stress-timing, and with the use of weak forms and certain connected speech changes. In contrast, most of the items in the LFC are teachable, with classroom teaching leading to learning. The consonants are the obvious example of this, especially if we remember that the two most difficult consonants, the dental fricatives /θ/ and /ð/, are not ELF requirements. Vowels, of course, are notoriously unteachable, but because the LFC focuses on vowel length rather than exact quality, learners are once again offered a more achievable goal.

Intonation is one of the least teachable aspects of pronunciation, although with the part of intonation that is included in the LFC (nuclear stress placement) the situation is not thought to be so impossible:

> As far as nuclear syllable placement is concerned, the rules, both unmarked and contrastive, are simple enough for learners to master in the classroom, 'carry around' with them, and automatize as procedural knowledge. ... Rules can be taught overtly, though with the caveat that it is not sufficient to tell students simply to stress the 'most important' word – they need help in working out how to identify this word.
> (Jenkins 2000: 155)

What Jenkins is saying here is that nuclear stress placement can be described in the classroom in simple rules, and that teaching these rules can bring about a change in the way learners use nuclear stress when they speak.

Not everybody agrees with her on this point, and certainly learners whose first language has no parallel system to the nuclear stress placement of English usually find it difficult to generalize about the way it is used. As a result, they find it hard to relate the nucleus they have detected to a logical reason for that particular placement. In addition, their own attempts to place nuclear stress often fail, even when they believe that they have done it correctly.

To sum up, nuclear stress placement is teachable in the sense that the rules are simple enough for learners to master in the classroom, although for some learners there may be a noticeable gap between receptive and productive competence. As a result, our primary aim in the classroom will be to make learners aware of the existence and importance of nuclear stress. This should make them more sensitive to its use by other speakers, and consequently more likely to acquire competence in its use themselves. How we can do this will be tackled in Chapter 4. Overall, though, it is fair to say that in the majority of learners' cases the items in the LFC are more achievable than those that make up traditional pronunciation programmes, and this achievability generates an important sense of progress.

Benefit 3 – Accent addition instead of accent reduction

Type the term 'accent reduction training' into an Internet search engine and you will get literally hundreds of links. In the USA particularly, publicity invites immigrants and US-born citizens with one of the less prestigious American accents, to 'reduce' their accent and so gain social or economic success. There are a number of problems, however, with this concept of accent reduction.

The first problem is that it causes us to see the learner's accent in a negative light – as a fault or imperfection. Where English is not the speaker's first language, this is to perceive the mother tongue, the probable source of any accent, as a problem. In practice, the speaker's L1 can be an invaluable resource, as we will see in Benefit 5.

The second problem is that accent reduction implies that some other accent represents the ideal state that the learner should strive to attain. In the case of commercial accent reduction courses in the USA this refers to GA. In the UK, it is RP. But for ELF communication neither of these accents represents an ideal, partly because native speakers have no special status in ELF, and partly because native-speaker accents are not necessarily as intelligible as non-native speaker accents in lingua franca situations (see Chapter 1).

In contrast to the problems posed by accent reduction, ELF pronunciation leads learners through a process of accent 'addition'. In this process, the learner's L1 pronunciation is compared to the requirements of the LFC. Any LFC features that are not already present in the mother tongue are added to the learner's accent. Any features of the learners' mother tongue that do not impact negatively on intelligibility are left untouched, even when they are not part of any native-speaker accent. Last of all, any features of the mother-tongue accent that are damaging to international intelligibility are brought to learners' attention so that they avoid using them in ELF contexts. Transfer from his L1 phonology, for example, means that Speaker Q pronounces 'lamb' as [læmp] (Track 12: lines 5 and 6).

The switch from 'reduction' to 'addition' is important. Firstly it helps both teachers and learners to see the mother-tongue pronunciation in a more positive light. Rather than being an imperfect or an interfering system that requires repair or reduction, it is the starting point from which they can work towards international intelligibility. In addition, because accent addition makes no attempt to eliminate the first-language features that do not interfere with ELF intelligibility, speakers can retain their identity through their accent in English, which in turn may help to increase their confidence as users of English.

Benefit 4 – Identity through accent

Chapter 1 explained how our identities are linked to our accents, even though this may be at subconscious levels. Because of this, some learners display ambivalent feelings about sounding like native speakers of English, and yet taking pride in their nationality. The Russian and Argentinean speakers on Track 3 begin by saying that they would be pleased if people thought that they were British or American, but ended by admitting that they would not like to lose their accents, since it is part of their identity.

To a large extent an ELF approach removes any conflict between accent and identity, since it allows ELF users to indicate their first-language identity through their second-language accent without any loss in intelligibility. We can see how this works in practice if we take the case of Greek learners of English. Two of the traditional 'problems' these learners are said to have with English vowels are that:

1 Schwa is replaced either by /ɛ/ as in 'bed' or the Greek vowel /a/.
2 The Greek /r/ is midway between a 'd'-like flap and a trill.

In Track 17, for example, Speaker Q consistently replaces schwa with /a/ in the words 'metal' and 'mineral'. However, neither of these 'problems' is an obstacle to ELF intelligibility. More importantly, they are good examples of how ELF speakers can be intelligible whilst at the same time retaining their identity through their accent.

Without a doubt, some learners enjoy the other 'self' that they discover as they become proficient in a new language. Other students, however, can feel threatened by being made to sound like a native speaker. This is true of adolescents. They are at a difficult age, and are often struggling to define their own mother-tongue identity, especially in front of their peers. This would not appear to be the best moment to ask them to take on a new identity through their pronunciation. Adults, on the other hand, are often comfortable with their identity, and as a result may not feel attracted by the idea of discovering a different 'self'. They are quite content with the 'self' that they have spent a life time developing.

A key question that we can ask ourselves with respect to accent and identity is: Why would a Chinese speaker of English, talking to a Brazilian speaker of English want to be perceived as coming from the UK or USA? Similarly, when you speak to other delegates at the United Nations, would you want your accent to tell the audience that you were British or American, when in fact you represent an Outer or Expanding Circle nation? In this sense, an important benefit of an ELF approach to pronunciation is that it does not try to eliminate all traces of the learner's mother tongue. Instead, it uses the mother tongue accent as its starting point.

Benefit 5 – Mother tongue as friend

Experts now agree that not all errors made by second language learners can be explained exclusively in terms of transfer from the first language. They also agree that transfer is not automatically negative. In her studies of ELF speakers' pronunciation, Jennifer Jenkins examined the effect of transfer on intelligibility. She concluded that phonological transfer from the first language was 'deep-rooted and can be of benefit to learners; it is not to ... be abandoned easily or willingly, unless there is very good reason to do so' (2000: 119).

Where the first and second language share parallel structures, transfer will be positive, and will facilitate learning. Despite this, it is common to hear language teachers talking about 'mother-tongue interference', and it is widely recognized that pronunciation is the area where this 'interference' is most noticeable. While the concept of 'interference' has a negative connotation, the transfer of sounds and other pronunciation features need not be negative. It is exactly this sort of transfer, for example, that gives speakers their unique accents, the importance of which we saw in Benefit 4.

First language transfer can be useful in another way, too. Teachers can deliberately use the learner's mother-tongue pronunciation to help learners to attain a good command of the features in the LFC. For example, the English sound /ŋ/ is not a recognized phoneme in many languages. However, it is present in those languages whenever the consonant 'n' is followed by a /k/ or /g/ sound. This is the case with 'tengo' in Spanish or 'tankować' in Polish, for example. By referring learners to the pronunciation of the 'n' in these words, the teacher uses the mother tongue to help learners access a sound they thought they did not make in their L1.

Another example of the way the mother tongue can help is through the variations that can be found in the language's different regional accents. If a Brazilian learner is having difficulty with the /tʃ/ and the /dʒ/ sounds, the teacher can refer them to the pronunciation of the words 'tia' and 'dia'. In the accents from São Paulo, Carioca, and Mieiro, the initial 't' and 'd' are pronounced /tʃ/ and the /dʒ/ respectively. Learners who can imitate these regional accents are well on the way to being able to use the two problem sounds in English.

The exact ways in which the first language can be exploited to help learners to gain competence in the LFC is explained in detail in Chapter 5 for a range of different L1 backgrounds. This benefit works best with the monolingual groups. This represents the most frequent teaching situation around the world. With such groups, teachers who share the learners' first-language background have an advantage over their colleagues who do not. That is to say, non-native speaker teachers are potentially better instructors for ELF pronunciation than their native speaker colleagues. We now turn to this very important benefit of an ELF approach to pronunciation.

Benefit 6 – Non-native speakers as instructors

In a traditional approach to pronunciation the learner's goal is a native- or near-native speaker accent. With such a goal it is only natural that the native-speaker teacher should be seen as the ideal instructor. Who better than someone with a native-speaker accent? In contrast, non-native-speaker teachers cannot be 'ideal' instructors, since inevitably they will have traces of their L1 accent in their English pronunciation.

However, when we are talking about ELF communication, there are a number of reasons why the non-native speaker teacher is potentially the better instructor.

Performance

A native-speaker teacher of English can model a native-speaker accent in class. However, since this accent is not an ELF goal, nor is it especially intelligible in ELF interaction (see Chapter 1), this advantage is of no real value. In contrast, non-native speaker teachers who are competent ELF users will automatically provide an excellent example of precisely the sort of internationally intelligible accent that their learners aspire to. Moreover, the non-native speaker teacher represents what learners can realistically be expected to achieve. 'If my teacher can do this, so can I' might summarize the learner's thinking. This, however, is not possible when the teacher is a native speaker of English, something the learner can never be.

Knowledge

An ELF approach with a monolingual class works best when the teacher has a good working knowledge of the phonologies of both English and the learners' first language. This is needed partly in order to be able to understand the source of any problems that learners encounter in their attempts to master the requirements of the LFC. More importantly, as I explained in the previous Benefit, this knowledge is central to the use of learners' first language pronunciation as a strategy for attaining competence in the LFC. Sadly, many native-speaker teachers enter the profession with little or no knowledge of the phonology of English, and very few study the phonology of their learners' mother tongues. In contrast, in many countries a degree in English includes the study of the phonologies of both English and their own corresponding first language. As a result, in terms of teacher knowledge, the non-native speaker teacher is inevitably better placed to teach ELF pronunciation.

Experience

Through personal experience, a non-native speaker teacher of English understands the physical and psychological difficulties in acquiring a second pronunciation. They have been through the process and can remember the effort and the anguish that this involves. A native-speaker teacher, on the other hand, cannot do this. Of course, native-speaker teachers can be aware of the difficulties of perfecting second language pronunciation through their own experience of learning other languages. But precisely because they are native speakers, they can never really get under a learner's skin with respect to the pronunciation of English. In short, non-native speaker teachers share a common learning experience with their students in a unique way. This gives them maximum empathy with their students when they have problems. It also allows them to draw on their own learning experience and use this to show learners how to overcome these problems.

Effectiveness

Because they are ELF-users themselves, non-native speaker teachers frequently know which approximations or variations on the LFC will prove intelligible internationally, and which will not. They know this through experience; they have already gone out and used their pronunciation successfully to communicate in ELF contexts. Because of this real-life experience, non-native speaker teachers are better placed to decide when a learner's versions of target LFC features will work in practice, and when they will not. Clearly it is much less easy for the native speaker teacher to do this. Native speakers do take part in ELF communication, and some are successful at evaluating what is or is not intelligible in ELF. Those who have this ability can note down the instances in which they have used their native-speaker accent in ELF interactions successfully and, more importantly, when their accent has caused problems. In this way, they will be able to modify their own speech in class and become better models for their learners. The problem for most native-speaker teachers, however, is that they find it very difficult to put their native speaker intuitions to one side.

The best teacher for ELF pronunciation, especially for monolingual groups, is the bilingual speaker of both English and the learner's L1. This can be a native speaker of English who has learned the local first language or it can be a non-native speaker teacher who has learned English. However, even when both teachers understand the phonology of both languages, the non-native teacher has an advantage over the native-speaker colleague because of shared experience as a learner, and because of their more likely real-life experience as an ELF user. The teacher who is in the worst position to teach ELF pronunciation is the native speaker who is neither fluent in the learners' mother tongue, nor understands the phonologies of either English or the learner's first language.

Summary

This chapter has looked at some of the concerns and benefits of adopting an ELF approach to pronunciation. In Part A it explored some of the concerns that surround the adoption of ELF. Some of these, such as a possible lowering of standards, or the incompatibility of ELF with native-speaker oriented institutional goals, are general concerns, and might be expressed equally by learners, teachers, trainers, managers, and parents. Other concerns are more specifically related to how the teachers might react to ELF, whilst a third group are concerns that learners themselves might express. In each case, however, we saw that the concern is either founded on a misconception about ELF, or that it does not constitute a strong enough argument for the outright rejection of ELF.

In Part B we looked at a number of potential benefits of an ELF approach to pronunciation. These include a lighter workload and increased levels of achievability. These will inevitably translate into increased learner motivation towards pronunciation. Motivation will be further increased for many learners when they see that an ELF approach is about accent addition rather than accent reduction, and that an ELF accent will allow them to hold on to their first-language identity when speaking in English. Also in Part A, we saw how the learners' mother tongue is a valuable resource in the ELF pronunciation classroom, as opposed to being an 'obstacle'. Finally, we discovered how non-native speaker teachers who share their learners' first language background are ideal instructors for ELF pronunciation.

In Chapter 5 we will look at a range of different first-language backgrounds in much greater detail in order to see exactly how the learners' mother tongue pronunciation can be brought into the classroom to help learners to achieve full competence in the requirements of the LFC. Before that, in Chapter 4, we will examine a range of classroom techniques and activities that can be used to teach pronunciation for English as a Lingua Franca.

Further reading

On non-native teachers

Llurda, E. (ed.). 2006. *Non-Native Language Teachers: Perceptions, Challenges and Contributions to the Profession.* New York: Springer Science+Business Media, LLC.

On attitudes to accents

Jenkins, J. 2007. *English as a Lingua Franca: Attitude and Identity.* Oxford: Oxford University Press.

Lippi-Green, R. 1997. *English with an Accent: Language, Ideology and Discrimination in the United States.* London and New York: Routledge.

On learner preferences

Scales, J., A. Wennerstrom, D. Richard, and **S. Hui Wu.** 2006. 'Language learners' perceptions of accent'. *TESOL Quarterly* 40/4: 715–738.

4 TECHNIQUES AND MATERIALS FOR TEACHING ELF PRONUNCIATION

Introduction

In this chapter we look at techniques and materials for teaching ELF pronunciation. Many of these will be familiar to you if you regularly teach pronunciation. This should not come as a surprise, since teaching pronunciation for ELF is primarily about re-thinking goals and re-defining error, as opposed to modifying classroom practice. However, a re-appraisal of existing activities and techniques is necessary. As we saw in Chapter 1, for example, the less proficient listener in ELF depends significantly on bottom-up processing. Because of this, activities designed to develop competence in the pronunciation of individual sounds are important. This contrasts with the emphasis current approaches place on connected speech.

Another area in which ELF pronunciation differs from existing approaches is in the clear separation of receptive and productive competence. For most learners there is a gap between what they can pronounce and what they understand in the pronunciation of fully competent speakers. Until now, this gap has been seen as a sign of incomplete learning. In an ELF approach, in contrast, learners will have to be able to deal receptively with features of pronunciation that they themselves do not produce. Mark Hancock discusses this in his teacher's notes to *English Pronunciation in Use:* '[s]ome of the pronunciation points in the book are potentially irrelevant to some learners. For instance, for learners whose aim is mainly to communicate with other non-native speakers of English, accurate production of the sounds /θ/ and /ð/ is probably not necessary' (2003a: 8).

Listening is a third area in which an ELF approach to teaching pronunciation differs to some extent from others. On the one hand, ELF listening materials must help learners to accurately identify and reproduce the items in the LFC. This is similar to the role listening plays in traditional approaches. Up to now, however, listening materials for pronunciation have exposed learners mainly to a few native-speaker accents, whereas an ELF approach has to prepare them for quite significant variation. The CD accompanying this book can be used to start giving learners experience of listening to a range of non-native speaker accents.

A skill that is not found in traditional programmes but which is central to pronunciation for ELF is that of accommodation. In terms of ELF pronunciation, speakers accommodate productively to listeners by making small changes in how they pronounce certain sounds or where they place nuclear stress. At the same time, listeners can accommodate receptively to speakers by being flexible in their expectations and interpretations of what they hear.

One final issue that needs taking into account when considering an ELF approach to pronunciation is the make-up of a group – whether it is monolingual or multilingual. Although there is a great deal of overlap in the teaching of pronunciation in these two different contexts, with ELF there are certain significant differences.

With all of these points in mind, this chapter is divided into:

Part A: Raising learner awareness: In order to make informed choices about goals, learners will need to know about both ELF and EFL in the world today.
Part B: Guidance in how to help learners to achieve competence in the items in the LFC.
Part C: Activities designed to develop accommodation skills.
Part D: How best to exploit working with a monolingual group.

Part A: Raising learner awareness

The sociolinguistic facts

Most learners will only have a vague notion of the concept of English as a Lingua Franca, and very few will have any idea as to the size of the different native-speaker and non-native speaker populations. As a first step in the process of raising awareness of how English functions in the world today, you can show students data such as that in Table 4.1 and ask them to use the estimates in the first column in order to guess the populations of each of the different speaker groups. Students should discuss their guesses in pairs or groups, using their mother tongue where appropriate and if necessary. After seeing the answers, the whole class can discuss the chances of NNS–NNS interactions (i.e. ELF) taking place around the world, as opposed to NS–NNS interactions (EFL).

Possible populations	Speaker group	Actual population	Actual population
		Your guess	Official*
1200 million	American English		
400 million	British English		
230 million	BBC English		
200 million	Indian English		
57 million	Native speakers		
1 million	Non-native speakers		

Table 4.1   The English speaking populations of the world

Photocopiable © Oxford University Press

*ANSWERS: American English = 230 million; British English = 57 million; BBC English = 1 million; Indian English = 200 million; Native speakers = 400 million; Non-native speakers = 1200 million. (Data from Crystal 2003)

It might be useful at this stage to look at a world map or an atlas and try to highlight parts of the world where English is most likely to act as a lingua franca. Next, you can introduce the idea of the Inner, Outer, and Expanding Circles (see Chapter 1), and invite students to place their own country in one of the circles. Finally, students can discuss any experiences that they person-ally have had of using English both as a foreign language, and/or as a lingua franca. These experiences might have been through tourism, through busi-ness, or at international conferences and similar events. On the CD, Speakers A and B (Track 1), and Speaker K (Track 7) talk about their experiences as ELF users.

The roles of English

Although many learners will have come across the term 'English as a Foreign Language' and will have seen the acronym 'EFL', the majority will not have stopped to think about what the term means, and how it relates to other terms such as ENL, ESL, or ELF. As with the previous section, rather then simply tell students what these acronyms mean, it will be more productive to ask them to work together and complete a chart such as the one in Table 4.2.

Acronym*	Full name	Meaning
EFL	English as a (1)_____ language	English when it is used by (5)_____ speakers to communicate with native speakers.
ELF	English as a (2)_____ franca	English when it is used between two or more (6)_____ speakers who do not have the same first language.
ENL	English as a (3)_____ language	English when it is used between two or more (7)_____ speakers.
ESL	English as a (4)_____ language	English when it is used in countries that were once colonized by the (8)_____. English when it is used by immigrants to countries where (9)_____ is the native language, (USA, UK, etc.).

Table 4.2 The roles of English

Photocopiable © Oxford University Press

*ANSWERS: 1 = foreign; 2 = lingua; 3 = native; 4 = second; 5 = non-native speakers; 6 = non-native; 7 = native; 8 = British; 9 = English

After giving the answers, clarify that the different roles that English plays depend on who is speaking to who, rather than where English is being used (see Chapter 1). This could lead into a discussion as to who decides what is correct and incorrect English in each of the four situations in the table. In the case of ESL in countries like India, Nigeria, or Singapore, for example, you can explain how these countries have gradually developed their own rules on what is or is not correct. This could lead to the question as to who decides what is correct in ELF communication in the absence of native speakers. There are no 'right' or 'wrong' answers to this type of discussion. The aim is simply to increase learner awareness of how English works in different ways, one of which is as a lingua franca.

Standard accents and accent variation

To elicit ideas on standard accent, on accent variation, and on the generally subjective nature of attitudes towards different accents, ask students to name accents in their own country. With a list of accents on the board, students can say which ones they prefer, and try to explain why. At this point you could present the conclusions of research such as that of Sarah Hannam (see Chapter 3). Students can then comment on how they feel about the standard accent in their own country, if there is one.

With a monolingual group, students can talk to each other in their mother tongue and try to decide where each class member comes from on the basis of their accent. Jorge Suárez finds that this works especially well with a group of students who do not know each other and who come from different areas of the same country (Suárez 2000). As a follow up activity, or when learners in a group know each other already, he suggests asking the class to listen to film, television, or radio extracts of people from around the country speaking in their mother tongue. 'These activities are beneficial in that they allow students to talk about their personal linguistic experiences in their own L1 and freely express their likes, dislikes, and even prejudices about language' (Suárez 2000: 33).

By the end of any discussion students should begin to understand that:

- accent variation is completely normal
- in some countries one accent has become the standard for various reasons, usually social, political, or economic
- attitudes to different accents may be personal, and are more often based on feelings than on rational arguments
- attitudes to different accents may also be based on social prejudices and stereotypes.

(NOTE: This can be a delicate topic and needs to be handled sensitively. In a local context where accent is a socially or politically conflictive issue, this discussion is probably best avoided.)

As a complement to this activity (or as an alternative if you feel that a discussion of mother-tongue accents will not be productive), you can let students hear a number of the recordings on the CD that accompanies this book. The standard text (Tracks 21–30) will be the easiest way to help learners to notice the variation from one speaker to another, especially if these are from phonologically different languages, such as Japanese, Portuguese, and Russian, or Arabic, Malay, and Polish.

As they listen, students might want to guess the first-language background of each speaker, but the main aim for you at this point is to bring out the idea of how accent variation is normal. It is also useful to point out how accent and intelligibility are not the same thing (see Chapter 1). As a conclusion to this discussion, students could be invited to talk about how they feel when they hear their mother tongue being spoken by non-native speakers. They might mention which sounds or other features of their mother tongue non-native speakers do not usually pronounce well, and what sort of deviations by non-native speakers cause problems of intelligibility.

For further opportunities to compare different accents, students with Internet access can visit the *Speech Accent Archive*. This website provides audio clips of speakers from a wide variety of native and non-native backgrounds. The speakers all read a short, standard text, and this allows users to compare different accents. Two other websites (*OM Accents* and the *International Dialects of English Archive*), both provide similar access to native and non-native speaker accents, although the first of these does not use a set text. A third website (*English Listening Lesson Library Online*), provides over 1,000 short conversations, a number of which involve non-native speakers (see Further reading below for website details.)

Part B: Teaching the LFC

Although problems with individual sounds are often directly related to a particular first-language background, a number of problems are common to learners from a wide range of first languages. This section offers general guidance as to how to deal with these.

Basic techniques

Minimal pairs

When the difference in the pronunciation of two words is limited to a single sound, these words form a minimal pair. The words 'pit' and 'bit', for example, differ only in the sound of the initial consonant. Minimal pairs have been used for a long time in pronunciation teaching, but the arrival of the Communicative Approach in the 1980s, and the corresponding shift in focus towards connected speech, meant that they became much less popular. However, as we saw in Chapter 1, competence in individual consonant sounds is important in ELF, and in this area of pronunciation, teaching minimal pairs is a valuable classroom technique. Jenkins, in fact, calls for an 'extensive focus on the LFC sounds, including drilling and tailor-made minimal pair work' (2000: 189).

By 'tailor-made' she is referring to the need to generate minimal pair exercises that focus on contrasts that are difficult for learners from specific first-language backgrounds. For German learners this could be the /w–v/ contrast, as in 'wine–vine', for example. For Brazilian learners, this could be the contrast between /h/ and /r/, as in 'hope' and 'rope'. Adapting ideas originally put forward by Adam Brown (1995) for communicative practice using minimal pairs, Jenkins produced exercises for Korean learners, who confuse /p/ and /f/. (See Table 4.3.)

Knowledge of the learners' first-language backgrounds is vital in order to prepare exercises of this sort. In addition, work on selected sound contrasts

Student A	Student B
1 (a) Can I make you a coffee?	Yes, black with two sugars, please.
1 (b) Can I make you a copy?	Yes, please – I'll read it later.
2 (a) Your cat's purr is lovely.	But it keeps me awake at night.
2 (b) Your cat's fur is lovely.	Yes, I'm always stroking it.

Table 4.3   Tailor-made minimal pair exercises for consonants

is only meaningful to all of the students in class when working with mono-lingual groups, for example, Korean learners in the case of /p/ and /f/. With multilingual groups it is more important to help individual learners diagnose their own problems with reference to the items in the LFC, and then to direct them to self-access facilities. I discuss some ways of doing this in Part B of Chapter 6 when I look at diagnostic testing.

Drills

Pronunciation involves developing automatic speech habits. For sounds or features that do not exist in the learner's mother tongue, these will be completely new habits. For features from the mother tongue that are not desirable in English, the learner's task is to modify existing habits. Whatever the situation, habit formation requires learners to be given multiple opportunities to practise articulating the new item so that its pronunciation becomes as automatic as possible. In this respect, the use of drills is openly encouraged in ELF, although their value may have been somewhat discredited by communicative approaches to language teaching.

Drills do not have to be tedious and demotivating, as is usually argued. A tongue-twister, for example, is a disguised drill. But as Mark Hancock points out, it is also a piece of language play (Hancock 2006), and language learners are just as likely to enjoy such play as native speakers. Tongue twisters can be found on a number of Internet web sites such as http://www.esl4kids.net/tongue.html or http://thinks.com/words/tonguetwisters.htm.

A variation on traditional tongue-twisters is to ask learners to produce their own, focusing on the sounds that are hardest for them. Rhymes, chants, and songs, especially when they have a chorus, also often provide repeated practice of specific language features. At the same time they are generally motivating for students, although obviously it will be necessary to take age and other factors into account before choosing material like this.

Thinking about Spanish learners of English, Hancock came up with 'This is my very best berry vest', which contrasts /b/ and /v/. (See Figure 4.1 on page 78.)

This is my very best berry vest!

Figure 4.1   A tailor-made tongue twister (From Speak Out! 36: 20)

Consonant sounds

Individual consonants

A great deal has already been written about the teaching of individual consonants, and there are a number of pronunciation manuals on the market that offer clear guidance to the teacher in this area (see Celce-Murcia 1996; Kelly 2000; Hancock 1995; and Hewings 2004). These all assume intelligibility in EFL or ESL as the learner's goal, and so include work on consonants that are not part of the LFC (see Chapter 2). But where ELF and traditional approaches coincide, these manuals will be of great value, especially to teachers new to pronunciation.

All work on consonants requires learners to have a minimum knowledge of how they are made. This in turn supposes a basic knowledge of the parts of the mouth (**articulators**) involved in making them. A diagram such as the one in Figure 4.2 is a useful teaching tool in this respect.

In general, describing how a sound is made should refer to three factors:

1   where in the mouth the airstream is obstructed (i.e. place of articulation)
2   how the airstream is obstructed (i.e. manner of articulation)
3   the presence or not of vibration in the vocal chords (i.e. voicing).

One way of helping learners to feel comfortable with this information is to take each of the three points in turn and look for examples in the pronunciation of the mother tongue. Ask students to find mother-tongue consonant sounds that are voiced, for example, or that involve either or both lips. They can look for consonants that can be pronounced for as long as you have breath in your lungs (i.e. fricatives /f/, /v/, /θ/, /ð/, /s/, /z/, /ʃ/, /ʒ/, nasals /n/,

/m/, /ŋ/) or approximants (/w/, /l/, /r/, /j/), or consonant sounds that cannot be kept going in this way (i.e. plosives /p/, /b/, /t/, /d/, /k/, /g/ and affricates /tʃ/, /dʒ/).

Activities such as these have the double aim of:

1 equipping learners with the knowledge they need in order to be able deal with the consonants of English
2 relating the consonants of English to those of their mother tongue.

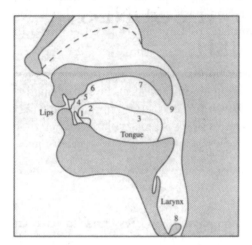

Articulators
1 Tip of tongue
2 Blade of tongue
3 Back of tongue

Places of Articulation
4 Teeth
5 Tooth (alveolar) ridge
6 Hard palate
7 Soft palate (velum)
8 Glottis
9 Uvula

Figure 4.2 The articulators and places of articulation (From Avery and Ehrlich 1992: 12)

Voicing

English consonants are usually described as voiced or voiceless. The vocal chords in the throat vibrate when we make voiced consonants. The sounds /b/, /d/, /g/, /v/, /z/, /ʒ/ are the voiced 'partners' of /p/, /t/, /k/, /f/, /s/, /ʃ/ respectively, for example. Some languages do not have as many voiced consonants as English, but they do have the voiceless partner. The /v/ sound is not a phoneme of Arabic, for example, but the sound /f/ is. Learners can be shown how to make /v/ by asking then first to make /f/ and by then 'adding' voice.

To introduce voicing, pronounce a long 'sssssss'. Hold the palm of your hand against your throat while you do this. Ask your students to do the same. Now switch to 'zzzzzzz'. With their hand on their throat learners should be able to feel the vibration of their vocal chords. Now get them to switch voicing off and on by switching between the two sounds to make 'sssszzzzsssszzzz'.

Once learners can control voicing at will, turn their attention to the problem voiced consonant. If a learner cannot pronounce /v/, for example, get them to make a long /f/ and ask them to 'add' voicing so as to produce 'ffffffvvvvv'. Repeat this process making the 'f' phase shorter and shorter until finally the learners make /v/ by itself. The same process can be used to teach the pronunciation of /ʒ/ starting from /ʃ/.

Devoicing of final consonants

One of the characteristic features of English is the presence of voiced consonants at the ends of words, such as in 'cab', 'bad', 'bag', 'save', 'peas', and so on. Some languages do not have final voiced consonants and learners from these L1s tend to end words with the voiceless equivalents. This makes 'cab', 'bad' and 'bag' sound like 'cap', 'bat', and 'back' respectively, and that is true for German, Polish, or Russian speakers of English. This can be heard in Tracks 3, 15, 16, and 18 of the CD.

It is tempting to focus learners' attention on the voicing itself and to get them to exaggerate this. However, voicing is quite weak at the end of English words, and it is more effective to draw attention to the length of the vowel immediately before the final consonant. Vowels are always longer when they are followed by a voiced consonant than when followed by a voiceless one.

Another technique is to practise phrases where a final voiced consonant is followed by a vowel such as:

- Along a tube into a tank (final voiced /b/ in 'tube')
- They followed a car (final voiced /d/ in 'followed')
- A bag and a coat (final voiced /g/ in 'bag')

In such phrases, the vowels after the voiced consonant in each example serve to reinforce the voicing.

Aspiration

The consonant sounds /p/, /t/, /k/ are aspirated in English when they occur at the beginning of one-syllable words, as in 'pen', 'tea' or 'cat', and also when they occur at the beginning of a stressed syllable in words with more than one syllable, such as in 'repeat', 'attend', and 'because'.

To introduce aspiration, hold a piece of paper in front of your mouth and pronounce the word 'pen'. The puff of air that accompanies the /p/ will cause the paper to flutter momentarily. The effect is most obvious to the students if you stand so that the students see the side of your face.

The demonstration can be repeated using other English words beginning with /p/, followed by words beginning with /t/ and /k/. It is especially effective if the English words are contrasted with words from the learners' first language beginning with the same three consonants (see Chapter 5). The absence of aspiration will be made clear by the fact that the paper does not flutter when those words from the mother tongue are pronounced.

You can continue the demonstration by putting your hand in front of your mouth and asking the students to do the same. They can then try the sample words from English and contrast them with the words chosen from their mother tongue. Finally, the teacher can put the learners into pairs and give them a list of English words where /p, t, k/ are aspirated. The learners pronounce the words while their partners 'test' for aspiration with their hand.

Consonant clusters

Initial clusters

The correct pronunciation of consonant clusters at the beginning of words is very important for ELF intelligibility. As we saw in Chapter 2, learners who find initial clusters difficult employ one of two strategies: deletion of one of the consonants, or insertion of a short vowel before the cluster. Because deletion is far more damaging to ELF intelligibility than vowel insertion, practice in this area of the LFC needs to concentrate on avoiding deletion.

Celce-Murcia et al. (1996) suggest that teachers begin work on initial consonant clusters by raising students' awareness as to which combinations are possible. They can do this by getting students to come up with words for two- or three- consonant combination. In the process of offering examples of different clusters aloud, learners will inevitably encounter difficulties with their pronunciation. This will allow the teacher to comment on the strategies of deletion and vowel insertion, and on the importance of avoiding deletion.

Clusters that are especially difficult can be dealt with by getting learners to build up the cluster one consonant at a time:

lace	place	
lie	fly	
port	sport	
tone	stone	
ray	tray	stray
ray	pray	spray
rain	train	strain

Another teaching strategy with clusters is to get students to 'prolong' the first consonant until they are ready to articulate the next one (e.g. 'ffffffffly', 'ssssssssport' or 'sssssssstrain').

Learners who have received traditional training in English pronunciation may be reluctant to use the strategy of vowel insertion in order to facilitate the pronunciation of clusters, and you need to be sensitive to this. Vowel insertion is a useful option, but should not be forced on learners who are able to pronounce initial clusters adequately without resorting to insertion.

Medial and word-final clusters

It is possible for a syllable in English to end with up to four consonants as in 'tempts' or 'texts'. This is rare, but syllables ending with two or three consonants are common, especially with the plural of nouns (ants, hands, facts), the third person singular of the present simple of verbs (asks, builds, helps), and the past simple of regular verbs (asked, braked, controlled). The clusters /sps/, /sts/, /sks/, and /kts/ are notoriously difficult for learners whose first language has a simpler syllable structure. Fortunately, for ELF intelligibility the consonant clusters in the middle or at the end of English words are not as important as clusters at the beginning of words, and so require less attention.

As with word-initial clusters, learners will generally apply the strategies of insertion or deletion to simplify medial and final clusters. Vowel insertion is still preferable, but the addition of a vowel at the end of a word should be avoided. This is typical of a number of first-language backgrounds (see Chapter 5), and the effect is to create an additional syllable so that 'fast', for example, will sound like 'faster'.

Vowel sounds

Length

Work on the length contrasts of English vowels is especially important for learners whose mother-tongue vowels are all approximately equal in length. Practice should start with discrimination exercises so that learners begin to perceive the difference. Minimal pairs can be used to do this, both in isolated words and in short sentences:

1 Listen. Which word do you hear?

Short	Long
sit	seat
sell	sail
cat	cart
pull	pool

2 Listen and then respond with a or b.

1 Can you feel/fill them?	a Yes, they're a bit like wood.
	b No, I don't think I have enough.
2 They gave her a new coat/cot.	a Then we'll get her some gloves.
	b Then we'll get her a blanket.
3 When do you hope to sell/ sail?	a When the market gets better.
	b When the weather gets better.

This type of minimal pair practice does not need to make any distinction between pure vowels and diphthongs; the focus is on length rather than exact quality, and long vowels and diphthongs are similar in length.

The American pronunciation expert, Judy Gilbert (1993), recommends the use of rubber bands as useful way of using kinaesthetics to reinforce differences in vowel length/tension. Alternatively, students can hold their thumb and first finger close together for short vowels, and stretching them as far apart as possible to accompany long vowels. Initially, the length of long vowels can be exaggerated whilst performing these hand actions.

Vowel length and following consonants

Minimal pair exercises can be used to develop perception and production of the effect of voiced and voiceless consonants on the length of the preceding vowel (Chapter 2). As with vowel length in general, these can be done first with isolated words and then with words in sentences.

1 Listen. Which word do you hear?

Short	Long
peace	peas
ice	eyes
cap	cab
wait	wade

2 Listen and then respond with a or b.

1 Can you get him a cap/cab?	a I'll ring for one now.
	b He can have mine.
2 We'll have to wade/wait.	a Yes, the water's rising fast.
	b That's OK. I'm not in a hurry.

3 What do I like most? Peas/Peace!   a I prefer carrots.

b I prefer a busy city centre.

Vowel quality

Exact vowel quality is not a feature of the LFC. However, learners do have to establish a consistent set of vowel sounds for ELF intelligibility. In addition, many learners will have already been given traditional pronunciation instruction and could be disconcerted by their teachers simply ignoring quality. In addition, learners who regularly see IPA transcriptions in their coursebooks or dictionaries will want help in interpreting the symbols for vowel sounds.

Any treatment of vowel quality for ELF should begin by raising learners' awareness as to the extent of variation in vowel quality among native speakers. Examples such as those given in Chapter 2 can be discussed in class, although it is more effective to get students to describe their own experiences. Learners at intermediate level and beyond will probably be able to talk about the differences that they have encountered when travelling. My own students regularly comment on the way 'bus' is pronounced in different parts of the UK, for example.

In terms of classroom models for vowel consistency for ELF, we can opt for one of three approaches:

1 Continue to use the standard native-speaker accent most widely encountered in the teaching material and publications found in our local area, but using the NS accent as a model as opposed to a norm. That is to say, the NS accent acts as a target for our learners to aim at, but is no longer seen as a unique, correct variation that must be perfectly imitated. In practice, this is what most of us have been doing in the classroom up to now, but we have inevitably assumed that anything less than the perfect imitation of the NS vowel quality is inadequate. This is both frustrating and demotivating for teacher and learner alike. In an ELF approach this is not the case, and provided vowel length values are retained, students will have relatively little difficulty in using NS models to produce good ELF vowel qualities. Naturally, no work should be done on schwa or vowel reduction, because of the negative impact that these have on ELF intelligibility (see Chapter 2).

2 Use the mother tongue vowel system as your starting point and extend this to include other qualities that learners can easily produce. Spanish L1 learners, for example, come into the class with five pure vowels and seem to have little difficulty in making good approximations to the long vowels /ɑː/, /ɔː/, and /ɜː/. This gives them an eight-vowel set. If we then include the five Spanish diphthongs that are closest to English diphthongs, and

work on the /iː/–/ɪ/ contrast, we will have produced a consistent set of vowels adequate for most ELF communication.

3 Be the model yourself. Competent non-native speaker teachers can use their own accents as a model. If they have reached a point where their own pronunciation is fully intelligible in ELF communication, their vowel qualities are, by definition, an ideal model for their students to imitate. This approach not only offers learners an achievable target in that they are following a path their teacher has already negotiated successfully; the approach also means that instead of seeing themselves as modelling English vowels from the position of 'failed' native speakers, non-native speaker teachers are now doing so from the position of fully successful ELF users.

Intonation

Word groups

Word grouping can be a problem: some learners tend to pause after almost every one or two words, whilst others pause only to draw breath. In either case, ask your students to listen for pauses in short spoken texts or dialogues, and to mark the pauses they hear on a transcript of the text. A discussion of where they heard pauses should help them to see that good pausing benefits both the listener and the speaker (see Chapter 2), and that these benefits are especially valuable in ELF interactions.

As a follow-up exercise, students can be asked to predict pauses in similar texts, and then check their answers by listening to the recorded version. Coursebook dialogues are an excellent source of material for these exercises, as is the standard text recorded by ten of the speakers on the CD accompanying this book (Tracks 21–30). As a further activity, students can be asked to make their own recordings of a set text, and this can either be marked by you, or played to other members of the class for comment. It is also interesting to ask students to mark the pauses in preparation for reading a short story. Poetry and extracts from plays also provide excellent, natural, communicative contexts for practising pausing. In fact, badly paused, poems and plays are usually meaningless.

Nuclear stress placement

Because of its impact on intelligibility, nuclear stress placement is a key aspect of pronunciation teaching for ELF settings. Exercises on nuclear stress placement are not new, however, and once again the only requirement for ELF is for learners to be competent in both detecting and placing nuclear stress. Hancock (1995) offers a number of activities that are well suited to practising nuclear stress placement. The pairwork exercise in Figure 4.3 on page 86, for example, requires good placement on the part of the speaker, and good perception on the part of the listener.

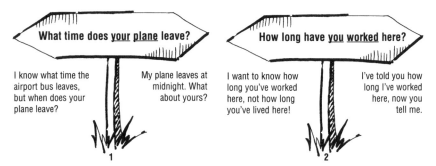

Figure 4.3 Pairwork exercises in perceiving and placing nuclear stress (Hancock 1995: 105)

The speaker asks the question on the signboard with the nuclear stress on one of the two words underlined. The listener says 'left' or 'right' to indicate which of the two 'explanations' he or she understood. For example, if the speaker says, 'What time does your PLANE leave?' the listener would reply 'left'.

In general, work on nuclear stress placement should lead learners towards the idea that:

1 One word in a word group will be stressed more than any of the others.
2 This stressed word is frequently a content word (i.e. noun, verb, adjective, or adverb).
3 This stressed word is frequently the last content word in the word group (i.e. unmarked stress).
4 The stressed word can come earlier in the word group in order to make a special meaning (i.e. contrastive stress).

Point 4 is illustrated in the following dialogue, where the Head Receptionist uses contrastive stress as a way of correcting a mistake in the hotel room list.

Junior Receptionist: I've put Ms Hesse in Room two one SEven.

Head Receptionist: TWO one seven? She should be in THREE one seven.

Junior Receptionist: But that's where the Weinbergers are.

Head Receptionist: No, no. They're in three FIVE seven, remember?

Junior Receptionist: Oh yes. Sorry. I'll just update the room list then.

Nuclear stress naturally falls on the last item in a word group in many languages and this tendency will transfer through into English. This usually creates problems for learners when trying to use contrastive stress. In the exercise in Table 4.4, for example, matching Parts A and B correctly is not normally too difficult for learners. Nor will they find A1 difficult to say since the stress is on the last word. But as the stress moves closer and closer to the beginning of the word group, many students will find it difficult to place it correctly in this 'early' position, and may unconsciously create a double nuclear stress, producing 'I LIKE their new FLAT'.

Match statement A with response B.

Part A (what the speaker says)	Part B (what the speaker means)
1 I like their new FLAT.	a But I'm not in love with it.
2 I like their NEW flat.	b It's very nice.
3 I like THEIR new flat.	c But Michel doesn't.
4 I LIKE their new flat.	d I didn't like the one they were in before.
5 *I* like their new flat.	e It's a pity I don't like ours.

Table 4.4 Practice in placing contrastive stress

A useful technique to help learners place nuclear stress in the right place is back-chaining. The learners begin by pronouncing the word which carries the nuclear stress, several times if necessary, and then continue by adding the remaining words in the word group first towards the end of the group, and then, if necessary, towards the beginning. Thus, A4 would be practised beginning with the word 'like':

1 LIKE
2 LIKE their
3 LIKE their new
4 LIKE their new flat
5 I LIKE their new flat.

If necessary, you could also point out that the stressed word is louder than the others. Finally, as with all practice of this nature, eventually allow students to work in pairs, listening to and evaluating each other's efforts. You act as the 'referee' in case of any disagreement as to what was said or heard.

Another idea for working on both word groups and nuclear stress at the same time comes from Wayne Rimmer (1997). He suggests that the teacher dictate a short text from the class coursebook. The students use slashes (/) instead of punctuation to mark the end of each 'chunk' that the teacher dictates to them. These chunks should correspond to the word groups of natural speech. When the teacher finishes dictating the text, the students work in pairs or groups and use the slashes to help them insert the punctuation. The teacher then reads the text again, and this time the learners circle the nuclear stress in each word group.

Part C: Improving accommodation skills

Phonological accommodation

One of the ways that Jennifer Jenkins gathered data for her research on intelligibility between non-native speakers was to observe them as they performed communication tasks. In one of these tasks a Japanese speaker was describing a scene to a Swiss-German listener. The listener had a set of six pictures, and based on what he heard, he had to decide which of the six coincided best with what his partner was describing. When the speaker mentioned a 'gley house' the listener frowned. On seeing this, the Japanese speaker quickly adjusted her pronunciation to 'grey' (Jenkins 2000: 82). This small adjustment allowed the listener to understand the speaker[1], and the pair were able to continue with the activity.

Deliberate adjustments in pronunciation like this are known as phonological accommodation. Native speakers make such adjustments without thinking as they change from one setting or region to another. They usually do this as a means of identifying with each other, although occasionally speakers may subconsciously adjust their pronunciation away from that of the listener as a way of distancing themselves from the other person.

Phonological accommodation is also important in ELF. However, whereas the pronunciation of native speakers changes for essentially sociolinguistic reasons, ELF users need to be able to accommodate to their listeners in order to be intelligible to them. Moreover, ELF users will need to make any adjustments based on an awareness of sounds that they have difficulties with in terms of the requirements of the LFC. The Japanese speaker, for example, was conscious of her problems with /r/ because of a breakdown in communication between herself and the same Swiss-German partner four weeks earlier (see Chapter 2, page 28). Because of this, she was quickly able to identify the [l] in [glei] as the problem, and adjust her pronunciation accordingly.

For optimum efficiency in ELF communication, it is not enough that speakers adjust their pronunciation. Listeners need to be more flexible in interpreting what they hear. By doing so, they will be able to deal more comfortably with the variations in accent that are characteristic of ELF. The remainder of this Part C looks at activities aimed at improving both productive and receptive phonological accommodation skills.

Dictation

Although Communicative Language Teaching has marginalized dictation, in practice it 'requires great concentration on both segmental and suprasegmental level, it has a definite goal, and feedback can be immediate' (Rimmer 1997: 36). For ELF pronunciation, however, rather than the teacher dictating to the whole class using a single, standard accent, it is far more effective if students work in pairs and dictate to each other. The students in each pair ideally need to be from different mother-tongue backgrounds, partly because over time this will expose them to a range of different accents, and partly because students with the same first language can understand each other even when their pronunciation of the LFC items is incorrect. However, if no one with a different first language is available, short extracts from the unscripted recordings on the CD (Tracks 1–20) could be used for dictation purposes.

Used correctly, dictation contributes to improving pronunciation in a number of ways:

- Firstly, it leaves a written record of any 'breakdowns' in communication. Differences in the learners' respective texts will immediately reveal where they failed to understand each other. If necessary, you can help them to determine if the breakdown was caused by the speaker's productive skills or the listener's receptive skills.
- Secondly, the written records of the activity allow learners to accurately identify the pronunciation items at fault. This will raise their awareness of problem areas for them at an individual level, at the same time as making it easier for you to suggest effective remedial work.
- Dictation also allows listeners time to think about context and make adjustments to what they thought they heard on the basis of what seems reasonable in terms of the context that is developing as the dictation proceeds. In this respect, it is a valuable tool for encouraging listeners to accommodate receptively to the speaker.

Dictation need not be the intimidating activity it was when teachers dictated to the whole class. Where the technology is available, for example, students with mobile phones can ring each other up and leave a voice message. The receiver then listens to the message and writes it down, before comparing what he or she understood with what was intended. Numerous low-tech, enjoyable dictation activities can also easily be set up, such as a running dictation, or Chinese whispers (see Davis and Rinvolucri 1988).

Negotiation of meaning

One of the keys to successful communication between competent language users is their ability to work together to construct understanding. Speakers and listeners do this by signalling that they understand each other. When they do not understand each other, they attempt to repair the breakdown by repeating or rephrasing what has just been said. This process of negotiation of meaning should be practised in ELF classrooms, particularly if you want to involve learners in communication activities of the sort described in Part C, under Communication activities.

One way of giving learners practice in negotiating meaning is to encourage them to intervene in the listening process. Tony Lynch, for example, suggests the use of what he calls 'indirect negotiation' (1996: 98–102) as a means of providing this practice. Working in groups, learners listen to a recorded text, completing a task sheet as they do. Before listening, the teacher explains to the learners that if they have any problems understanding the text, they can ask to stop the recording. If they do this, first they discuss in groups what they think they have understood. Then they can ask to hear the problematic section again, they can ask the teacher for additional information, or they can ask to go on to see if the next part of the recording clarifies what they have not yet understood.

In another activity designed to introduce the concept of negotiation of meaning, Lynch gave each learner one sentence from a short paragraph about the luxury cruise ship, the Queen Elizabeth II. After memorizing their sentences, the learners tried to reconstruct the whole paragraph by 'dictating' their sentences to each other. As can be seen in the following transcript, the pronunciation of the word 'world' caused a problem.

E   the Queen Elizabeth second

A   hm?

E   sorry + I mistook + Queen Elizabeth the second

A   hmhm

H   it's the second

E   is the largest passenger in the

H   in the?

E   in the world

A   yeah in the

H   in the?

J   in the boat?

E   in the world

H   in the bar?

E   world

J   in the w-o-r-l-d (stretching the vowel)

E   in the world yes

H   oh w-o-r-l-d

[laughter]

(Lynch 1996: 114)

Three things are interesting about this interchange in terms of ELF pronunciation and what we saw about intelligibility and the LFC in Chapters 1 and 2:

- the learners were clearly relying heavily on the acoustic signal, and when this failed, as was the case with the pronunciation of 'world', they were unable to use top-down processing to fill the 'gap' in their understanding. Despite E saying 'is the largest passenger in the', and their knowledge of the broad content of the text, neither J nor H were able to suggest plausible options for finishing the phrase. Neither 'boat' nor 'bar' makes much sense here.
- J stretched (i.e. lengthened) the vowel in 'world' in order to check that this was the word that E was trying to pronounce.
- the sound involved in the negotiation was /ɜː/, which is the only vowel quality that is specified in the LFC.

Tasks like this, then, provide natural opportunities for learners to negotiate meaning. Also, because they are working in groups and not performing in public in front of the whole class, this practice will take place in a relaxed, supportive atmosphere. Most important of all in terms of this handbook, many breakdowns will stem from problems of pronunciation, and the process of repairing these will provide excellent practice in developing and using phonological accommodation skills.

Communication activities

Communication activities such as information-gap or problem-solving tasks came into the language classroom with the arrival of Communicative Language Teaching in the early 1980s. They are now regularly used in order to promote fluency, and as a means of getting learners to use their English in order to interact with each other in ways that reflect communication outside the classroom. The interesting thing about such activities for ELF is that as they attempt to complete them, learners 'discover themselves where their faulty pronunciation or faulty reception has caused a breakdown in communication' (Jenkins 2000: 189). We saw earlier, for example, how the Japanese speaker was able to repair her first, faulty pronunciation of 'grey' and so become intelligible to her interlocutor.

More importantly, if the two learners from different mother-tongue backgrounds try to repair a breakdown in communication due to pronunciation, they can only do this by converging on the correct production of the items in the LFC. In other words, successful completion of a communication task by learners from different mother-tongue backgrounds automatically signals successful ELF pronunciation. In this case, you have no need to intervene. In contrast, if the learners fail to complete the task, you can intervene as an observer and help the learners to identify faulty pronunciation or faulty reception.

Typical simpler communication tasks include:

- Guessing games – one learner has some information and the other tries to guess what the information is.
- Describe and draw – one learner describes a picture or arrangement of shapes while the other tries to draw exactly what they hear.
- Spot the difference – two learners describe almost identical pictures to each other and attempt to spot any differences.
- Discover missing information – two learners complete gaps in complementary tables of information by asking each other questions.
- Giving directions – one learner gives directions to another based on a street map or road map.

At higher levels, learners can be set more complex tasks, including ones where they share information in pairs or small groups, and then process the joint information in order to find the best solution to a problem.

Whatever the exact nature of the game or activity, they will be most effective if the information exchange is reciprocal; that is to say, if all of the learners involved are required to get and give information, and therefore act as speakers and listeners. In addition, learners should be encouraged to make notes as to any pronunciation problems they had during the activity, both as speakers and listeners.

Part D: Working with monolingual groups

Accommodation in monolingual settings

In Part C we saw that accommodation skills are of great importance for ELF communication, and that communication tasks are effective, natural ways of developing these skills. Unfortunately, this is only true for multilingual groups, where speakers from different mother-tongue backgrounds converge on the LFC as they make adjustments in order to be intelligible to each other. In monolingual groups, exactly the opposite happens.

In their desire to understand each other and complete the task, learners in monolingual classes adjust their pronunciation towards the common ground of their first-language phonology. As a result, their pronunciation frequently moves further and further away from the LFC. For example, I have heard Spanish speakers of English converge on [roaθ] when carrying out a task involving giving street directions (Walker 2005: 551). Although what is happening here is a good example of phonological accommodation, this convergence on the speakers' common L1 phonology is problematic for two reasons:

- it stops the speakers from acquiring an ELF-intelligible pronunciation of the word, and so extending their command of the LFC
- for most non-Spanish users of ELF, [roaθ] would be unintelligible.

The situation is summed up in Table 4.5.

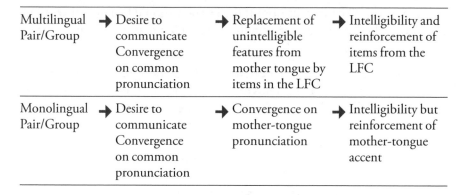

Multilingual Pair/Group	➜ Desire to communicate Convergence on common pronunciation	➜ Replacement of unintelligible features from mother tongue by items in the LFC	➜ Intelligibility and reinforcement of items from the LFC
Monolingual Pair/Group	➜ Desire to communicate Convergence on common pronunciation	➜ Convergence on mother-tongue pronunciation	➜ Intelligibility but reinforcement of mother-tongue accent

Table 4.5 Communication tasks and pronunciation with multilingual and monolingual classes (Adapted from Jenkins 2000: 192)

In addition to the problem of convergence on the L1, learners in a monolingual environment receive only limited exposure to the accent variation that is commonplace in a multilingual class. Nevertheless, monolingual groups are the reality in most of the world's classrooms and, as we saw in Chapter 3, the fact that students share the same mother tongue can be used to their advantage. We look more closely at how to do this in Chapter 5. Before that, we look at ways of dealing with the problems of convergence on the mother tongue, and with the absence of natural exposure to different accents.

Student recordings

As a partial solution to the problem of learners in monolingual groups converging on their L1 pronunciation, I have suggested the use of recordings (Walker 2005). Working individually or in pairs, learners prepare a text for recording. Before doing the recording, focus their attention on a small number of pronunciation points from the LFC, and practise these in class through drills, minimal-pair activities, and so on.

At the recording stage, students work in small groups, even when the texts are monologues. By doing this, they can listen to each other and offer feedback on the correctness of each other's production of the target items. Using this feedback, speakers can make deliberate adjustments to their pronunciation, and so gain practice in phonological accommodation. You can also encourage learners to repeat their recording as often as they wish until they are satisfied with it. Repeated, focused practice like this helps to make the production of individual pronunciation features automatic.

Monologues and dialogues both lend themselves well to recording in this way, and the text can either be from a coursebook or be written by the learners themselves. Whatever its origin, the learners should be familiar with the text so that they are free to focus on the pronunciation issues involved during the recording session.

When marking recordings you need to follow a marking scheme that rewards the correct production of the items of the LFC that the learners were required to focus on. If the students hand in their own copy of the transcript, you can indicate on the transcript where their pronunciation has or has not been satisfactory. This makes individual students aware of the extent to which they have progressed in their pronunciation of a problem LFC item.

Exposure to a range of ELF accents

As we saw in Part A of this chapter, the Internet provides different sites that give learners access to English spoken with different non-native speaker accents. In addition to these dedicated sites, it is also a source of authentic, unscripted non-native speaker English. Podcasts, YouTube, online news programmes, and similar Internet features all provide relatively easy access to interviews with international figures from the world of sport, entertainment, business, and politics. And of course the CD that accompanies this book offers unscripted recordings of speakers from a range of different L1 backgrounds.

Regardless of the source, these recordings are ideal for activities such as analysing and comparing the accents heard. This is the approach Julie Scales and her colleagues propose. They conclude a study on learners' perceptions of accent by suggesting that rather than listen to a single, standard accent, 'English language learners could hear, analyse and compare key features among a variety of accents. Such an approach would address both intelligibility and listening comprehension, increasing communication flexibility and respect for accent diversity' (2006: 735). That is to say, by listening to a range of different accents, learners not only come to accept the reality of accent variation, but also equip themselves to deal with it better, thanks to increased familiarity with given accents. John Field has shown that familiarity is a key factor in a listener's ability to understand an accent (Field 2003). The more listeners hear different accents, the better they are at dealing with them.

During early work on accent variation, learners should be exposed to scripted texts such as the standard text on the CD with this book (Tracks 21–30), or the texts used on the *Speech Accent Archive* and *IDEA* web sites. A typical teaching sequence with such texts could be:

- Invite learners to read the scripted text prior to the listening work. In this way they will be familiar with its content, and their attention will not be drawn away from pronunciation issues during the listening phase.
- Listen to four or five versions of a standard text, preferably with noticeably different accents.
- Try to match each accent to a country in a list of possible nationalities. This is not that easy to do, but it gives a clear purpose to listening, which focuses the learners' attention.
- Listen to each version again, stopping as appropriate to compare the speaker's accent (and any pronunciation difficulties) with the learners' own.

Short, scripted texts such as those on the CD can also be used as a way of getting students to focus closely on specific aspects of pronunciation that a particular mother-tongue group finds difficult. As part of work on word-initial consonant clusters, for example:

- Ask learners to find examples of these clusters in the transcript of a recording.
- Invite them to listen to speakers with different accents, and to comment on how each speaker deals with the clusters, and, in particular, on how the pronunciation of each speaker compares with their own.
- Decide which speaker dealt best with the clusters. This speaker can now be used as a model for the class's own work on the pronunciation of clusters.

This last activity can also be done using unscripted texts. As before, it is necessary to focus on a limited number of features of the LFC. If this is not done, listeners will be swamped by the amount of information they receive. Also, prior to any work on pronunciation, it is essential that learners hear unscripted texts first of all for their meaning. To do this, it is enough to give the class a little background information about the speaker(s) in the recording (see Introduction, pp. xvi–xx), and about the topic itself (see individual CD transcripts). The class can brainstorm possible contents, and then listen for the first time to see which of these are actually mentioned. On listening for a second time, learners can answer standard comprehension questions and, where necessary, can ask for the recording to be repeated until they are satisfied that they understand the content.

Listening for meaning is best carried out in pairs or small groups. This is 'to engage students in some kind of verbal interchange about what they have heard. This will ensure that they are thoroughly involved with the content, that is to say with what was being said, before they go on to attend to how it was said' (Brazil 1994: 3). Once learners are happy with the content, they can then go on and focus on the pronunciation point you have selected to work on.

A variation on this last activity is to put students into pairs or groups, and to invite each pair/group to find an example of a non-native internationally known figure speaking in English. News websites on the Internet are a good source of interviews. The students:

- Transcribe the recording.
- Make notes about where the celebrity's pronunciation is different from their own – worth imitating, unintelligible, etc.
- Present the video or audio clip to their classmates, along with their findings about their chosen celebrity's accent.

Summary

In this chapter we have seen how we can raise learners' awareness of English as a Lingua Franca by discussing with them the reality of the language in the world today. This discussion will include data showing the numbers of speakers of English, the proportion of first to second language speakers, the different roles English now fulfils, and its current importance as a lingua franca. We have looked at a range of teaching techniques, with special emphasis on those that facilitate the teaching of the items in the LFC. Chapter 4 has also revealed the importance of accommodation in ensuring success in spoken interaction in ELF. Dictation, activities stimulating the negotiation of meaning, and communication activities have been proposed as ways of developing accommodation skills. Finally, we have seen that with monolingual groups, communication tasks can have a negative impact on pronunciation, since they cause learners to converge on their mother-tongue phonology and thus often become less intelligible internationally. This problem can be remedied to an extent by activities designed specifically for monolingual groups, such as the use of student recordings, or the exposure to ELF accents such as those on the audio CD that accompanies this book.

Further reading

On drills, minimal pairs, and activities for the pronunciation of individual sounds

Avery, P. and **S. Ehrlich.** 1992. *Teaching American English Pronunciation.* Oxford: Oxford University Press.

Bowen, T. and **J. Marks.** 1992. *The Pronunciation Book.* Harlow: Longman.

Hewings, M. 2004. *Pronunciation Practice Activities.* Cambridge: Cambridge University Press.

Kelly, G. 2000. *How to Teach Pronunciation.* Harlow: Pearson Education Limited.

On consonant clusters

Avery, P. and **S. Ehrlich.** 1992. *Teaching American English Pronunciation.* Oxford: Oxford University Press.

Celce-Murcia, M., D. M. Brinton, and **J. M. Goodwin.** 1996. *Teaching Pronunciation. A Reference for Teachers of English to Speakers of Other Languages.* Cambridge: Cambridge University Press.

Kelly, G. 2000. *How to Teach Pronunciation.* Harlow: Pearson Education Limited.

On nuclear stress placement

Gilbert, J. 2005. *Clear Speech* (3rd edn). Cambridge: Cambridge University Press.

Hancock, M. 1995. *Pronunciation Games.* Cambridge: Cambridge University Press.

On accommodation, communication activities, and dictation

Davis, P. and **M. Rinvolucri.** 1988. *Dictation. New Methods and New Possibilities.* Cambridge: Cambridge University Press.

Jenkins, J. 2000. *The Phonology of English as an International Language.* Oxford: Oxford University Press (Chapter 7).

Hadfield, J. 2000. *Intermediate Communication Games* (2nd edn.). Harlow: Pearson Education (also available at beginner and advanced levels).

Websites

English Language Learning Library Online: http://www.elllo.org, accessed 23 August 2008.

International Dialects of English Archive: http://www.ku.edu/~idea, accessed 25 May 2009.

OM Accents: http://www.ompersonal.com.ar/omaccents/contenidotematico.htm, accessed 25 May 2009.

Speech Accent Archive: http://accent.gmu.edu/browse_atlas.php, accessed 25 May 2009.

Endnote

page 88. In the discussion after the task, the listener admitted that he had initially understood 'a clay house', which had not made sense in the context of the activity.

5 ELF AND THE LEARNER'S FIRST-LANGUAGE PRONUNCIATION

Introduction

In Chapter 3 we saw that one of the benefits of taking an ELF approach to pronunciation is the change in the value it places on the learner's first language. In this chapter we will look at this benefit in detail. The chapter begins with a brief account of the thinking behind the existing lists of pronunciation problems for speakers of different L1s. The bulk of the chapter, however, offers detailed descriptions for ten L1 backgrounds on how their respective phonologies can help or hinder learners of ELF. These sections will be useful to:

- teachers who work in a monolingual environment with students from one of the L1s described
- teachers working with multilingual groups. This can be quite problematic for pronunciation teaching, but the 'ELF and selected first languages' section below should make it easier for you to give individualized attention to learners from the different backgrounds covered.

If you work in a monolingual environment that is not covered in this book, you can adopt the approach demonstrated here to your own situation. To do this, you might need to get help with your students' L1 phonology. You can help yourself, however, by listening carefully to different accents of this language. In particular, try to identify features of local accents that are also requirements of the LFC. You can then refer to them in class and get your students to imitate them. At the same time, try to recognize any non-core features of your learners' pronunciation, and 'train' yourself to leave these alone – they are part of the speaker's L2 accent.

Traditional lists of pronunciation difficulties

If you think about non-native speakers resident in your country, you will realize that almost without exception they have traces of their mother tongue in their accent when they speak your language. Until now this has usually been viewed as a sign of failure or incomplete learning. Consequently, the long-term aim of most pronunciation teaching has been to eliminate all traces of 'foreign' accent. However, as I explained in Chapter 1, accent and intelligibility are separate issues – accent is part of identity, and speaking with an accent is normal. More important still, the concept of 'foreign' is not actually applicable to accents in ELF communication as there is no such thing as a non-native (or native) speaker of ELF. Because of this, we need to reassess the contents of existing lists of pronunciation problems for learners of English.

Up to now these lists have generally been put together using an approach known as **Contrastive Analysis (CA)**. This approach has compared the learner's first-language pronunciation with that of a standard English accent (usually RP or GA). The comparison has predicted problems where certain phonemes or features that are present in a particular standard English accent are not present in the learner's first language.

CA has not proved to be as good at predicting problems as linguists originally thought it was going to be. In practice, some problems that it predicts do not actually arise. Others are found to exist that CA has not predicted. More importantly, when we marry the lists of problems generated by CA to the goal of native-speaker pronunciation, there is a strong tendency to see our learners' attempts at English principally in terms of what they cannot do. There is also the danger of assuming that the L1 pronunciation is the cause of any deviation from the NS target, and therefore the root of any 'foreign' accent. One result of this is that the mother tongue has largely been excluded from pronunciation practice, and teaching strategies have focused predominantly on what the native speaker does. Another result is that phonological transfer from the L1 has inevitably been described as 'interference'.

In an ELF approach, however, the value of the first language changes. It is no longer simply an obstacle to good pronunciation, nor necessarily a barrier to intelligibility. Instead, it is a resource that learners and teachers can take advantage of as they work towards ELF competence. This shift from 'L1 as foe' to 'L1 as friend' changes the emphasis in pronunciation teaching from what our learners cannot do, to what they can do. The first outcome of this is an increase in learners' motivation towards work on pronunciation. A second outcome is that teachers obtain a powerful teaching resource – the learners' first-language pronunciation. This can also improve motivation towards pronunciation.

The remainder of this chapter will try to demonstrate how this re-conceptualization of the learner's first language works in practice. For each of ten different first-language backgrounds you will find:

1 An introduction to the general features of the pronunciation of the L1 in question, and any broad positive or negative effects that the transfer of these features has on the learner's ELF pronunciation.

2 Language-specific ELF pronunciation notes explaining the relationship between the items in the LFC and the speaker's L1 pronunciation. As a minimum, these notes will contain an indication of the potential problems for ELF intelligibility. In addition, wherever possible suggestions are given on features of L1 accents and variants that can be used in class to achieve competence in the LFC.

The ELF pronunciation notes do not give detailed guidance on how to deal with common problems such as aspiration, voicing, treatment of consonant clusters, or vowel length, all of which have already been covered in Chapter 4.

ELF and selected first languages

Arabic (Mustafa Moubarik)

Arabic is currently the sixth most widely spoken language in the world, with approximately 186 million native speakers, spreading from North Africa to the Middle East. It is the official language of some 17 countries. The term 'Arabic' has two referents: literary Arabic on the one hand, and the many regional varieties commonly called 'colloquial Arabic' on the other. There are significant linguistic differences between these varieties, and intelligibility between users of different varieties depends largely on geographical closeness.

Interestingly, this situation favours native speakers of Arabic when they embark on foreign language acquisition because of:

- their knowledge of Arabic in its high and low varieties
- their awareness of coexisting languages in the same setting
- the limited promotion of Arabic outside the Arabic-speaking world, which forces them to learn languages that can be used as lingua francas. In this respect, Arabic native speakers are a very good example of ELF users.

Both the segmental and suprasegmental phonologies of Modern Standard Arabic (MSA) (and other languages or varieties known to the Arabic speaker) can be exploited in order to achieve high levels of competence in ELF pronunciation. For example, /g/ is not part of the consonant set of MSA, but it is represented in some North African regional varieties, where [g] is a phonetic variant for the phoneme /q/. Another instance is the sound /v/, which is absent from MSA, but is present in some loan words in regional varieties. In cases in which neither MSA nor local varieties offer near-equivalent targets, allophonic variation is sometimes the answer. The sound [dʒ], for example, although not a consonant of Arabic, is encountered as an **allophone** of /ʒ/ in words such as [madʒar] meaning 'shop'.

The distinction between long and short vowels in MSA is very important for correct pronunciation and spelling, because MSA contains minimal pairs that differ from each other only by vowel length. In addition, syllable stress in MSA is determined by syllable length, which crucially depends on vowel length. This is a great asset for achieving competence in ELF pronunciation.

Arabic has two kinds of syllables: open syllables (CV and CVV), and closed syllables (CVC, CVVC, and (CVCC). Every syllable begins with a consonant or else a consonant is borrowed from a previous word. English consonant clusters can be a little problematic, however.

ELF pronunciation for learners with Arabic as their first language language (Tracks 6, 8, and 21)

Consonants

Arabic has equivalent or near-equivalent sounds to the English phonemes /b/, /t/, /d/, /k/, /f/, /s/, /z/, /ʃ/, /h/, /m/, /n/, /l/, /j/, w/, so these should not be problematic for ELF intelligibility.

/p/   This phoneme can be problematic as it tends to be replaced by [b]. Learners should be reminded that a variant of [b] occurs in Arabic words. The [b] in 'kabch' [kapʃ] (lamb), for example, is similar to English /p/. It also emerges in loan words such as 'pasta'. In class teachers should emphasize aspiration since the lack of aspiration can interfere with intelligibility.

/g/   This is not part of the phonemic set of the Arabic language. However, [g] is an allophonic variant of the uvular voiceless stop /q/ in North African vernaculars, or of /ʒ/ in some Arabic vernaculars, such as those of Egypt or Lebanon.

/tʃ/   This can be problematic as it is not a consonant of standard Arabic. Nevertheless, the sound occurs in Arabic words when /t/ and /ʃ/ are adjacent, as in [tʃæmær] (to get ready). In addition, Arab speakers are familiar with this sound in loan words like 'champions', as well as in some local varieties.

/dʒ/   This can be problematic, as this phoneme is not a consonant of standard Arabic. Nevertheless, the sound occurs, especially where /d/ and /ʒ/ are adjacent in some Arabic vernaculars, such as in 'majar' [madʒar] (shop).

/v/ This can be problematic as it is not a consonant of standard Arabic. Nevertheless, in some Arabic vernaculars the sound occurs in loan words from French such as 'villa', 'virage', or 'vodka'.

/ʒ/ Arabic has a near-equivalent sound to /ʒ/. This sound may be problematic in some areas such as northern Morocco, where /ʒ/ tends to be replaced by [dʒ].

/ŋ/ This phoneme is not a consonant of standard Arabic. However, [ŋ] emerges as a variant of /n/, especially when it is preceded by /k/, as in 'in kana' [ɪŋkaːna], (if he was), or [fɪŋkaɪːn], (where is it/he).

/r/ In Arabic, this is a voiced alveolar trill. A flap is also common in some Arabic words, especially in non-stressed environments such as 'marara' or 'rajae' (bitterness, wish). Neither variant is problematic for ELF.

Consonant clusters

Clusters, whether they occur in word initial or final position, do not present serious problems for Arabic L1 speakers, except when one member of the cluster is /p/, such as in 'sport'. Arabic dialects, which work differently from MSA, allow the occurrence of two-consonant clusters. Three-consonant clusters might present problems. There is a tendency to insert a vowel in these clusters for ease of pronunciation, but this is not problematic for ELF.

Vowel length

Length in vowels is not a major problem either from the productive or from the receptive points of view. This is because Arab speakers of English are aware that length is a contrastive feature of their own language.

Nuclear stress placement

Word grouping is similar to English and is not a problem for ELF intelligibility. In addition, a key feature of Arabic is that content words are stressed just as they are in English. However, in order to mark contrast, Arabic uses a change in word order. This phenomenon could have a negative impact on the production of contrastive stress in English by Arabic L1 speakers, resulting in a loss of intelligibility because of the message being distorted, or because of the omission of the required contrastive stress.

Chinese (David Deterding)

Chinese represents a family of languages, including Mandarin (Pǔtōnghuà) in the north, and Cantonese (Yue) and Hokkien (Min) further south. Sociolinguistically, these last two are dialects, as they have no written form and most speakers accept Mandarin as the standard. Linguistically, however, being mutually unintelligible, they are separate languages. Whether they are called languages or dialects, the varying pronunciations throughout China raise different issues for English pronunciation. Here, most reference will be made to Mandarin, but reference will also sometimes be made to problems faced by speakers elsewhere in China.

The structure of a Chinese syllable is CGVF, where C is an optional consonant, G is an optional glide, V is the obligatory vowel, and F is an optional final, either /n/ or /ŋ/. A syllable with all these elements is 边 'biān' (side). One with just the vowel is 饿 'è' (hungry).

Although there are many different initial consonants in Chinese, there are fewer choices at the end of the syllable, so Chinese people struggle with final consonants in English, especially consonant clusters. Some speakers are so concerned about dropping final consonants that they always carefully produce all the sounds, and then an extra vowel occurs, so 'fast' sounds like 'faster'. ELF pronunciation allows for some simplification of medial and final consonant clusters, but persuading native Chinese speakers that it is OK to drop some sounds, such as the /t/ in 'postman' or in 'best man', is often difficult.

A second issue with Chinese pronunciation of English is that there are no voiced fricatives in Chinese, and many speakers struggle with /v/, /z/, and /ʒ/.

Finally, Chinese is a tonal language, so changes in tone affect the lexical identity of a syllable. This restricts the role of intonation in Chinese, and learners may struggle with English intonation. We do not need to focus on tonal contrasts in English, as they are exempted from ELF pronunciation; but placement of nuclear stress can be problematic, as speakers from China tend to stress the final word in English, even if it is a function word such as a pronoun.

ELF pronunciation for learners with Mandarin Chinese as their first language (Tracks 5, 14, and 22)

Consonants

Chinese has equivalent or near-equivalent sounds to the English phonemes /p/, /b/, /t/, /d/, /k/, /g/, /s/, /m/, /ŋ/, /j/, /w/, so these should not be problematic for ELF intelligibility.

/tʃ/   Chinese has a similar consonant, though the tongue is generally curled back in the mouth. It is spelled <ch> in Pīnyīn, and it occurs at the start of words such as 虫 'chóng' (insect). One problem is that speakers in Southern China, including Taiwan, often do not have this retroflex sound, so for them /tʃ/ and /ts/ may be merged, so 虫 'chóng' (insect) may sound the same as 从 'cóng' (from). For them, some work may be needed for English /tʃ/.

/dʒ/ Chinese has a similar consonant at the start of words such as 竹 'zhú' (bamboo). One problem is that some speakers in south China conflate the sounds that are represented by the Pinyin letters <zh> and <z>, with the result that 竹 'zhú' (bamboo) and 足 'zú' (foot) can sound the same. For these speakers, use of /dʒ/ in English may need some work.

/f/ Standard Chinese has /f/, so this sound is not a problem. However, some southern varieties of Chinese, such as Hokkien, conflate /f/ and /h/, and in this case some work may be needed for /f/, especially in Taiwan.

/v/ Chinese has no voiced fricatives, so /v/ can be a real problem. Some speakers use [w] in its place, so 'never' becomes [newə]. One effective teaching strategy is to get students to use [f] instead of /v/. Although [nefə] is not exactly correct, it sounds a lot better than [newə]. This strategy is less applicable for initial /v/ in English, so some careful work is needed here.

/z/ The absence of voiced fricatives makes /z/ a real problem for many speakers from China. This issue is compounded as <z> in Pīnyīn, for example at the start of 字 'zì' (character), is actually pronounced as an affricate [dz] not the fricative [z], and as a result, the English word 'zoo' may be pronounced as [dzuː] by some speakers. In final position, /z/ is often omitted, so 'has' may be [hæ] and 'because' may be [bɪkɒ]. For final position, getting students to use [s] instead is quite effective. It really does not matter too much that standard English has /z/ at the end of 'as' and 'because'. However, in initial position in words such as 'zoo', work on getting the /z/ correct is important.

/ʃ/ Chinese has a similar consonant, spelt <sh> in Pīnyīn, at the start of words such as 树 'shù' (tree). For the Chinese sound, the tongue may be curled back in the mouth, but it is generally fairly similar to the English sound. The main problem is that speakers in Southern China, including Taiwan, often do not have this retroflex sound, so for them /s/ and /ʃ/ may be the same, with the result that 树 'shù' (tree) may sound the same as 速 'sù' (speed). For them, some work may be needed to differentiate /ʃ/ and /s/, to ensure 'sheet' is distinct from 'seat'.

/ʒ/ Although this is the least common of the 24 consonants of English, it constitutes one of the biggest problems for speakers from China, especially in the word 'usually' which many speakers, especially in Shandong and elsewhere in the north of China, pronounce as [jurəli]. The problem arises because the Pinyin letter <r> is a voiced fricative in most varieties of Mandarin, but it may be [r] in other varieties, and even quite proficient speakers of English then conflate English /ʒ/ with /r/ and are quite stunned to be told that [jurəli] is not an appropriate pronunciation. One strategy is to get them to say 'you Shirley' – although it is not exactly right, [juʃəli] is a lot more intelligible than [jurəli]. Alternatively, one could go for an avoidance strategy and say 'generally' instead of 'usually'. One way or another, /ʒ/ is a problem.

/h/   Chinese has /h/, but in many parts of China it is pronounced as [x] (a velar fricative, similar to the sound at the end of the Scottish pronunciation of 'loch'), and students often use this sound for /h/ in English. This does not matter too much, as [x] can be understood as /h/ reasonably easily.

/n/   Chinese has /n/, so this is not generally a problem. However, in some southern provinces, such as Guangdong and also Sichuan, /n/ and /l/ are conflated, and students from these places may have real problems separating them, pronouncing 'law' as [nɔː] or 'knife' as [laɪf]. For these students, lots of work is needed to differentiate /n/ and /l/ at the start of a word. One helpful strategy is to place a small mirror under the nose: for /n/, the mirror should steam up (because air is coming out of the nose), but for /l/ it should not.

/l/   Chinese has /l/, so this sound is not generally a problem, except for some speakers from south China who many conflate it with /n/ (see /n/ above). At the end of a word, many speakers pronounce the dark /l/ in words such as 'call' and 'fool' as a vowel; but use of a [ʊ] in place of dark /l/ is acceptable in ELF, so this replacement is not a problem.

/r/   Chinese does not have /r/, and the sound represented by the Pīnyīn letter <r> is generally a voiced fricative instead of an approximant. But most Chinese speakers of English do not seem to have a problem with /r/.

Consonant clusters

Chinese does not have consonant clusters, but it is only the final clusters in English that all Chinese learners find really problematic. Mandarin Chinese only allows two final consonants: /n/ and /ŋ/. Other dialects of Chinese, such as Cantonese and Hokkien, allow a few more (/m/, /p/, /t/, and /k/), but never have final clusters. Some speakers drop consonants, others insert a vowel, so that 'mist' sounds like 'mister', which can interfere with intelligibility.

Vowel length

Chinese has no distinctions in vowel length, so making a distinction between the long and short vowels of English, between 'beat' and 'bit' and also between 'fool' and 'full', is something that needs lots of work.

Nuclear stress placement

Chinese is a tonal language, so the English system of intonation is problematic, including the placement of the main nuclear stress. There is a tendency, for example, for emphasis to be placed on final function words such as pronouns, possibly to signal the end of a sentence. Work is needed to ensure that pronouns do not receive prominence in this way.

German (Armin Berger)

German is the most widely spoken mother tongue in the European Union. As with any other language, it has not just one form of pronunciation, but a number of regional accents. These can differ so sharply that local varieties from one part of the German-speaking area are not readily understood by other German speakers and vice versa. What is usually considered the 'standard' is commonly referred to as Hochdeutsch or Standardlautung. However, it must be remembered that German has in fact more than one standard. As a result, pronunciation is not uniform, and most speakers have some distinct regional characteristics in their speech. Nevertheless, some general features of the phonology of German and their effects on the pronunciation of English for ELF communication can be described.

Comparing the German and English phonemic systems, we find quite a number of equivalent or near-equivalent phonemes in both languages. This is particularly true for the consonants, and most German consonants are adequate for use in ELF communication. One major problem for German learners of English, the production of /θ/ and /ð/, is not essential in ELF communication, which is a great relief for learners and teachers alike. Possible threats to intelligibility arise not so much because of difficulties in articulation but rather as a result of different distributions of the phonemes in the two languages. For example, the distinction between voiced and voiceless consonants in some contexts might be problematic. In German, voiced consonants cannot occur in word-final position, where they are replaced by their voiceless counterparts. This devoicing of final consonants is often transferred into English. A more important threat to intelligibility stems from the lack of voiceless plosives /p/, /t/, /k/ in word-initial positions in southern parts of the German-speaking area.

Although the German vowel sounds differ slightly from their English counterparts, the German vowel inventory is sufficient for ELF communication. The English vowel sound /ɜ:/, which is considered important for ELF, does not exist in German and might need some practice. In addition, German vowels are not shortened before voiceless consonants or lengthened before voiced consonants. This will be problematic for ELF.

Word grouping and the placement of nuclear stress follow very similar principles in English and German, so are unlikely to cause major problems.

ELF pronunciation for learners with German as their first language (Tracks 1, 4, 15, and 23)

Consonants

German has equivalent or near-equivalent sounds to the English phonemes /tʃ/, /f/, /ʃ/, /h/, /m/, /n/, /l/, /j/, so these should not be problematic for ELF intelligibility.

/p/   German /p/ in 'Pass' (passport), 'Papier' (paper), or 'Lippe' (lip) is very similar to English /p/ in terms of place and manner of articulation. Whereas Northern German maintains a distinction between /p/ and /b/ in word-initial positions, southern German varieties such as Austrian German sometimes do not make this distinction. Speakers of these varieties, therefore, tend to produce English /p/ as an unaspirated sound at the beginning of words, making 'pin' sound like 'bin'. Stress the difference in meaning between these words and focus on the aspiration of English /p/.

/b/   German /b/ is very similar in word-initial positions. However, word final <b> is pronounced [p]. Demonstrate the difference by contrasting word pairs like 'rib' and 'rip'. Insist on a longer duration of the preceding vowel.

/t/   German /t/ is very similar. However, what was said about the aspiration of /p/ is also true for /t/ (see above). Demonstrate aspiration if necessary by contrasting the English words 'town' and 'down'.

/d/   /d/ is very similar in the two languages and does not generally cause problems. However, in German <d> is pronounced [t] in word-final positions. Insist on /d/ at the end of words. Guide learners to the difference between English words like 'got' and 'god', and stress that the vowel is a little longer before final /d/.

/k/   German /k/ is very similar to its English counterpart. In some varieties of the central and southern German-speaking area, /k/ might be either very weakly aspirated or completely unaspirated. Point to the difference in aspiration between words like 'came' and 'game'.

/g/   /g/ is very similar in both languages. There is a tendency to substitute [k] for /g/ in word-final positions. Demonstrate the difference by contrasting word pairs such as 'back' and 'bag'. Insist on the lengthening of the vowel before /g/.

/dʒ/   /dʒ/ is not a phoneme of German; it occurs only in loan words, principally from Italian. German speakers therefore tend to pronounce English /dʒ/ as [tʃ]. Practise the difference with minimal pairs such as 'gin' and 'chin'. Draw attention to Italian loan words such as 'adagio'.

/v/   /v/ does exist in German words such as 'Wetter' or 'Vase'. However, the spelling of Modern German might cause problems. Since German /v/ is most frequently represented by the letter <w>, German learners tend to pronounce /w/ for [v], resulting from an over-generalization of the use of English /w/. Draw attention to the misleading spelling. Another difficulty is the voiced–voiceless distinction in word-final positions. Insist on the use of /v/ particularly at the end of words, together with a longer vowel before /v/.

/s/   /s/ is very similar in English and German. Problems for German speakers are more likely to occur because of the different distributions of this sound. German speakers may use [z] for /s/ in initial positions.

/z/   Just like /s/, /z/ is similar in terms of production. In many southern varieties, however, /z/ is devoiced and thus not clearly distinguished from /s/. Encourage pronunciation which adds voicing to /s/. Another problem is the voiced–voiceless distinction in final positions.

/ʒ/   /ʒ/ does exist in German. In southern parts of the German speaking area, however, /ʒ/ does not occur; also many other German speakers tend not to use /ʒ/ at all, replacing it with [ʃ]. Draw attention to the sound in loan words of French and Italian origin such as 'Genie' or 'Girokonto'.

/ŋ/   The articulation of /ŋ/ is the same in English and German. Some northern and south-eastern forms of German have /ŋk/ in place of final /ŋ/.

/r/   /r/ is the most varied German consonant sound. It can be a trill, flap, fricative, or approximant, most of which are intelligible in ELF. Discourage the use of a uvular fricative [ʁ], which might not be as readily intelligible.

/w/   /w/ is not a phoneme of German, so learners tend to substitute unrounded /v/ for it. Demonstrate the difference by contrasting the German word 'Wein' and the English 'wine'. Invite students to produce the sound /uː/ to get the feel for lip rounding, followed by the sound /ə/. Tell students to put the two sounds together and keep them short.

Consonant clusters

Consonant clusters are not normally problematic for speakers of German in any position. Neither deletion of one of the consonants in the cluster nor insertion of a vowel sound between the consonants will generally occur. A vowel sound might be inserted between fricative sounds in words such as 'breathes', 'clothes', or 'loathes'.

Vowel length

German distinguishes between short and long vowels, so learners of English should be able to produce the basic short–long distinctions. However, German vowels are not shortened before voiceless consonants, so German learners of English will need some practice in producing different vowel quantities in word pairs like 'feed' and 'feet', 'hid' and 'hit', or 'advise' and 'advice'.

Nuclear stress placement

Word grouping in German is very similar in English and German, so that the transfer should not generally cause problems for German learners of English. In addition, the placement of nuclear stress in German follows rules very similar to those of English, so German speakers do not have major problems with this either. In German, as in English, emphasis is given to a particular item in the word group by shifting the nuclear stress to that word.

Greek (Bill Batziakas)

The Greek language is currently used by around 16 million people. Around 11 million of them are the residents of Greece, and around 800,000 of Cyprus. It is also used by around 4 million expatriate Greeks and Cypriots, mainly in the USA, Australia, Germany, and England. It is the sole official language in Greece, and with some variation, Greek is one of the two official languages in Cyprus, Turkish being the other. It has been one of the official languages of the European Union since 1981.

Greek belongs to the Indo-European family of languages. From a chronological point of view, it is essentially divided into Ancient Greek and Modern Greek. Until 1976, Modern Greek drew heavily on Ancient Greek and thus was considered prestigious and was called 'katharevousa' ('pure language'). Then the growing everyday variety, called 'demotiki' ('language of the populace'), was recognized. This was simpler than 'katharevousa' and was considered less prestigious. Despite this, 'Demotiki' has been the official variety ever since, and nowadays it is referred to simply as 'Greek' unless there is the need to differentiate it from the other varieties.

This mosaic of temporal and spatial variation in Greek offers advantages for teaching and learning the regularities of ELF pronunciation. Notably, speakers of Greek have taken part in spoken exchanges characterized by accent variation that did not compromise successful communication, and such positive accent-related experiences can be recalled and emulated in work on pronunciation. Also, speakers with regional accents may find it easier to deal with English sounds that occur in their own accents.

The sounds and the other pronunciation features discussed below are important for English teachers and learners in Greece for one more reason. In 2006, the Paidagogiko Institouto of Greece (the official educational policy-making body of the Ministry of Education of Greece) came up with two volumes of guidelines for Greek state schools: *Training of School Counsellors and Teachers of Primary and Pre-school Education in DEPPS and APS* for primary schools; and *Training Material Issue* for secondary schools. In the corresponding chapters of both manuals, state school teachers are instructed to teach English as a lingua franca.

ELF pronunciation for speakers with Greek as their first language (Tracks 12, 17, and 24)

Consonants

Greek has equivalent or near-equivalent sounds to the English phonemes /b/, /d/, /g/, /f/, /v/, /z/, /m/, /n/, /j/, and so these should not be problematic for ELF intelligibility.

/p/   The Greek /p/ as in 'παραλία' (beach) is similar, but it is not always aspirated strongly enough, so 'pin' can sound like 'bin'. Demonstrate the difference in aspiration by contrasting the Greek 'πάντοτε' (always) and the English 'pan'.

/t/   The /t/ in Greek as in 'τοίχος' (wall) is not always aspirated strongly enough. Demonstrate the difference in aspiration using the Greek word 'του' (of) and the English 'too'.

/k/   The Greek /k/ has two allophones, but both are intelligible for ELF. However, /k/ in Greek is not always aspirated strongly enough. Demonstrate the difference in aspiration using the Greek word 'κίτρινο' (yellow) and the English 'kit'.

/tʃ/   /tʃ/ is not a phoneme of Greek and is substituted by [ts]. However, Cretans produce /tʃ/ as in 'τσαμπί' (cluster). Encourage learners to imitate Cretans with regard to this, or to produce the fat 's', as it is called in Greece.

/dʒ/   /dʒ/ is not a phoneme of Greek and is substituted by [dz]. However, Cretans produce /dʒ/, as in 'τζόγος' (gamble). Encourage learners to imitate Cretans with regard to this, or to produce the fat 'z'.

/s/   The /s/ in Greek as in 'σημασία' (importance) is very similar. However, when /s/ occurs between vowels, the Greeks will tend to pronounce it as [z] as in 'Vaseline'.

/ʃ/   /ʃ/ is not a phoneme of Greek, and is often substituted by [s], so words like 'shame' and 'same' can sound the same. Tell learners to make their /s/ fatter by raising the front of their tongue close to their hard palate.

/ʒ/   /ʒ/ is not a phoneme in Greek, which only has /z/, so words like 'leisure' and 'lesser' can sound the same. Tell learners to make their /z/ fatter, by raising the front of their tongue close to their hard palate.

/h/   Instead of the English /h/, Greeks in general have [x] as in 'χορός' (dance) and [ç] before /ɪ/ and /e/ as in 'χυμός' (juice) and 'χέρι' (hand), respectively. These are similar to /h/ and no action is needed. Cretans, however, have /tʃ/ before /ɪ/ and /e/, which is problematic. Demonstrate the difference to these learners, and insist on /h/.

/ŋ/   /ŋ/ is not a phoneme in Greek. Invite students to pronounce /n/ and then slowly /k/ so as to raise the back of their tongue and make it touch their soft palate.

/l/   /l/ in English and in Greek as in 'καλά' (well) are very similar. Speakers from Laconia and Eastern Romylia pronounce /l/ in the middle of words as [ʊ], but this is intelligible in ELF, so these speakers can use this local feature instead of dark /l/.

/r/   Greek has a rhotic accent, with the <r> in the spelling being pronounced clearly as /r/. This does not affect ELF intelligibility.

/w/   /w/ is not a phoneme in Greek. In words like 'whisky' it is substituted by [ʊ] as in 'ουρά' (tail), in words like 'wet' it is substituted by [ɣ] as in 'γάμος' (marriage), and in words like 'Hawaii' it is substituted by [v] as in 'φόβος' (fear). Demonstrate the difference, and insist on /w/.

Consonant clusters

In Greek, /s/ becomes [z] before /m/ followed by a vowel as in 'σμήνος' (flock), so, 'smile' becomes 'zmile'. Practise exaggerating the 's' before producing the /m/.

In Greek, /p/, /t/, /k/ are voiced and are pronounced as [b], [d], [g], respectively, when they come after nasal consonants with the same place of articulation. Words like 'ampere', 'centre' and 'ankle' will be pronounced 'amber', 'sender' and 'angle'. Demonstrate the difference, and use minimal pairs to practise it.

In Greek, /m/, /n/, /ŋ/ are elided before voiced consonants with the same place of articulation. Words like 'gamble', 'pounder', and 'jungle' will be pronounced 'gabble', 'powder', and 'juggle' respectively. Demonstrate the difference, and get students to lengthen the first consonant as a practice strategy: 'gammmmble', 'pounnnnder', 'junnnngle', etc. This process can occur in reverse; words like 'gabble', 'powder', and 'juggle' can be pronounced as 'gamble', 'pounder', and 'jungle' respectively. In addition, the two previous features can co-occur. For instance, 'simple' can be reduced to 'Sybil' (/p/ is pronounced as [b] because of the nasal /m/, and /m/ is deleted before /b/.)

With the exception of the clusters already covered in this section, other clusters should not be problematic. Combinations of three consonants exist in Greek as in 'στρατός' (army). These can become four consonants with the addition of a prefix, as in 'εκστρατεία' (campaign).

In Greek, there are no word-final clusters, but only word-final single consonants as in 'καλός' (good). Greeks learners of English tend to add an [ə]-like sound at the end of a word, so that 'cold' will sound like 'colder' in English. Demonstrate the difference, and point out the possible impact on intelligibility.

Vowel length

In Greek, there are no short or long vowels per se, and their length lies roughly midway between the short and long vowels of English. An exception occurs in the Greek of the islanders of the Ionian and the Aegean seas, who tend to lengthen the last vowel of a word, especially when this word is the last one in a sentence, making it even longer than the English long vowels. Use this local feature to make learners aware of the different vowel lengths of English as in 'it' versus 'eat' and 'sit' versus 'seat'.

In Greek, vowels are lengthened when their syllable is stressed as in 'ανδριάντας' (full size statue). Make learners aware of this, and refer to it when working on vowel length in English. Vowels are also lengthened when they are followed by a voiced consonant, as in 'πάντως' (anyway) versus 'πάτος' (bottom). If necessary, refer to this when dealing with the length of English vowels. In contrast, in rural Thessaly, a vowel is often elided when it occurs in an unstressed syllable between different consonants as in 'κάνεις' (you do) and 'σκυλί' (dog), and when it occurs in an unstressed final syllable as in 'σκουλήκι' (worm) and 'κορίτσι μου' (my girl). This can be problematic, because a word like 'giraffe' can sound like 'graffe', and 'graffiti' can sound like 'graffit'. Insist on learners giving these vowels their full value.

Nuclear stress placement

In Greek, words are grouped almost in the same way as in English, so this should no present problems. In both English and Greek nuclear stress can be shifted, in order to create a change in the intended meaning, so with regard to nuclear stress placement, no special action should be needed. Note how the five Greek sentences below resemble their equivalent English sentences in that both the sets are written in the same way but can be pronounced differently, thus signifying shift of attention to a different element of the sentence:

ΕΣΥ δεν διάβασες σήμερα. (YOU didn't study today.)

Εσύ ΔΕΝ διάβασες σήμερα. (You DIDN'T study today.)

Εσύ δεν ΔΙΑΒΑΣΕΣ σήμερα. (You didn't STUDY today.)

Εσύ ΔΕΝ ΔΙΑΒΑΣΕΣ σήμερα. (You DIDN'T STUDY today.)

Εσύ δεν διάβασες ΣΗΜΕΡΑ. (You didn't study TODAY.)

Japanese (Atsuko Shimizu)

Japanese is a language of unknown origin. It is not related to Chinese, despite the fact that a large number of Chinese characters are used in its writing system. Two other kinds of characters are employed in the writing system, with each letter representing a mora consisting of a consonant and a vowel or a vowel alone, which reflects the basic Japanese (C)V construction as described below.

Japanese has a wide range of regional accent variation, and some of the vowel realizations that are absent from Tokyo Japanese but present in regional accents are similar to English vowels. For example, [uː] in Kansai (western) accents accompanies lip-rounding and is thus similar to English /uː/, and [i] in Tohoku (north-eastern) accents often sounds similar to English /ɪ/.

Japanese is a language of open syllables. No consonant can appear without preceding a vowel, with the only exception of the syllable-final uvular nasal /ɴ/. Consequently, Japanese students tend to add a vowel to every consonant other than /n/ if it is not preceding a vowel. The vowel added is usually /u/, though /o/ is regularly added to /t/ and /d/. As a result of this strategy, English words containing consonant clusters and/or syllable-final consonants often end up as much longer words than the original, and this can threaten intelligibility.

Most of the English consonants have equivalents or near-equivalents in Japanese. The notorious problem concerning consonants is the lack of distinction between /l/ and /r/ in Japanese (see 'Consonants' below). Palatalization of consonants before /i/ is regular in Japanese, and its effect is especially notable with /s/, /z/, /t/, /d/, /n/, /h/ (see 'Consonants' below). This can threaten intelligibility when transferred to English consonants preceding /iː/ and /ɪ/. The weakness of aspiration of /p/, /t/, /k/ is another potential threat to intelligibility.

Japanese students tend to give equal length to every syllable without reducing vowels in English unstressed syllables. This alone may not threaten intelligibility very seriously, but when it is combined with the addition of extra vowels as discussed above, the result will be utterances far longer than the original, which are sometimes very hard to understand even in ELF contexts.

ELF pronunciation for learners with Japanese as their first language (Tracks 7, 20, and 25)

Consonants

Japanese has equivalent or near-equivalent sounds to the English phonemes /tʃ/, /dʒ/, /ʃ/, /m/, and so these should not be problematic for ELF intelligibility.

/p/   Japanese /p/ is very similar, but is only slightly aspirated, and can sound rather like /b/ in English. Demonstrate aspiration by contrasting the Japanese loanword 'pen' and the English 'pen'.

/b/   Japanese /b/ in words like 'boku' (I) and 'tonbo' (dragonfly) is similar, but when this consonant occurs between vowels as in 'abunai' (dangerous) in fast and/or casual speech in particular, it is often pronounced as a fricative, which can sound more like /v/ than /b/ in English. Insist on the use of the /b/ in 'boku'.

/t/   Japanese /t/ is dental before /e/, /a/, and /o/, with only weak aspiration. This dental articulation does not threaten intelligibility, but the lack of aspiration can make /t/ sound like /d/ in English. Demonstrate aspiration by contrasting the Japanese loanword 'toppu' and the English 'top'.

Japanese /t/ is realized as [tʃ] before /ɪ/ or /i/, making 'tip' and 'tease' sound like 'chip' and 'cheese'. Also, /t/ is realized as [ts] before /u/, and so /t/ in words like 'tour' and 'tool' can become [ts], which can be heard as /s/ by English speakers. Similarly, the Japanese loanword 'tsunami' (tidal wave) is often heard and pronounced as [su:na:mi] by English speakers. Insist on the use of the /t/ in 'toppu' with appropriate aspiration.

/d/   Japanese /d/ is dental before /a/, /e/, and /o/. However, this does not threaten ELF intelligibility. /d/ does not normally occur in Japanese before /i/ or /u/ except in loanwords, but students do not have much difficulty pronouncing /d/ in words like 'disc' or 'doom'.

/k/   Japanese /k/ is very similar to /k/ in English, but is only weakly aspirated. Demonstrate aspiration by contrasting Japanese loanword 'kuru' and the English 'cool'.

/g/   Japanese /g/ in words like 'gohan' (meal) is very similar, but when it occurs between vowels, as in 'kagi' (key), it is often realized as a fricative or as [ŋ]. Insist on the use of the /g/ in 'gohan'.

/f/   Not a phoneme of Japanese, /f/ is often substituted with a fricative sound made with the airflow escaping from between closely rounded lips, as heard in 'foto' and 'Fuji'. Raise awareness by pronouncing 'photo' and 'Fuji' with English /f/ and invite students to bring their lower lip into light contact with their upper teeth.

/v/   Not a phoneme of Japanese, this is often substituted with [b] or a fricative sound as heard in 'abunai'. Raise awareness by contrasting the Japanese loanwords 'besuto' and 'kaba' with the English 'vest' and 'cover'. Invite students to bring their lower lip into light contact with their upper teeth.

/s/   Very similar to Japanese /s/ as in 'sake'. However, this consonant is realized as [ʃ] before /ɪ/ or /i/, and so words like 'sip' and 'seat' can sound like 'ship' and 'sheet'. Insist on the use of /s/ in 'sake'.

/z/   Very similar to Japanese /z/ between vowels as in 'kaze' (wind). However, /z/ is realized as [dz] in word-initial contexts and after /N/, as in 'zen' and 'banzai' respectively, and sometimes also when between vowels as in the above-cited 'kaze'. This is not normally problematic for ELF, although students have difficulty differentiating between /z/ as in 'cars' and /dz/ as in 'cards'. Raise awareness to the difference by adding voice first to /s/ and then to /ts/ several times. In addition, /z/ is realized as [ʒ] or [dʒ] before /i/, so English /z/ can become [dʒ] in 'New Zealand', and [ʒ] or [dʒ] in 'easy'. Insist on the use of /z/ in 'kaze'.

/ʒ/   Not a phoneme of Japanese, but the 'j' between vowels as in 'niji' (rainbow) or 'kanojo' (she) is mostly pronounced as [ʒ]. As in the case of /z/, students have difficulty differentiating between /ʒ/ and /dʒ/, so that the second consonants of 'vision' and 'region' are pronounced alike, often as /dʒ/.

/h/   Very similar to Japanese /h/ before a vowel, as in 'hana' (flower). Before /i/, this consonant is realized as a voiced velar fricative as heard in German 'ich' (I) or Spanish 'giro' (turn), and before /u/ as a fricative [ɸ] pronounced with the airflow escaping from between the lips. Raise awareness by contrasting the Japanese loanwords 'hi:to' and 'hu:do' with the English 'heat' and 'hood', and insist on the use of /h/ in 'hana'.

/n/   Japanese /n/ is not normally problematic for ELF. However, Japanese has an /n/-like sound, transcribed as /N/, which is made deep in the throat in word-final contexts. This sound often substitutes English final /n/, giving the impression that it has been dropped in phrases like 'in an hour' and 'on air'. Insist on the use of /n/ in 'nuno'(cloth).

/ŋ/   Not a phoneme of Japanese, but it regularly occurs in words like 'iNku' (ink) and 'saNgai' (third floor) and sometimes in words like 'kagi'.

Japanese students have difficulty pronouncing /ŋ/ between vowels as in 'singer' without adding /g/ after it. However, this does not appear to be problematic for ELF.

/l/   Not a phoneme of Japanese, but Japanese /r/ following /ɴ/, in words like 'aɴraku' (ease) and 'hoɴɴrui' (base) is realized as a consonant very similar to /l/. Invite students to prolong this kind of /r/ in order to learn how to produce English /l/.

/r/   Japanese has /r/, but it is different from English /r/ in that the tip of the tongue always comes into contact with the alveolar ridge, making Japanese /r/ sound like something between English /l/ and /r/. Consequently, Japanese students have difficulty differentiating the English /l/ and /r/, both in production and reception. Raise awareness by pronouncing the English 'right', 'light' and the Japanese loanword 'raito' (meaning either 'right' or 'light'). Invite students to try pronouncing Japanese /r/ without their tongue-tip touching anywhere, which will produce English /r/.

/j/   Japanese has /j/ in words like 'yasui' (inexpensive) and 'yoru' (night), but this semi-vowel never occurs before /i/ or /e/. Japanese students tend to pronounce 'yeast' and 'year' just like 'east' and 'ear'. Raise awareness by contrasting the English 'yeast' and 'year' with the Japanese loanwords 'i:suto' and 'iya:'.

/w/   Japanese has /w/ pronounced without lip-rounding as in words like 'wa' (ring) and 'kawa' (river). This semi-vowel appears only before /a/, so Japanese students have difficulty pronouncing /w/ in words like 'wool' and 'wound'. Raise awareness by contrasting the English 'wool' and 'woman' with the Japanese loanwords 'u:ru' and 'u:ma'.

Consonant clusters

No clusters are permitted in Japanese, and so Japanese students often break up clusters through the insertion of a vowel. Words such as such as 'spray', 'taxi', and 'breakfast' can become /supure:/, /takushi:/ and /burekkufasuto/ respectively. Even if no consonants are deleted, this strategy often produces words far longer than the original, which can affect intelligibility. Raise awareness by contrasting the English 'spray', 'taxi', and 'breakfast' with the Japanese loanwords 'supure:', 'takushi:' and 'burekkufasuto'.

Vowel length

Japanese has five short vowels and five long counterparts to them, which can also be analysed as successions of the same two short vowels. Consequently, Japanese students tend to pronounce English long vowels twice as long as their short counterparts regardless of contexts. Japanese has successions of two vowels similar to English diphthongs. They are pronounced with equal weight for both vowels, though this will not threaten intelligibility.

Nuclear stress placement

Japanese sentence structure is quite different from that of English, and so Japanese students have considerable difficulty with word grouping, often producing unnecessary pauses. This needs considerable work.

Japanese mainly uses changes in pitch as well as the choice of postpositional particles to produce the effect achieved by shifting stress in English. Japanese students will have difficulty deciding where to place nuclear stress, often stressing pronouns or other function words. However, once they have learned to tell where to put nuclear stress, they can do it easily because nuclear stress always involves pitch change as well as intensity, and they have a very sensitive ear for pitch change.

Malay (David Deterding)

Malay is a member of the Austronesian family of languages that are spoken in Malaysia and throughout the Indonesian archipelago.

Standard Malay (Bahasa Melayu) is the official language in Malaysia, Brunei, and the Malay population of Singapore. It differs somewhat from Indonesian (Bahasa Indonesia), though the two are (mostly) mutually intelligible. In fact, Standard Malay is spoken as a first language by few people, so throughout Malaysia there is widespread variation in pronunciation. Nevertheless, Standard Malay will be taken as the point of comparison here.

Malay learners of English complain about English spelling, insisting the pronunciation of Malay words is predictable from their spelling. This is not entirely true, as the pronunciation of some Malay words is not predictable. For example: 'perang' can be pronounced as [peraŋ] (brown) or [pəraŋ] (war); and 'capai' (achieve) is bisyllalbic but 'mulai' (beginning from) is trisyllabic. Nevertheless, Malay spelling is certainly more straightforward than English, and we can empathize with Malay speakers who struggle with the vagaries of English spelling.

The syllable structure of Malay is quite simple: CVC. So there are no consonant clusters either at the beginning or end of the syllable. However, Malay speakers of English find initial clusters easier than final ones, partly because in many Malay words the first two syllables may be combined into a single syllable in actual speech. For example: 'diam' (quiet) might underlyingly be bisyllabic, but it is generally pronounced monosyllabically as [djam]; and 'sekali' (once), which in careful speech is [səkali], nearly always gets pronounced as [skali]. Furthermore, there are some borrowed words that start with /pr/ (so they violate the basic CVC syllable structure), including 'program' and 'projek', and this helps make initial clusters easy for Malay speakers of English.

Final clusters are more difficult, and it is common for learners to drop the final consonant. This tendency is reinforced by borrowings from English into Malay in which the final consonant is omitted: 'lif' (lift), 'setem' (stamp), and many more. However, ELF pronunciation allows for some simplification of final consonant clusters, so this is not too problematic.

ELF pronunciation for learners with Malay as their first language (Tracks 1, 4, 15, and 26)

Consonants

Malay has equivalent or near-equivalent sounds to the English phonemes /s/, /h/, /m/, /n/, /ŋ/, /l/, /w/, /r/, /j/, so these should not be problematic for ELF intelligibility.

/p/   Malay has /p/. However, this consonant is unaspirated, and it can sound like /b/ in English. Work is needed to ensure the English sound is aspirated.

/b/   Malay has /b/, so this sound is not a problem in initial position. In final position, there is no /b/ in Malay, so some work is needed to distinguish final /b/ from /p/.

/t/   Malay has /t/. However, this consonant is unaspirated, and it can sound like /d/ in English. Work is needed to ensure the English sound is aspirated.

/d/   Malay has /d/, so this sound is not a problem in initial position. In final position, there is no /d/ in Malay, except in a few borrowed words such as 'kad' (card), so some work is needed to distinguish final /d/ from /t/.

/k/   Malay has /k/. However, this consonant is unaspirated, and it can sound like /g/ in English. Work is needed to ensure the English sound is aspirated.

/g/   Malay has /g/, so this sound is not a problem in initial position. In final position, there is no /g/ in Malay, except in borrowed words such as 'beg' (bag), so some work is needed to distinguish final /g/ from /k/.

/tʃ/   /tʃ/ is a consonant in Malay, represented by the letter 'c'. Although it mainly occurs in initial position, a few borrowed words have it in final position, such as 'Mac' (March), and it does not seem to be a problem for most speakers.

/dʒ/   /dʒ/ is a consonant in Malay, represented by the letter 'j', so is not a problem. Although it mainly occurs in initial position, a few borrowed words have it in final position, such as 'imej' (image), where it does not seem to be problematic.

/f/   /f/ was not originally a consonant of Malay, though a number of borrowed words use it, including quite common words from Arabic such as 'faham' (to understand) and some words from English such as 'fail' (file). However, many speakers pronounce these words with /p/ instead, and confusion between English /f/ and /p/ is widespread for less-proficient learners. This needs considerable work.

/v/   /v/ is not a basic consonant of Malay, and it just occurs in a few borrowed words such as 'visa'. Many speakers use /b/ instead, and this requires some work in English.

/z/   /z/ in Malay mainly occurs in words of Arabic origin such as 'zakat' (tithe). For some speakers, it is a problem and needs some work. For example, some pronounce 'zoo' with [dʒ] at the start.

/ʃ/   /ʃ/ was not originally a sound in Malay, but it occurs in so many words of Arabic origin that it is not a problem in initial position for most speakers. It is represented by the letters 'sy', as in 'syarikat' (a company). However, it never occurs in final position, so this is a problem for many speakers.

/ʒ/   Malay does not have /ʒ/, so it can be a problem for learners of English.

Consonant clusters

Initial clusters do not seem to be a problem, as in fast colloquial Malay initial clusters are common, even if they do not exist in the underlying system. Thus 'sepuluh' (ten) is nearly always [spuluh]. Word final consonant clusters are very frequently simplified, and this is reinforced by the large number of words that are borrowed into Malay with the simplification of their final clusters. Examples include 'pos' (post) and 'sen' (cent).

Vowel length

Malay does not have vowel length distinctions, so differentiation between words such as 'beat' and 'bit', and also between 'pool' and 'pull', needs lots of work.

Nuclear stress placement

Word grouping is similar to English, so this is not a problem. There is sentence stress in Malay, but its placement is somewhat different from English. For example, some speakers stress pronouns, and this can result in them receiving unexpected stress in English, especially when in final position. This needs some work.

Polish (Grzegorz Śpiewak)

Polish is a member of the West Slavic language family, with notable similarities to Slovak and a degree of intelligibility with Croatian, Czech, Serbian, Russian, and Ukrainian. Polish is relatively homogeneous accent-wise; save for several varieties of rural Polish (considered substandard by the city folk) and the speech of south-western Poland (Silesia), southern Poland (highlanders' accent) and north-eastern Poland.

Pronunciation of Polish is as a rule predictable from spelling (a source of much complaining by Polish learners when they are confronted with English complexities in this domain). Note, however, that this causes initial problems with the letters 'w' and 'j' (mispronounced as [v] and [dż], respectively). Given this remarkable stability, Poles will expect every letter to be pronounced (including all 'r' letters before consonants and in word-final positions). This will in general constitute an advantage for learners aiming for ELF intelligibility.

As regards the sounds, quite a few English consonants have equivalents in Polish. There are also several near-equivalents with no major threats to EFL intelligibility (/t/, /d/, /n/ are all dental in Polish; /ʃ/, /ʒ/, /tʃ/, /dʒ/ are replaced with corresponding retroflex fricatives/affricates; 'r' is a trill). A potential threat to intelligibility is the lack of aspiration of the voiceless plosives /p/, /t/, /k/. Another threat is the obligatory devoicing of word-final stops, fricatives, and affricates, resulting in words like 'cap' and 'cab' or 'of' and 'off' sounding identical (see more on this when discussing vowel length below). Polish is notorious for its consonant clusters in all possible positions, so the English clusters are not a problem.

Polish only has six pure vowels, all short. It takes considerable time and energy to get Polish learners to hear vowel length contrasts, and longer still to get them to produce them. For instance, Poles will tend to approximate the /iː/ in 'sheep' and /ɪ/ in 'ship' with their single high front short vowel, which is very much like the final sound in 'happy' or the /i/ in 'react'.

ELF pronunciation for learners with Polish as their first language (Tracks 2, 13, 18, and 27)

Consonants

Polish has equivalent or near-equivalent sounds to the English phonemes /tʃ/, /dʒ/, /f/, /s/, /ʃ/, /ʒ/, /m/, /n/, /l/, /r/, /j/, w/, so these should not be problematic for ELF intelligibility.

/p/   Polish /p/ is identical to English /p/ before consonants and before word boundaries. Polish learners need help with the aspiration of English /p/ before vowels – to demonstrate aspiration, get them to compare the Polish 'papier' and the English 'paper', or 'Piotr' and 'Peter', etc.

/b/   Polish /b/ is the same. Draw learners' attention, though, to word-final contexts where Poles tend to devoice it.

/t/   Polish /t/ is never aspirated. To demonstrate this, compare the Polish 'Tomek' with the English 'Tom'.

/d/   Polish /d/ is dental but this is not problematic for ELF. However, draw learners' attention to word-final /d/, which Poles will otherwise devoice.

/k/   Polish /k/ is identical to English /k/ before consonants and before word boundaries. Polish learners need help with the aspiration on English /k/ before vowels – to demonstrate aspiration, get them to compare the Polish 'kort' and the English 'court'.

/g/   Polish /g/ is the same as in English. Draw learners' attention, though, to word-final contexts where Poles tend to devoice it.

/v/   Polish /v/ is the same as in English. Draw learners' attention, though, to word-final contexts where Poles tend to devoice it.

/z/   Polish /z/ is the same as in English. Draw learners' attention, though, to word-final contexts where Poles tend to devoice it.

/h/   Poles pronounce this as a voiceless velar fricative. Raise awareness by pronouncing the Polish 'cham' or 'cholera' with the English /h/. To a Polish ear, the English sound has a very soft quality, so a good laugh is guaranteed with Polish swearwords containing this sound!

/ŋ/   An equivalent sound can be demonstrated before /k/ in the Polish 'bank' or 'tankować' (to fill up a car), but most Poles will pronounce it together with /g/ in the middle of a word (e.g. 'tango') or with a /k/ word-finally. Raise awareness by showing that 'sting' and 'stink' are not identical in English.

Consonant clusters

Polish permits highly complex consonant clusters in all positions. Word-initial examples include 'roztrzaskany' (broken into pieces), 'tkwi' (is stuck), and 'drwina' (insult). Medial clusters in Polish can contain up to five consecutive consonants, e.g. 'przestępstwo' (crime), where the consonant cluster /mpstf/ occurs. All word-final consonant clusters with plosives, affricates, and fricatives are devoiced in Polish, so work is needed on the English 'rubbed', 'held', 'words', etc.

Vowel length

Standard Polish uses only six oral vowels, plus two nasal vowels, all short and uniform in length in all contexts. Therefore, Poles need to do a lot of work to achieve the appropriate length of English long vowels. There is no equivalent in Polish of the vowel-shortening effect before word-final voiceless consonants, because Polish simply devoices all plosives, affricates, and fricatives in this context. Consequently, words like 'bag' and 'back' will be judged as identical. Poles need a lot of help with length contrasts as in 'pea'/'peas'/'peace', etc. The second segment of the English diphthongs /ɪə/, /ɛə/, /ʊə/ will be short, but this will not matter much for ELF intelligibility, as the following 'r' in the spelling will regularly be pronounced anyway.

Nuclear stress placement

In terms of word grouping, the tendency with the great majority of Polish speakers at lower levels of English proficiency is to pause far more frequently than necessary, particularly on short grammatical words, which, coupled with the devoicing of word-final stops, fricatives, and affricates, makes it harder for the listener to decode the meaning structure of what is being said or read aloud.

Although the general principles of nuclear stress placement are similar in Polish and English, Poles may also resort to changes in word order more than English speakers to achieve emphasis in general and contrastive stress in particular. As a result, they need to be encouraged to take greater care to produce nuclear stresses in a more conspicuous manner.

Portuguese (Ricardo da Silva)

The two main varieties of Portuguese – European and Brazilian – both feature many different accents within the countries where they are spoken. Therefore learners of English in these countries will obviously display different L1 transfer in their pronunciation of English depending on the variety of Portuguese they speak. This section focuses on learners whose first language is Portuguese as spoken in Brazil, and considers pronunciation features that are generally present as a pattern in most accents all over the country. In some cases where there may be significant variation from this pattern in one region of the country, a specific comment is added.

The production of English consonants by Brazilians is not usually a source of unintelligibility. Most English consonants have equivalent or near-equivalent sounds in Portuguese, and there are a few which are not present as phonemes in Portuguese, but are usually produced easily enough by most Portuguese speakers. The main intelligibility problems most Brazilians face are the confusion of /h/ and /r/ in initial position (making 'hat' and 'rat' sound identical).

Also problematic is the replacement of /n/ and /m/ in word-final position with a sound very similar to /ŋ/, accompanied by the nasalization of the preceding vowel. An additional threat to ELF intelligibility comes from the lack of aspiration of the voiceless plosives /p/, /t/, /k/. Consonant clusters, in contrast, are not usually problematic.

Few English vowels pose difficulties for Brazilian Portuguese speakers. The main problem related to vowels has to do with final unstressed syllables, which are far more reduced than their equivalent in English. This often renders final syllables practically inaudible to non-Portuguese ears. This is especially true for English words ending in unstressed /i/, such as 'fancy', 'coffee', 'taxi', etc., that may be heard as 'fans', 'cough', 'tax'.

Word grouping is very similar in Portuguese and English. However, nuclear stress placement may be a problem if not taught appropriately, as nuclear stress position may or may not be used in Portuguese to indicate meaning.

ELF pronunciation for learners with Brazilian Portuguese as their first language (Tracks 10, 11, 19, and 28)

Consonants

Portuguese has equivalent or near-equivalent sounds to the English phonemes /b/, /g/, /f/, /v/, /ʃ/, so these should not be problematic for ELF intelligibility.

/p/   Portuguese /p/ is very similar to English /p/, but it is not aspirated when it comes at the beginning of words, so 'pin' can sound like 'bin'. Demonstrate aspiration by contrasting the Portuguese word 'pai' (father) and the English 'pie'.

/t/   Brazilian Portuguese /t/ is dental. This is not a problem for ELF. However, it is never aspirated, which is problematic. Raise awareness of this. In addition, when /t/ is followed by /iː/ or /ɪ/, or at the end of words, many speakers of Brazilian Portuguese replace it with /tʃ/. Raise awareness using minimal pairs such as 'tear/cheer', 'eat/each'.

/d/   Portuguese /d/ is dental. This is not a problem for ELF. However, when /d/ is followed by /iː/ or /ɪ/, or comes at the end of words, most speakers of Brazilian Portuguese replace it with /dʒ/. Raise awareness by using minimal pairs such as 'deep/Jeep', 'head/hedge'.

/k/   Portuguese /k/ is very similar to English /k/, but it is not aspirated when it comes at the beginning of words, so 'cut' may sound like 'gut'. Demonstrate aspiration by contrasting the Portuguese word 'quer' (whether … or) and the English 'care'.

/tʃ/ Although /tʃ/ is not a Portuguese phoneme, speakers of Portuguese learn it easily and can produce it quite naturally. (See comments on /t/ above.)

/dʒ/ /dʒ/ is also not a Portuguese phoneme, but speakers of Portuguese learn it easily and can produce it quite naturally. (See comments on /d/ above.)

/s/ Portuguese /s/ is the same as in English. However, spellings with the letter 's' may cause confusion, and lead learners to pronunciation errors, since in Portuguese an 's' between vowels is always pronounced /z/. Make learners aware of this fact and be alert to the mispronunciation of words like 'basic', 'buses', and 'case'.

/z/ Although Portuguese /z/ is the same as in English, it is important to make learners aware of its use in plural endings, as most tend to use /s/ or even /ʃ/, following Portuguese pronunciation patterns.

/ʒ/ Portuguese /ʒ/ is the same as in English. However, learners have to be made aware that it occurs in combinations of the letter 's', such as in 'vision', otherwise they may pronounce it [vɪzjən] rather than [vɪʒən], not because they are not able to, but because they are misled by the spelling.

/h/ /h/ is a common sound in Brazilian Portuguese, and can be easily learnt and produced by learners. However, as it is not associated with the letter 'h' in Portuguese, and so learners have to be made aware of this. (See comments on /r/ below.)

/m/ Portuguese /m/ is the same as in English, but it never occurs in final position in Portuguese. Because of this many learners omit it at the end of words, and replace it with a version of /ŋ/, and nasalize the preceding vowel, making 'beam' sound [bĩŋ]. Raise awareness by showing how the Portuguese word 'sim' (yes) sounds almost like 'sing' in English. Practice using minimal pairs such as 'Kim/king'.

/n/ Portuguese /n/ is the same as in English, but it never occurs in final position. As with /m/, many learners replace it with a version of /ŋ/, and nasalize the preceding vowel, making 'lean' sound like [lĩŋ]. Raise awareness by using minimal pairs such as 'ban/bang' or 'sin/sing', and insist that learners produce /n/ at the end of words. Also contrast /m/, /n/, and /ŋ/ with minimal 'trios' such as 'rum/run/rung'.

/ŋ/ Although /ŋ/ is not a phoneme of Portuguese, learners usually produce it easily.

/l/ Portuguese /l/ is the same as the English clear /l/. However, /l/ in final position is pronounced [ʊ] by Brazilians, so 'ball' will sound [bɔːʊ] (some parts of the South of Brazil excluded). This will only cause problems of intelligibility when the word is followed by a vowel, so insist that learners pronounce /l/ when a word ending in 'l' is followed by a word starting with a vowel, as in 'tell us'.

/r/   Brazilians can usually produce the English /r/. It is a common variant of the letter 'r' between vowels or in clusters in many parts of Brazil, and people from other parts can usually imitate it. However, most Brazilians use the sound [h] to pronounce the letter 'r' in initial position (some areas of the South of Brazil excluded), and transfer this to their English. Make learners aware of this from the beginning, and insist on the production of /r/ to pronounce the initial 'r' in words like 'restaurant' or 'real'.

/j/   Although not a Portuguese phoneme, /j/ is usually learnt and produced quite easily, except when it precedes /iː/, when it is usually omitted, so 'year' sounds exactly like 'ear'. Tell learners to see it as two Portuguese [i] sounds pronounced quickly.

/w/   Although not a Portuguese phoneme, /w/ is usually learnt and produced quite easily, except when it precedes /uː/ or /ʊ/, when it is usually omitted, so 'would' sounds like [ʊd]. Tell learners to see it as two Portuguese [u] sounds pronounced quickly.

Consonant clusters

With clusters that begin /s/ + consonant (e.g. 'speak') or /s/ + consonant + consonant (e.g. 'stroll'), learners will add an initial very short /i/, producing 'ispeak' and 'istroll', respectively. This is not problematic for ELF. In general there are no intelligibility problems related to medial and word-final clusters for speakers of Portuguese.

Vowel length

Although differences in length are not phonological distinctions in their language, Portuguese-speaking learners do not seem to have problems of intelligibility arising from this, except for the distinction between the long /iː/ and the short /ɪ/ vowels. Raise awareness by using minimal pairs, and insist that they lengthen /iː/.

Nuclear stress placement

Word grouping in Portuguese is very similar to English, and it rarely causes breakdown in communication. Portuguese uses a mix of changes in syntax and nuclear stress shifting to emphasize different parts of an utterance. For example:

Where are you GOing?/Aonde você VAI?

Where are YOU going?/Aonde voCÊ vai? or VoCÊ vai aonde?

WHERE are you flying to?/Você vai aONde?

Because the word receiving the emphasis always gets a nuclear status, no matter where it is in the sentence, it is not difficult for the learners to understand how nuclear stress placing works in English.

Russian (Mikhail Ordin)

Russian is one of the Indo-European East Slavic Languages, and the most-widely spoken Slavic language. Although there are many regional accents in Russia, these accents are used in remote areas and are not familiar to most Russian speakers. Two pronunciation standards are recognized – Moscow and Petersburg – but the differences are minor for learners of English, and both varieties have similar influence on the English pronunciation of Russian native speakers. Wherever differences between Russian regional varieties might be influential enough to affect ELF pronunciation, they will be mentioned.

There are many native Russian speakers in former USSR republics, e.g. Georgia, Ukraine, Uzbekistan, etc. Their Russian is influenced by local national languages, and native speakers of Russian in these countries use some variety of the language that is quite distinct from the variety spoken in the Russian Federation. Such local varieties will have their own influences on ELF pronunciation.

Russian spelling is much closer to the spoken form than English spelling is, which can make it difficult for early learners to cope with the irregularities of English sound–spelling correspondences. Mispronunciations induced by the spelling of English are very common and may obstruct communication more strongly than accented pronunciation.

The Russian language allows very complex consonant clusters, with up to five consonants being normal. All the clusters found in English can occur in Russian, which is why consonant combinations are unlikely to cause problems for learners in terms of ELF intelligibility.

In final position, fricative and plosive consonants in Russian are fully devoiced, and this is transferred into English. Together with the lack of differences in the duration of the vowels before voiced and voiceless consonants, this feature eliminates the differences between 'back' and 'bag', or 'log' and 'lock', or 'bus' and 'buzz'. Other problems for ELF learners are the consonant /w/ (see 'Consonants' below), the aspiration of /p/, /t/, /k/, the consonants /ŋ/ and /h/, and the palatalization of consonants before /i/ and /e/.

Problems with vowels are important for ELF learners. Lack of phonological distinctions between short and long vowels may be a frequent cause of misunderstandings. A lot of work may be required to ensure quantitative distinctions.

ELF pronunciation for learners with Russian as their first language (Tracks 3, 16, and 29)

Consonants

Russian has equivalent or near-equivalent sounds to the English phonemes /tʃ/, /f/, /ʃ/, /ʒ/, /m/, /n/, j/, so these should not prove problematic for ELF intelligibility.

/p/   This consonant is not aspirated, and might sound like /b/. Demonstrate aspiration contrasting Russian 'петь' (to sing) and English 'pet'.

/b/   Russian /b/ is fully devoiced at the end of words, which might cause difficulties in ELF. Work is required to ensure that final devoicing is eliminated when learners speak English.

/t/   Russian /t/ is not aspirated, and might sound like /d/. Demonstrate aspiration contrasting Russian 'тонна' (ton) and English 'ton'.

/d/   Russian /d/ is fully devoiced at the end of words, which might cause difficulties in ELF. Work is required to ensure that final devoicing does not occur when learners speak English.

/k/   This consonant is not aspirated, and might sound like /g/. Demonstrate aspiration by contrasting Russian 'конь' (horse) and English 'cone'.

/g/   This consonant could cause difficulties in ELF. Work is required to ensure that final devoicing does not occur when Russian learners speak English. Some speakers with regional accents might use velar voiced fricative [ɣ] instead of /g/ in initial positions. If that is the case, work is required to ensure proper pronunciation of /g/ in English.

/dʒ/   Although this consonant does not exist in Russian, the cluster of /d/ and /ʒ/ is quite frequent. /dʒ/ is not likely to cause intelligibility problems in ELF, even if Russian speakers insert a very short schwa between /d/ and /ʒ/.

/v/   Production of this consonant usually causes no problems. Sometimes it is used instead of /ð/, which should not be problematic, and sometimes instead of /w/, which can be. In addition, because of phonological transfer, speakers of some regional accents might use the voiced bilabial fricative [β] at the beginning of words instead of /v/. This requires some work to ensure the labiodental pronunciation of /v/ in this position.

At the end of words in Russian, this consonant is fully devoiced, which might cause difficulties in ELF.

/s/ Russian /s/ is similar to English /s/. Sometimes [s] is used instead of /θ/ but this should not cause problems for ELF.

/z/ Russian /z/ is similar to English /z/. Sometimes /z/ is used instead of /ð/ but this should not cause problems. At the end of words in Russian this consonant is fully devoiced, which might cause difficulties. Ensure that final devoicing does not occur.

/h/ Russians substitute English /h/ with the velar fricative [x]. This substitution is very noticeable to the ear, although it does not cause intelligibility problems.

/ŋ/ This sound is problematic because no similar sound exists in Russian. Even **assimilation** processes never trigger a velar nasal. Russians tend to use the /ng/ cluster instead of /ŋ/. Although this is not likely to cause intelligibility problems, some work is recommended to ensure /ŋ/ is acquired.

/l/ There is no distinction between clear and dark /l/ in Russian, all /l/s being dark. This is not problematic for ELF.

/r/ The English approximant sound is difficult for Russians. Russian features a trill or one of its variants, but these are acceptable for ELF intelligibility.

/w/ At the beginning of a word some learners substitute this sound with [v] or with a bilabial voiced fricative [β]. Although some work is needed to ensure proper pronunciation of /w/, it is usually easy to acquire.

Consonant clusters

Neither initial nor medial clusters seem to be a problem because Russian allows much more complex clusters, and all possible clusters of English are encountered in Russian as well. Word-final clusters are problematic because Russian tends to devoice final consonants fully.

Vowel length

The vowel system in Russian is very simple compared to English. Russian vowels do not differ in length, nor in tension. A lot of work is required to ensure distinctions between vowels in terms of length. Teaching vowel shortening before the voiceless consonants is even more difficult.

Nuclear stress placement

Word grouping is similar to English. Russian features free nucleus placement, and so nuclear stress placement is not usually a problem to ELF learners.

Spanish (Robin Walker)

There are numerous accents of Spanish, both in Spain and throughout South America. This situation brings two advantages. Firstly, learners are already aware of the notion of accent variation, although some learners hold the view that only the Castilian Spanish accent is 'correct'. Secondly, a number of English sounds that are absent from the Castilian Spanish can be found in regional accents. A small number of closely related languages are spoken in different areas of Spain. Learners familiar with these languages can often imitate specific sounds that they need for ELF from these languages.

Several English consonants have equivalent or near-equivalent sounds in Spanish. The main threats to intelligibility are the confusion of /s/, /z/, /ʃ/, /ʒ/, and of /tʃ/, /dʒ/, /ʒ/, /j/. Two additional threats to intelligibility come from the lack of aspiration of the voiceless plosives /p/, /t, /k/, together with the tendency for the voiced plosives /b/, /d/, /k/ to be pronounced as fricatives when they come between two vowels.

Many clusters are common to both Spanish and English and are not normally problematical. In Spanish, however, clusters are limited to two or three consonants, and where there are three, one of them is usually deleted, which can be problematic for ELF communication when the cluster is word initial.

The pronunciation of Spanish is entirely predictable from its spelling. With lower-level students this will cause them to pronounce every letter, and this can lead to problems of intelligibility. More importantly, the uniform length of Spanish vowels means that learners do not perceive the different lengths of English vowels, finding them particularly hard to produce. The situation is true for both diphthongs and pure vowels.

In Spanish nuclear stress placement is almost always on the last or the penultimate syllable of a word group. Moreover, there is no relationship between meaning and the position of the nuclear stress. Despite this, many learners are quick to understand the concept of English nuclear stress placement, although it is a long time before their understanding is transferred to their spoken English.

ELF pronunciation for learners with Spanish as their first language (Tracks 3, 14, 16, and 30)

Consonants

Spanish has equivalent or near-equivalent sounds to the English phonemes /tʃ/, /f/, /n/, /l/, so these should not prove problematic for ELF intelligibility.

/p/   Spanish /p/ is very similar to English /p/, but it is not aspirated at the beginning of words, so 'pin' can sound like 'bin'. Demonstrate aspiration by contrasting the Spanish word 'papi' and the English 'paper'.

/b/   Spanish /b/ in 'basta' (enough) or 'ambos' (both) is similar to English /b/. However, the 'b' between vowels (e.g. 'cabe' (fits), 'haba' (broad bean) is pronounced as a fricative sound [β] that does not exist in English. Guide learners to the difference between the two ways of pronouncing 'b' in Spanish. Insist on use the /b/ in 'basta' for English.

/t/   Spanish /t/ is a dental plosive. This is not a problem for ELF, but Spanish /t/ is never aspirated, which is a problem for intelligibility in ELF. Demonstrate aspiration by contrasting the Spanish 'té' and the English 'tea'.

/d/   Spanish /d/ is dental. This is not a problem for ELF. However, it is only pronounced as a plosive at the beginning of words, e.g. 'debe' (must, owes). Between vowels, e.g. 'lado' (side) or when word-final, e.g. 'Madrid', it is pronounced as the fricative [ð]. This is problematic. Raise awareness by getting learners to feel the two different articulations of /d/ in the word 'dedo' (finger). Insist on the use of the plosive /d/ for English.

/k/   Spanish /k/ is similar but it is not aspirated at the beginning of words such as 'keep'. Demonstrate aspiration by contrasting Spanish 'qué' (what) and English 'key'.

/g/   Spanish /g/ in 'gana' (earns, wins) is similar to English /g/. However, between vowels, e.g. 'pago' (payment/I pay), it is pronounced as a fricative, [ɣ]. Help learners feel the difference between these two ways of pronouncing /g/. Insist on use the sound from 'gana' for the English /g/.

/dʒ/ /dʒ/ is not a phoneme of Spanish, and is often substituted with [j], making 'jaw' sound like 'your'. Approach /dʒ/ by adding voicing to /tʃ/.

/v/   /v/ is not a phoneme of Spanish. Spanish speakers tend to produce a sound between [b] and [v] and often cannot hear the difference. This makes 'vote' sound like 'boat'. It is important for learners to differentiate between the bilabial plosive /b/, and the fricative /v/, which is made through light contact between the top teeth and the bottom lip. Approach /v/ by adding voicing to /f/.

/s/   Spanish /s/ is similar to English /s/, although in some accents the Spanish sound is rather close to [ʃ], which can be problematic. In some regions of Spain and Latin America, /s/ at the end of words is pronounced [h], which is problematic. Insist on the use of /s/.

/z/   /z/ is not a phoneme of Spanish, but the /s/ in words like 'desde' (since) or 'asno' (donkey) is pronounced as [z]. Alternatively, add voicing to /s/.

/ʃ/   /ʃ/ is not a phoneme of Spanish and is often substituted by [s] or [tʃ]. Fortunately, /ʃ/ is present in various regional accents or languages. In some parts of Andalusia, 'muchacho' (young man) is pronounced [muˈʃaʃo]. In Galician, the <x> is pronounced [ʃ] in words like 'xunta' (assembly). The same is true for the <x> in Catalan and Portuguese in words like 'caixa' (box).

/ʒ/   /ʒ/ is not a phoneme of Spanish, so 'leisure' can be confused with 'lesser'. /ʒ/ is used in Southern Latin America for the 'll' in 'llegar' (to arrive) or 'calle' (street). Alternatively, approach /ʒ/ by adding voicing to /ʃ/.

/h/   /h/ is not a phoneme of Spanish, but it is present in the Andalusian accent in the pronunciation of the letter <j> in words like 'jamón' (ham) or 'caja' (box).

/m/   Spanish /m/ is the same as in English, but in word-final position this sound is usually substituted by [n]. This makes 'comb' sound like 'cone'. Insist on /m/.

/ŋ/   /ŋ/ is not a phoneme of Spanish, but the sound occurs naturally in words like 'tengo' (I have), where /n/ is followed by /g/. Invite students to pronounce 'tengo' and hold the /n/ until they can feel the back of the tongue raised to the back of the roof of the mouth.

/r/   The Spanish trilled or tapped /r/ in words like 'roto' (broken), 'caro' (expensive) or 'carta' (letter) is intelligible in ELF.

/j/   The Spanish /j/ in words like 'yo' (I), 'yerno' (son-in-law) or 'hielo' (ice) is similar to the English sound.

/w/   /w/ is not a phoneme of Spanish, and can be problematic, especially in words like 'would', where a [g]-like sound is made in the throat. A sound like /w/ occurs naturally in Spanish in words like 'puerta' (door) or 'suave' (smooth, soft), but with insufficient lip-rounding. Approach /w/ through these words but focusing on greater lip-rounding.

Consonant clusters

With clusters that begin /s/ + consonant (e.g. 'Spain') or /s/ + consonant + consonant (e.g. 'stroll'), learners add an initial vowel producing 'eSpain' and 'estroll' respectively. This is not problematic for ELF. With medial or word-final clusters the commonest strategy used is deletion, making both 'nests' and 'next' sound like [nes], or 'sold' like [sol]. Encourage the insertion of a short vowel between consonants if this facilitates pronunciation.

Vowel length

Spanish vowels have a length roughly midway between that of the short and the long vowels of English. This is problematic. The vowel in 'sit', for example, is usually too long, while the vowel in 'see' is too short. Diphthongs are generally too short. There is nothing in Spanish that corresponds to the shortening effect that the voiceless consonants have on the length of English vowels. Vowel length differences in words like 'bit' and 'bid', or 'price' and 'prize', are difficult for learners to hear, and even more difficult to produce. This is problematic for ELF.

Nuclear stress placement

Although word grouping in Spanish works in much the same way as in English, it does not seem to transfer successfully from the mother tongue. Learners often produce pauses that are inappropriate for English, which can be problematic. Often these are the result of pronunciation problems with some part of the word group, especially consonant clusters.

Spanish uses changes in syntax to produce the effect created by shifting nuclear stress in English. For example:

Where are you FLYing to?/¿A dónde vuelas?

Where are YOU flying to?/¿A dónde vuelas tú?

WHERE are you flying to?/¿Que vuelas a dónde?

In addition, the nucleus in word groups in Spanish is almost always on the penultimate or the last syllable. Placing the nucleus earlier in the word group is unnatural, and as a result, even when learners succeed in placing the nucleus early, they frequently place a 'second' nucleus on the last item in the word group. This gives a double focus to the utterance, which can be confusing. Spanish L1 learners of English, therefore, need abundant practice in detecting and producing nuclear stress.

Notes on the contributors

Armin Berger is a graduate of Vienna University where he read English and theology. He currently works as a language teacher and lecturer in language teaching at the English Department of Vienna University.

Atsuko Shimizu teaches phonetics and phonology as professor at Meiji University, Tokyo, and has written a coursebook and several English–Japanese dictionaries. Her interest has been focused on the English pronunciation of non-native speakers.

Bill Batziakas was until recently a teaching assistant at the University of Athens, and is currently a researcher of English as a Lingua Franca at King's College, University of London.

David Deterding teaches at the University of Brunei Darussalam. His research has focused on the description of Englishes in South-East Asia, particularly the pronunciation of English in Singapore and China.

Mustapha Moubarik has an MA in Linguistics and ELT from Leeds University, and a PhD at the University of Seville. Mustapha Moubarik is currently teaching at the Facultad de Ciencias de la Educación in Seville.

Mikhail Ordin is an EFL teacher and pronunciation trainer from Moscow Academy of Humanities and Technology, and a research associate at Bangor University, UK, with interests in monolingual and bilingual acquisition of prosody and cross-linguistic transfer in L2 learning.

Ricardo da Silva Sili has been an EFL teacher and trainer for years, and recently a coursebook writer and editor for Learning Factory (Cultura Inglesa, Rio de Janeiro, Brazil). He holds an MA in ELT Management, University of Southampton.

Grzegorz Śpiewak is a teacher, teacher trainer, adviser, and author; Lecturer at the Institute of English Studies, University of Warsaw; Former President of IATEFL Poland; and President of DOS-Teacher Training Solutions. He is Head ELT Consultant for Macmillan Poland.

Further reading

Pronunciation manuals with lists of pronunciation problems for specific L1 backgrounds

Avery, P. and S. Erhlich. 1992. *Teaching American English Pronunciation.* Oxford: Oxford University Press.

Swan, M. and **B. Smith.** 2001. *Learner English: A Teacher's Guide to Interference and other Problems* (2nd ed.). Cambridge: Cambridge University Press.

On specific first language phonologies

Watson, J. C. E. 2002. *The Phonology and Morphology f Arabic.* New York: OUP.

Deterding, D. 2006. 'The pronunciation of English by speakers from China'. *English World-Wide,* 27, 175–198.

Wiese, R. 2000. *The Phonology of German.* Oxford: Oxford University Press.

Lytra-Papaefthymiou, S. 2001. 'Greek learners' in M. Swan and B. Smith (eds.): *Learner English: A Teacher's Guide to Interference and other Problems* (2nd ed.). Cambridge: Cambridge University Press.

Vance, T. J. 2008. *The Sounds of Japanese.* Cambridge: Cambridge University Press.

Deterding, D. and **G. Poedjosoedarmo.** 1998. *The Sounds of English: Phonetics and Phonology or English Teachers in Southeast Asia.* Singapore: Prentice Hall.

Śpiewak, G. 2001. 'Polish speakers', in M. Swan and B. Smith (eds.): *Learner English: A Teacher's Guide to Interference and other Problems* (2nd ed.). Cambridge: Cambridge University Press.

Godoy, S. et al. 2007. *English Pronunciation for Brazilians.* São Paulo: DIS – DISAL Editora.

Monk, A. and **A. Rurak.** 2001. 'Russian speakers', in M. Swan and B. Smith (eds.): *Learner English: A Teacher's Guide to Interference and other Problems.* (2nd ed.) Cambridge: Cambridge University Press.

Quilis, A. and **J. A. Fernández.** 1996. *Curso de fonética y fonología españolas.* Madrid: Consejo Superior de Inverstigaciones Científicas.

6 ELF PRONUNCIATION: PLANNING AND ASSESSMENT

Introduction

This chapter looks at two areas that are important for the successful implementation of an ELF approach to pronunciation – planning and assessment. Part A of the chapter looks at planning and considers some of the variables that teachers need to think about before using an ELF approach in their own classes. This part also shows how the broad goal of ELF intelligibility can be broken down into a teaching syllabus adaptable to different teaching situations. Part A ends with a look at how to integrate ELF pronunciation into the rest of the language syllabus.

Part B is about testing ELF pronunciation. It begins with a brief overview of pronunciation testing up to the present time, before going on to offer ideas about how to test pronunciation within an ELF framework, both at the level of individual features of pronunciation, and at the level of overall intelligibility.

Part A – Planning

Variables and planning

Planning for an ELF approach to pronunciation requires us to look at the same variables as for other approaches, but to do this from a different perspective. The kinds of variables that we need to consider are issues like the setting or the institution where the teaching will take place. Marianne Celce-Murcia and her colleagues (1996) offer useful insights into these and other variables from an EFL/ESL perspective. In this review of variables, for example, they describe the EFL setting as one where:

> the language teaching occurs within a school or institutional setting to
> homogeneous groups of first-language learners. Examples might be Thai
> secondary school students learning English as a school subject or Mexican

tourist industry personnel taking a "brush up" English language course to
improve their oral fluency
(Celce-Murcia 1996: 321)

However, the two examples that Celce-Murcia gives of an EFL setting are
equally valid for ELF. For Thai secondary school students, English is just
as likely to be a means of communication with fellow non-native speakers
from the ASEAN countries as it is to be a means of communication with
native speakers from the USA, Australia, or New Zealand. 'In the ASEAN
community, therefore, a Thai or an Indonesian may choose to communicate
with each other using English as their lingua franca or common language'
(Kirkpatrick 2007: 7–8). Similarly, although Mexico may represent an exception because of its proximity of the USA, workers in the tourist industry do
not normally learn English solely for communication with native speakers.
In fact, in most parts of the world, tourism encounters in English are far
more frequent between non-native speakers than they are between native
speakers and non-native speakers. In other words, what Celce-Murcia and
her colleagues classify as an foreign language setting of English, is frequently
a lingua franca one in practice.

In terms of institutional variables, an ELF approach to pronunciation also
requires us to look at issues from a new perspective. With respect to teachers, Celce-Murcia asks '[i]f they are nonnative speakers of English, does their
own pronunciation in English provide an adequate model for students?'
(1996: 322). The implication here is that for EFL and ESL, a native speaker
teacher automatically provides a good model for students. In contrast, a non-
native speaker may be problematic. However, as I explained in Chapter 3
(Benefit 6), in ELF settings, it is the non-native speaker teacher who can
actually provide the better model, and the native speaker teacher who can be
problematic.

This is not to say that an ELF approach is automatically better than a traditional approach in terms of institutional variables. Individual teachers, for
example, are seldom free to act as they wish in the institution or teaching
centre where they work. Colleagues and Directors of Studies will need to
be consulted, and both might object to an ELF approach on the basis that
the institution favours a native-speaker accent. Directors of Studies might
be concerned that a teacher using a different approach can confuse learners.
Similar objections might also come from Principals or parents. This is especially likely in private language schools where marketing has announced that
the school employs native speakers and promotes native-speaker models.

These sorts of pressures help to explain why some teachers who responded
positively to the concept of ELF accents at a theoretical level, 'did not think
that it would be feasible to implement the teaching of ELF accents in classrooms in their own countries' (Jenkins 2007: 224). The situation is further

complicated by the fact that the testing of spoken English with most international examining boards assesses pronunciation in terms of the presence or absence of a 'foreign' accent (see Part B of this chapter). That is to say, proximity to the appropriate native-speaker accent is taken as the measure of good pronunciation. Until this changes, teachers preparing learners for these exams will need to take native-speaker accents into account.

In general, at an institutional level it is not possible to use an ELF approach without first seeking support from colleagues and/or permission from managers. Where permission is clearly not going to be given, teachers have little choice but to use the centre-approved model. It is likely, however, that the attitude to ELF at institutional level will change in the coming years, as the reality of the lingua franca role of English becomes more widely known. Referring to the situation for Assistant English Teachers in Japan, Sean Sutherland suggests that '[s]lowly, as awareness of ELF increases, students, their parents and other interested parties will realise that Japanese teachers should not be characterised as NNESs [Non-native English speakers], with all the negative associations implied by that term, but should instead be seen as proficient ELF speakers' (2008: 10).

A change in perspective is also necessary when we look at learner variables such as the amount and type of prior pronunciation instruction or the learner's linguistic background. With respect to prior instruction, learners who have progressed successfully within an EFL or ESL framework may react negatively to an ELF focus, perceiving it as simplified, inferior, non-standard, or simply incorrect. We looked at this reaction in Chapter 3 (Part A: Concern 10). In my own experience, however, many learners display a lack of confidence in their pronunciation because of repeated failure to acquire the native-speaker accent that is often implicitly laid down as the goal of EFL and ESL teaching. For these learners, the introduction of an ELF approach can bring about renewed interest in pronunciation and, correctly implemented, it can restore their confidence in their ability to achieve their pronunciation goals.

The importance of the learner's linguistic background also changes significantly when we shift from an EFL/ESL approach to an ELF one. Until now the learner's linguistics background has usually been seen as an obstacle to good pronunciation because of 'interference' from the first-language phonology. However, as we saw in Chapter 4, with an ELF approach, various teaching techniques and activities are based on the idea that the learner's linguistic background is a very valuable resource on which we can build success in ELF pronunciation. This concept of the learner's linguistic background as 'friend' rather than 'foe' is carried through in detail in Chapter 5, where the whole focus is about using the learner's first language in order to achieve competence in ELF pronunciation.

Programming for ELF pronunciation

EFL, ESL, and ELF approaches to teaching pronunciation all agree on the need to sequence the contents of the approach in question. At the end of Chapter 2 we saw how Jenkins had produced a five-stage programme for teaching ELF pronunciation. Table 6.1 on pages 142–3 shows how this programme can be used in order to develop a more detailed teaching sequence.

I have divided the contents of the table into phases rather than learner levels, which is how pronunciation syllabuses are traditionally organized. This is because learners will come to an ELF approach for the first time with very different levels of proficiency, both in terms of their English in general, and in terms of their pronunciation. In addition, by discussing an ELF approach in phases, it is easier to apply it to significantly different contexts, such as in secondary schooling, in private language schools, or with working adults who need to improve their pronunciation for professional reasons.

In the secondary school context, for example, which might typically involve four years' compulsory education from 12–16 years of age, plus two optional years from 16–18, Phase 1 could be carried out during the first two years, and Phase 2 during the last two years of compulsory education. Thus on leaving school at 16, successful students would have productive competence for ELF intelligibility, a basic idea of the need for accommodation in ELF communication, receptive competence in a range of ELF accents common to their environment, and receptive competence in one standard Inner Circle accent. Learners staying on from 16–18 would progress beyond this basic competence to Phase 3, where they would increase their ability to deal with less familiar ELF accents, and also extend the number of Inner Circle accents they are comfortable with. Additionally, they would have the chance to strengthen their understanding of nuclear stress, especially in terms of how it operates at the level of full discourse.

This same programme could be applied to other situations. For example, it could easily be applied to students entering tertiary education in fields such as business or technology, where English is often compulsory. As in secondary education, tertiary-level students could begin with Level 1 of Table 6.1, before progressing to higher levels. Alternatively, if only limited time is available, then Table 6.1 and the LFC can be adapted through the teacher's own experience in order to produce a tailor-made programme.

Working at the Shanghai Normal University (SNU), for example, Pedro Luchini decided to include pronunciation into a spoken English course that his students took to enable them to function in EFL or EIL contexts. He opted not to include the whole of the LFC.

Based chiefly on Jenkins's LFC (2000), and, on my own experience in China as a Non-Native Speaker of English (NNES), for reasons of practicality and time constraints, I decided to teach my Chinese students only some of the phonological items listed in Jenkins' LFC (2000).

This decision was not made arbitrarily, rather it was founded on those problematic phonological aspects that I came across when interacting in English with Chinese speakers.
(Luchini 2005:17).

The resulting programme was run over a period of approximately three weeks and was limited to:

• vowel length
• aspiration of initial /p/, /t/, /k/
• addition and deletion of sounds in initial clusters
• nuclear stress – unmarked and especially contrastive
• some basic characteristics of voice setting.

Luchini knew that the time constraints he was working under meant that his learners were unlikely to show a marked improvement in their pronunciation. But by the end of the programme, he felt he could:

fairly claim that the [pronunciation] goals were reached when considering that, after being explicitly taught some of the phonological core items listed in the LFC, most students were able to make interesting adjustments in their pronunciation. These enabled them to communicate in English more effectively with their peers and instructor alike, the latter being a NNES whose first language is Spanish.
(Luchini: 2005: 20)

That is to say, despite the limited time available, meaningful progress was made by adopting an ELF approach, since this focused his learners' attention on a manageable number of key pronunciation points.

Integrating pronunciation

The need to integrate pronunciation teaching into other skills and topics work has long been recognized. Kenworthy (1987) devoted a chapter to integrating pronunciation teaching into general class work, and argues that it is:

impossible to restrict pronunciation work to particular lessons or slots. Whenever a new word is met in a text, learners will ask how it is pronounced; when a learner says something and the teacher and/or class members don't understand, the intended word has to be discovered and its correct pronunciation presented; when learners are listening to taped material and misinterpret a speaker's intentions because they have missed some feature of stress or intonation, the teacher must draw their attention to it.
(Kenworthy 1987: 113)

	Phase 1	Phase 2	Phase 3
Broad aims	Introduction to the concept of ELF and its implications for learning English pronunciation. Presentation of the LFC. Addition of selected core items to the learner's productive and receptive repertoire.	Consolidation of competence in the LFC. Introduction to the concept of variation. Addition of a range of ELF English accents to the learner's receptive repertoire. Introduction to the concept of accommodation.	Moving beyond the LFC. Addition of selected non-core items to the learner's receptive repertoire. Increased familiarity with ELF accents. Addition of a range of Inner Circle accents to the learner's receptive repertoire.
Consonants	Basic competence in the LFC consonants that are problematic for learners depending on their first language background.	Full competence in production of the LFC consonants. Introduction of the concept of the aspiration of /p/, /t/, /k/ in word-initial position.	Aspiration of /p/, /t/, /k/ at the beginning of stressed syllables (e.g. 'repeat'). Use of BrE alveolar [t] as opposed to AmE flapped [r] in words like 'water'.
Clusters	Introduction to addition and deletion as strategies for dealing with word-initial consonant clusters. Insistence on vowel addition as preferred strategy in ELF.	Further practice in dealing with word-initial and medial consonant clusters that are difficult for a given first-language background.	Possible deletion of /t/, /d/ as for native-speaker norms, both in word-medial ('postman') and word-final ('aspects') position, as well as at word boundaries ('next week').
Vowels	Introduction to the idea of vowel length and vowel quality. Awareness of the relative impact of length differences on ELF intelligibility.	Introduction to the shortening of vowel length after voiceless consonants. Awareness-raising as to similarities between the learner's first language vowel system and BrE or AmE vowels.	More on vowel length, including length in diphthongs. Extension of the learner's L1 vowel repertoire by the addition of any vowel qualities readily available to the learner.

Nuclear stress	Introduction to the idea of nuclear stress. Perceiving nuclear stress in common lexical phrases and simple dialogues. Placing nuclear stress in the same contexts.	Practice in detecting nuclear stress in simple discourse. Introduction to the idea of unmarked and contrastive stress. Introduction to word groups. Detecting word group boundaries.	Further practice in detecting and placing word group boundaries. Nuclear stress in full discourse, especially contrastive stress. The concept of new and old information.
Accommodation skills	Presentation of the broad concept of accommodation and the role it plays in spoken communication. Introduction to the basic notion of phonological accommodation. Awareness raising as to the key features of the ELF accents that the learners are most likely to encounter, either because of regional proximity or because of presence of users of these accents in their own country.	Awareness raising as to which features of the learner's own pronunciation of English are most likely to prove problematic to listeners from other L1 backgrounds. Increased familiarity with ELF accents, including accents that learners are less likely to encounter and/or that differ substantially from the learner's accent. Guided exposure to standard Inner Circle accents. Negotiation of meaning – introduction to strategies for signalling non-comprehension. Activities that provide practice in accommodating productively.	Practice in perceiving variation of the substitutions of the dental fricatives, or /r/. Introduction to NS use of vowel reduction, weak forms, and other connected speech changes. Practice in understanding non-standard (regional) Inner Circle accents. Further practice in negotiating meaning and in accommodating productively to the listener, including practice in producing a range of pronunciations for the dental fricatives and /r/.

Table 6.1 A suggested syllabus for ELF pronunciation

Kenworthy's arguments also apply to the integration of ELF pronunciation into normal teaching programmes. As we have seen, Luchini integrated his pronunciation programme into a Spoken English course because of the circumstances in which he was working. However, it is generally better to find ways to integrate pronunciation into everyday classes, which, as Kenworthy suggests, will mean integrating pronunciation not only into the teaching of vocabulary, grammar, and speaking exercises, but also into skills work.

The most obvious area for integration is work that connects vocabulary and pronunciation. With vocabulary, the texts in a topic will provide learners with naturally occurring examples of consonants, consonant clusters, or contrasts in vowel length. Figure 6.1, for example, shows an activity on vowels that is integrated into a unit on transport in tourism. In keeping with an ELF approach, the focus of the exercise is on vowel quantity rather than exact vowel quality, and contrasts short vowels with long vowels and diphthongs.

Pronunciation

1 🎧 Look at the words about transport. Listen to their pronunciation. Write three words in each column.

| clean | ferry | leisure | safe | train |
| easy | jet | plane | scenic | |

ten /e/	see /iː/	day /eɪ/

2 Which column has the shortest vowel sounds?

3 Practise the words. Remember to make them short / long as appropriate.

4 🎧 Now do the same with these words. Listen and write them in the right column.

| car | drive | guard | harbour | track |
| craft | fast | guide | ride | |

hat /æ/	arm /ɑː/	five /aɪ/

Figure 6.1 Integrating ELF pronunciation into the teaching of vocabulary (Walker and Harding: Oxford English for Careers: Tourism 1: 46)

The exercise comes immediately after the introduction of the key vocabulary for the unit, and prior to any speaking activities on the same topic. This is a logical and useful place for pronunciation work for two reasons:

- students' success in speaking tasks is all too often limited because of problems they have with the pronunciation of key vocabulary
- speaking tasks provide a natural context for repetitive, contextualized use of key sounds, and this enhances the automatization of their pronunciation.

Going beyond individual words, lexical phrases can be used to provide integrated practice either in discrete sounds or groups of sounds, or in nuclear stress placement. The phrases in Table 6.2 are typical of those that speakers might use during a formal business meeting or discussion.

Introducing and starting a meeting	**Agreeing**
Good morning, everybody.	I think you're right.
Thank you for being here today.	I agree with Jane.
It's nice to see you all.	Yes, I'd go along with that.
Asking for an opinion	**Disagreeing**
Any thoughts about this?	I don't agree.
How do you feel about that?	I'm not so sure about that.
What do the rest of you think?	That's not how I see it.

Table 6.2 Integrating ELF pronunciation into the teaching of lexical phrases

For learners whose first language has no equivalent to nuclear stress in English, or which places nuclear stress on the last or penultimate syllable in a phrase, many of the phrases in the table provide an excellent opportunity to raise awareness of the importance of this central feature of ELF intelligibility. The exact meaning of 'I think you're right', for example, depends upon where the nuclear stress falls:

- I think you're RIGHT (i.e. unmarked stress) = an expression of general agreement
- I think YOU'RE right (contrastive stress) = I agree with you, but not with the other people
- I THINK you're right (contrastive stress) = I agree, but I still have certain doubts
- *I* think you're right (contrastive stress on 'I') = I agree with you even though the others don't.

Grammar, too, can lead to a consideration of different features of ELF pronunciation. The correct placement of nuclear stress is fundamental in order to differentiate between the affirmative and the negative when using 'can'.

In the affirmative the nuclear stress is on the main verb, 'sing' (He can SING), but in the negative 'can't' carries the nucleus, (He CAN'T sing). This is one way of integrating ELF pronunciation into the teaching of grammar.

An ELF approach to pronunciation needs planning just like any other approach. Planning will take into account a number of variables, some institutional, some to do with the learners, and so on. ELF pronunciation also needs programming if it is to be effective. The LFC can help us to carry out that programming, but the contents of an ELF pronunciation programme will be most effective if they are adapted to the local setting and are integrated into the learners' general classes.

Part B – Assessment

In Chapter 4 we saw how the change from EFL to ELF goals for pronunciation teaching meant a reappraisal of classroom teaching activities and techniques. However, we also saw that this reappraisal did not mean an automatic dismissal of previous techniques. Communication tasks, for example, were seen to retain their value when used with multilingual groups. In addition, with an ELF approach, activities that had been marginalized by communicative approaches to ELT, such as minimal pair work or dictation, were seen in a new light. At the same time, new activities were introduced, such as those aimed at raising student awareness of the sociolinguistic reality of English today, or those aimed at improving learners' accommodation skills.

The situation with regard to assessing pronunciation is similar to that of activities and techniques, and is more to do with reappraisal and evolution than with dismissal and revolution. But what exactly is current practice in the assessment of pronunciation, and what sort of evolution is required in order to respond to the requirements of assessment within an ELF framework? This part of Chapter 6 attempts to answer these questions.

Past and current practice

Despite its importance both in oral fluency and in listening, pronunciation has seldom been given the attention it warrants in the testing of these skills. It is not easy to say why this is, although a number of experts have pointed out that testing pronunciation is different from testing other areas of language learning. Unlike other areas, pronunciation has both strong 'knowledge' and strong 'skills' components. It is not only the application of relevant rules (e.g., when 's' endings are pronounced /s/, /z/ or /ɪz/); it is also a question of perception and production. Moreover, whereas the other language skills are generally viewed as either receptive (i.e. listening and reading) or productive (i.e. writing and speaking), pronunciation is both. Finally, unlike grammar or vocabulary, pronunciation cannot easily be graded into blocks that can be programmed and tested once a particular block has been taught. In practice, 'all features, (individual sounds, word stress, features of connected speech, intonation, etc.), will be present even in the very earliest lessons with beginner students, both in what they hear and in what they are required to say' (Hewings 2004: 18).

Another issue that needs to be taken into account when looking at testing pronunciation is the central role it plays in communication and intelligibility. People with poor pronunciation frequently fail to understand what others are saying to them. At the same time, because their pronunciation is poor, others find them difficult to understand. However, experience tells us that people can be intelligible to each other, even when their pronunciation of individual components of the system is not standard. Because of this, we have to ask ourselves if we should test discrete items of pronunciation, or if we should simply try to gauge the impact that a speaker's pronunciation is having on their ability to communicate freely and spontaneously with another person.

Teaching methods in the 1960s and 1970s favoured the former approach. For them the assessment of pronunciation frequently centred on the learner's ability to listen to and discriminate between pairs of individual sounds (minimal pairs), to recognize stress at word or sentence level, or to identify individual tones (fall, rise, fall–rise, etc.). The arrival of the Communicative Approach in the 1980s, however, shifted the emphasis away from the testing of discrete items, and began to take a more holistic approach. Testing increasingly used tasks that gave the candidates the opportunity to demonstrate their ability to communicate effectively. Testing discrete items of language competence, it was argued, did not provide 'convincing proof of the candidate's ability to use the language … to read, write, speak or listen in ways and contexts which correspond to real life' (Morrow 1979: 149). In 1990, for example, the oral interaction paper of the UCLES/RSA examination in communicative skills in English required candidates to complete different tasks and to demonstrate a degree of communicative competence that was measured at one of four different levels. Table 6.3 on page 148 shows the descriptors for the competence in pronunciation required for each level.

These four descriptors make no attempt to assess the speaker's ability to accurately produce individual sounds, stress patterns, or other isolated features of English pronunciation. In keeping with a communicative vision of language learning, their concern is entirely with the impact of the candidate's pronunciation on intelligibility, and the extent to which the influence of the first language phonology might make this impact more or less negative.

Level 1	Level 2	Level 3	Level 4
It is acceptable for pronunciation to be heavily influenced by L1 if it is generally intelligible.	Pronunciation must be clearly intelligible even if still obviously influenced by L1.	Pronunciation must be clearly intelligible even if some influences from L1 remain.	Pronunciation must be easily intelligible though some residual accent is acceptable.

Table 6.3 Descriptors of pronunciation competence for the 1990 UCLES/RSA Certificate in Communicative Skills in English (Adapted from Weir 1990: 177–8)

More recently, the online teaching resource for the Cambridge ESOL 'International Certificate in Financial English' describes pronunciation as:

> the candidate's ability to produce comprehensible utterances to fulfil the task requirements. This includes stress, rhythm and intonation, as well as individual sounds. Examiners put themselves in the position of a person who is not a language specialist and assess the overall impact of the pronunciation and the degree of effort required to understand the candidate.
> (Cambridge ESOL ICFE Teaching Resource – Focus on Assessment)

As before, and in keeping with the exams communicative focus, the emphasis is very much on the role pronunciation plays in facilitating (or not) the communication of meaning, rather than on the accurate production of individual items.

The two exams we have just looked at are examples of proficiency testing. This type of testing is typical of the testing done by the major external examination boards such as TOEFL, Cambridge ESOL, and so on. It attempts to describe what a learner is capable of doing in a foreign language, and often the results show if the candidate has a sufficient command of the language for a particular purpose. This could be banking, as with the ICFE exam, or engineering, law, university study, and so on. Because proficiency testing is usually done by exam boards, few teachers are responsible for them, or influence their format or assessment criteria. This is not to say that they will not be required to prepare learners to take such tests, and we will come back to the implications of this later in this chapter.

The two other common types of testing are diagnostic testing and achievement testing. The first of these is used to find out what problems the learner has with the language. In the case of ELF pronunciation, a diagnostic test would tell the teacher (and the learner) which features a student has problems producing. A diagnostic test at the beginning of a course will help teachers and learners to determine both group and individual priorities for the course.

Achievement testing is directly related to the specific contents of a course, and allows the teacher to determine to what extent students have been successful in their attempt to learn what has been taught. Achievement tests can be given at different moments throughout a course, and are then called progress achievement tests. They can also be given at the end of a course, and are then described as final achievement tests.

The assessment of pronunciation, then, can be seen in a number of different dimensions. Firstly, it has both a knowledge and a skill component. Secondly, it is both a receptive and a productive skill that is intimately related to speaking and listening. Indeed, if a speaker's pronunciation is very poor, it may be impossible for an examiner to determine their level of competence in areas such as grammar or vocabulary. Thirdly, the assessment of pronunciation can be either done at the level of individual features such as consonants, or it can be done holistically. Finally, it can be done with the purpose of determining a candidate's level of proficiency, to see what problems and priorities a learner or class has, or to measure what they have achieved over a given period of time. In the next section, I will try to show how these different dimensions can be brought together to produce a coherent framework for testing ELF pronunciation.

Assessing pronunciation for ELF – diagnostic testing

As we have seen, classroom teachers are primarily concerned with diagnostic and achievement testing. At the same time, they are concerned with assessing pronunciation within a communicative framework. These two concerns would seem to be in conflict with each other. Both diagnostic and achievement testing favour a discrete item approach to assessment. It is only through careful analysis of the individual features of a new student's pronunciation that the teacher can offer guidance as to where the student needs to improve. Similarly, if we teach a specific feature of pronunciation, an achievement progress test will only have any value if it demonstrates that the learner has a better command of this feature than before. However, at the end of a course in spoken English, what matters most is that speakers have become more intelligible to their interlocutors during the completion of communication tasks.

One answer to this conflict is for you, the teacher, to take advantage of both discrete item and holistic modes of testing. At the beginning of a course, you could carry out a diagnostic test to determine which discrete features require most attention. To do this, each student will need to produce a recording of a standard text. The elicitation paragraph used by the speakers on the CD (see Appendix 1) was written to illustrate the different items in the LFC, especially the consonants and consonant clusters (see Appendix 2). Hewings offers an alternative text (2004: 189), as do Celce-Murcia et al. (1996: 398–399). With local knowledge, however, you could prepare an elicitation paragraph that would take into account the learners' first language and the problems it supposes for ELF pronunciation. A standard text could be supplemented with two or three minutes' spontaneous speech from each student, using topics the students propose or topics that they are familiar with. The value of a sample of spontaneous speech is that many learners are very conscious of the need to be 'correct' when they read a standard text for a recording, and as a result tend to be especially careful with their pronunciation. When talking more freely about familiar topics, they tend to focus more on the content of what they are saying than on accuracy. As a result, any pronunciation problems become more noticeable.

Whatever text(s) you use to obtain a sample of a learner's pronunciation, marking the samples is not as onerous as might appear from looking at the word lists in the Appendices, especially if the learners all share the same first language. In this case, the lists in the two appendices can be vastly reduced to cover only the areas that are problematic for that particular first language. For learners whose first language is Greek, for example, Appendix 2 could be reduced to the consonants shown in Table 6.4. With /p/, /t/, /k/, for example, you would focus on appropriate aspiration, and with /s/ between vowels, the focus would be on the learner pronouncing /s/ and not /z/ (see page 111). The main focus, however, would initially be on the fricatives /tʃ/, /dʒ/, /ʃ/, /ʃ/, /ʒ/, at least with lower-level students.

You could draw up similar tables for diagnostic analysis with other first-language backgrounds, either using the data in the individual language sections of Chapter 5, or using your own local knowledge for learners from other first-language backgrounds. You could also prepare tables for other areas that are central to ELF pronunciation, such as consonants clusters, or nuclear stress placement.

Diagnostic testing has the primary value of helping you to determine priorities for a course. This value can be extended by going through a recording with a learner and pointing out any problems. In this way, learners become conscious of the problems, and consequently place greater value on classroom activities designed to correct them. In addition, they are now better situated to work on problem sounds on their own and in their own time.

Another way of raising learner awareness of their problems is to get them to work in groups. The members of a group would then be responsible for correcting each other's recordings, using the same mark sheet as yours. You would all then compare the peer-corrected mark sheets with yours and discuss any discrepancies. In my own teaching, I strongly encourage my students to work in groups when they are required to produce a recording of some sort. The presence of the other students can provide feedback about the correctness of target features as well as the effectiveness of any adjustments each student makes. By working in groups they can guide each other

Name					Group	Date
Sound	**Examples**	**✓**	**OK**	**✗**	**Comments**	
/p/	party pictures put					
/t/	truly take too invitation					
/k/	could course keep copies OK					
/tʃ/	charge pictures much					
/dʒ/	join just project message charge					
/s/	message depressing					
/ʃ/	shouldn't invitation wish					
/ʒ/	visuals					
/ŋ/	amazing depressing long getting					
/w/	what wish work					
Overall comments:						

Table 6.4 A marking sheet for diagnostic testing of consonants for Greek learners of English.

towards correct production of the pronunciation items that the task focuses on. Such peer input has a double value. On the one hand it pushes learners to be more active, reflective, and critical of their own attempts to improve their pronunciation, and on the other, input from peers is often more acceptable and more accessible than input from teachers (Celce-Murcia et al. 1996; Larsen-Freeman 1985).

Assessing pronunciation for ELF – progress achievement testing

If diagnostic testing allows us to set priorities, progress achievement tests that focus on recently taught items helps both teachers and learners to monitor progress and to carry out remedial work where necessary. This type of test can take the form of individual words or sentences, or you can use longer texts such as monologues or dialogues that involve repeated use of the item(s) being tested.

Although the students can read the test items aloud in real time to the assessor, it is preferable to record them. Digital recording facilities on modern computers greatly facilitate this process, but even with traditional media such as cassettes tapes, the use of recordings, both as a teaching and as a testing tool means that:

- Learners can prepare the sample in their own time and at their own speed.
- Learners can rehearse as much as they want before handing in a sample they are finally satisfied with.
- The speaker and the assessor do not have to be in the same place at the same time.
- The assessor has the opportunity to listen to the sample or part of the sample more than once.
- The assessor and the speaker can discuss the mark on the basis of a joint analysis of the recording.

At it simplest, a progress achievement test could involve students recording minimal pairs and then sentences involving minimal pairs. Aspiration of initial /p/, /t/, /k/, for example, is a problem for a speakers from many different first-language backgrounds. Table 6.5 shows a simple test sheet for this LFC feature.

An alternative to students recording both options in each part of the test is for them to record only one of them, and to make a note of which one they chose. You would then listen and mark the option you had understood. Comparing what you understood with what the student had intended not only gives a mark for the test, but also gives the learner an opportunity to receive individualized feedback and further guidance.

1 Pronounce each pair of words.	
pea	bee
peach	beach
tent	dent
coat	goat
cap	gap

2 Pronounce each sentence twice, once with each of the alternatives.

I can't stand peas/bees.
What an amazing peach/beach!
They found a large tent/dent.
She went to market to buy a coat/goat.
He didn't know what to do about the cap/gap.

Table 6.5 A simple progress achievement test for aspiration of initial /p/, /t/, /k/

Moving beyond individual words or sentences, students can be asked to record a short dialogue such as that shown below. This is similar to dialogues I regularly used with my own students in my work at Oviedo University School of Tourism in Spain (Walker 2005).

RESERVATIONS: Hotel Llastres Spa. Reservations. Can I help you?

CALLER: Yes, I'd like to make a reservation.

RESERVATIONS: Certainly. Could I have your name, please?

CALLER: Jardine. Ray Jardine.

RESERVATIONS: When would you like to stay, Mr Jardine?

CALLER: I'd like a double room for five nights from the 11th of June.

RESERVATIONS: So that's a double room, arriving June 11th, five nights. I'll just check availability … Yes, we can do that for you, Mr Jardine. Is this an individual booking?

CALLER: Yes.

RESERVATIONS: And have you stayed with us before?

CALLER: No, it's the first time.

RESERVATIONS: Would you like one of our suites? They're on the top floor and have wonderful views of the harbour and the jetty.

CALLER: Not really. In fact I was hoping we could have a room near the ground floor.

RESERVATIONS:	OK. I've made a note of that. When you check in, the receptionist will give you a room on the first floor.
CALLER:	Thank you.
RESERVATIONS:	Can I take your credit card details?
CALLER:	Yes, of course. It's VISA. It's in my name.
RESERVATIONS:	So that's VISA in the name of Mr Ray Jardine. And the card number?
CALLER:	4335 4000 3609 2014.
RESERVATIONS:	OK, Mr Jardine, that's reserved for you.
CALLER:	Thank you.
RESERVATIONS:	You're welcome, and we look forward to seeing you on the 11th.

Prior to recording the dialogue my students would previously have done work on the pronunciation of /v/, /dʒ/, and /d/ between vowels, all of which are problematic for Spanish L1 speakers of English. They would also have met and practised nuclear stress placement in set phrases such as 'Can I help you?'.

Before administering the test, I would normally give each student a copy of the marking sheet reproduced in Table 6.6. By doing this, they pay more attention to the items being tested, which has a number of beneficial effects. On the one hand, it gives a clear focus to any revision or practice that students might do before making their recordings. On the other, it means that during the recording they are not so easily distracted or discouraged by pronunciation items that they may find difficult, but which are not listed in the marking scheme. A third advantage of making the marking scheme 'public' prior to the test is the sense of 'fairness' that it generates amongst students – they can see that they are being tested on what they were taught.

One less obvious advantage of going through the marking sheet with the students is that this obliges teachers to attend only to what is on the scheme when doing the marking, and to ignore other 'errors'. These can be mentioned in the space for 'Comments' at the end of the marking sheet, if teachers feel it is appropriate. This is especially useful for native-speaker teachers, who can be drawn to mark students down for any deviation from a standard native-speaker pronunciation. Unconsciously, native-speaker teachers often tend to compare all aspects of a student's pronunciation to their NS norm, including features such as vowel quality, rhythm, or choice of tone, all of which lie outside the requirements of intelligible ELF pronunciation.

First name(s)	Family name(s)		
Partner's name			
Group	Date of recording:		

a) Consonants (20 x 0.25 points)

/v/	reservations	have	arriving	five
	availability	individual	have	views
	I've	give	VISA	reserved
/dʒ/	Jardine	June	just	jetty
/d/	Could I	Jardine	individual	made a

b) Sentence stress (5. x 1 point)

	Can I help you?
	Could I have your name, please?
	When would you like to stay, Mr Jardine?
	Is this an individual booking?
	And have you ever stayed with us before?

Final mark =

Comments:

Table 6.6 An example of a marking sheet for a progress achievement test

On preparing the recordings of a test like this, students have to work in pairs, with each student taking on the role of the caller, as well as that of the receptionist. For marking purposes, however, you only need to focus on the pronunciation of each student as the receptionist. With practice, it is perfectly possible to complete the marking for one student in two or three minutes. This compares very favourably with the marking of tests for other areas of language competence, such as grammar or vocabulary. More importantly, in my experience the backwash effect of progress tests like these is excellent, especially since there does not seem to be any direct correlation between students' competence in their pronunciation and their grammar. As a result, students who perceive themselves as poor at English are often pleasantly surprised to see that they have good marks for pronunciation.

Assessing pronunciation for ELF – final achievement testing

Although discrete item tests are very useful for diagnostic and progress achievement tests, at the end of a course a holistic test is more appropriate. This is because at this stage what we are interested in is not so much a learner's pronunciation in itself, but the impact this has on their intelligibility. A holistic test based on some type of communication task is better for several reasons, but especially because:

1 There does not appear to be any direct relationship between a learner's competence in the pronunciation of individual items and his or her overall intelligibility (Porter 1989a).
2 Discrete item tests largely ignore the role of the listener in intelligibility. However, as it is now accepted that '[i]ntelligibility presupposes participants. In other words, intelligibility has as much to do with the listener as with the speaker' (Kenworthy 1987: 14).
3 Students following a course based on a communicative approach to ELT will probably see greater face value in a communication task than in a test based on discrete items.

The communication tasks for the test would reflect the sort of tasks students had already performed during the course, and might include roleplays, problem-solving tasks, or presentations. Marking schemes would need to reflect the extent to which the learner's pronunciation has facilitated intelligibility or not. One way of producing these is to modify existing schemes from the major exam boards. The Cambridge ESOL *International Certificate in Financial English Test of Speaking*, for example, assesses candidates on four criteria: grammar and vocabulary, discourse management, pronunciation, and interactive communication. In terms of pronunciation, the examiner is required to 'assess the overall impact of the pronunciation and the degree of effort required to understand the candidate' (Cambridge ESOL 2009). In particular, the examiner is invited to consider:

STRESS AND RHYTHM:	the appropriate use of strong and weak syllables in words and connected speech, the linking of words, and the effective highlighting of information-bearing words in utterances.
INFORMATION:	the use of a sufficiently wide pitch range and the appropriate use of intonation to convey intended meanings.

INDIVIDUAL SOUNDS: the effective articulation of individual sounds to facilitate understanding.

(Cambridge ESOL 2009)

Parts of these descriptors are not appropriate to an assessment of intelligibility for ELF. By deleting or modifying these so that they come into line with an ELF approach, we might come up with:

STRESS AND INTONATION   the effective highlighting of information-bearing words in utterances to convey intended meanings.

INDIVIDUAL SOUNDS   the effective articulation of the LFC consonants to facilitate understanding.

CONSONANT CLUSTERS   the effective treatment of word-initial clusters to facilitate understanding.

These broad descriptors pay attention to three key aspects of the LFC – the use of nuclear stress placement, articulation of consonants, and the treatment of clusters. However, it is more in keeping with the idea of pronunciation as part of intelligibility if an even less analytical approach is taken. The International Civil Aviation Authority, for example, take a holistic approach to assessing the language proficiency of pilots and air-traffic controllers. Their rating scales describe pronunciation at six different levels from 'Pre-Elementary' (Level 1) through to Expert (Level 6). The descriptors for Levels 4–6 are:

Level 4 (Operational)

Pronunciation, stress, rhythm and intonation are influenced by the first language or regional variation, but only sometimes interfere with the ease of understanding.

Level 5 (Extended)

Pronunciation, stress, rhythm and intonation, though possibly influenced by the first language or regional variation, rarely interfere with the ease of understanding.

Level 6 (Expert)

Pronunciation, stress, rhythm and intonation, though possibly influenced by the first language or regional variation, almost never interfere with the ease of understanding.

(Civil Aviation Authority 2009)

Interestingly, these scales attribute pronunciation problems both to first-language influence and to regional variation. That is to say, the ICAO are aware that problems of intelligibility are not exclusively the result of first-language transfer by non-native speaker pilots and air-traffic controllers.

Native-speaker regional accents are also seen as problematic. This makes the ICAO scales especially useful as a basis for testing ELF pronunciation, given that almost all other currently available scales explicitly or implicitly imply that problems of intelligibility stem from the failure to approximate to a native-speaker standard.

We can adopt the ICAO scales to generate scales for judging intelligibility in communicative speaking tests to use in secondary schools, private language schools, or university departments around the world. With such scales the candidate's pronunciation is judged holistically using broad descriptors such as:

1   Pronunciation did not interfere with the listener's understanding.
2   Pronunciation occasionally interfered with the listener's understanding but any problems were quickly resolved by the speaker and/or the listener.
3   Pronunciation regularly interfered with the listener's understanding and required concentrated listening. Not all misunderstandings were easily resolved.
4   Pronunciation frequently interfered with the listener's understanding and required numerous repetitions by the speaker. Some misunderstandings were left unresolved.
5   Pronunciation constantly interfered with the listener's understanding and required frequent repetitions. Many misunderstandings were not resolved despite the listener's participation.

Scales like these may feel unprofessional when compared to the more analytic alternatives we saw earlier. However, the more analytical assessment scales are, the more they draw the assessor away from an evaluation of a speaker's intelligibility in a communicative context, and the more they pull it towards a rating of the accuracy of individual features of pronunciation. Secondly, the more analytical such scales are, the more sophisticated the training that is needed by the assessors who are using them. This inevitably makes them less accessible to ordinary teachers. Lastly, the more analytical the scales are, the more they begin to look like diagnostic or progress achievement tests, and the less they respond to the requirements I proposed earlier for end-of-course assessment.

An interesting alternative to a single test at the end of a course is to use portfolios as a form of continuous assessment. Magdalena Szyszka, experimented with this approach with students at the Foreign Language Teacher Training College in Opole, Poland. She encouraged her students 'to look for materials on their own, decide on the time and place of their work outside the classroom, identify their own problems and plan activities and techniques to be included in the portfolio' (2007: 22). The contents of the portfolios varied quite a lot and while some students included light-hearted samples of pronunciation such as tongue twisters, lists of homophones, and song lyrics, others included transcription exercises. Portfolios like these have a lot of potential. In particular, if they are part of the assessment system for the pronunciation component of an English course, they can become a tool for evaluation as well as for learning. Typically, a student's portfolio could include paper and audio copies of:

1 the diagnostic test from the beginning of the course, together with the priorities that student and tutor agreed upon on the basis of this test
2 progress tests taken during the course, together with the marks and the notes from any discussion of the test with the tutor
3 exercises done during normal course work
4 samples of ELF speakers found on the Internet
5 notes about any experiences the student might have had using English in an ELF context.

Ultimately, assessing pronunciation for ELF should be about assessing the impact of a speaker's pronunciation on the overall intelligibility when they are involved in some sort of communicative interaction. This favours a holistic rather than a discrete item approach. However, a judicious balance between both approaches through a combination of diagnostic and achievement testing will probably gives us the best results, and will make most sense to our students. Many existing assessment activities and methods can be adapted to suit an ELF approach.

Summary

This chapter looked at two areas connected with the successful implementation of an ELF approach to teaching pronunciation – planning and assessment. In terms of planning we saw that ELF requires us to take a different perspective on the variables that a traditional approach would consider. We looked at ways to programme the teaching of ELF pronunciation and at how to adapt that programming to different teaching contexts. Finally, we looked at examples of how to integrate ELF pronunciation teaching into our normal classes.

Part B described how the optimum way to assess ELF pronunciation is probably through a careful combination of diagnostic and achievement testing, and through the application of discrete item and holistic testing to each of these, respectively. Part B also showed how marking scales for existing proficiency tests can be adapted to provide holistic marking scales that we can use to gauge a speaker's overall intelligibility in end-of-course achievement tests.

Further reading

On planning pronunciation teaching

Celce-Murcia, M., D. Brinton, and **J. M. Goodwin.** 1996. Teaching *Pronunciation: A Reference for Teachers of English as a Second or Foreign Language.* Cambridge: Cambridge University Press.

Kenworthy, J. 1987. *Teaching English Pronunciation.* Harlow: Longman.

On assessment for pronunciation

Hewings, M. 2004. *Pronunciation Practice Activities.* Cambridge: Cambridge University Press.

Kenworthy, J. 1987. *Teaching English Pronunciation.* Harlow: Longman.

Vaughan-Rees, M. (ed.). 1997. 'Testing pronunciation'. *Speak Out!* 20.

TRANSCRIPTS

Track 1: Reactions to the concept of ELF

Speaker A is Malaysian (English L1) and Speaker B is German (German L1)

The speakers know each other, although not very well. The concept of ELF was explained to them briefly in a meeting prior to the recording session. Here they discuss their feelings about the new concept. Both speakers have regularly used English in ELF situations previously, but were unaware of the role their English was playing.

1	**A**	have you heard . about this idea of lingua franca before is it . new
2	**B**	well . I haven't heard about the name . and . well . also . the
3		theoretical concept . em . I've never heard about it . but . I've used
4		it quite a lot of times so now . when we were introduced . to it I
5		thought well . of course we're using
6	**A**	[hm]
7	**B**	[English] like that all the time . what do you think about it what's
8		your opinion on
9	**A**	(draws breath) ah . (both laugh) well it's pretty much the same for
10		me 'cos I hadn't really heard of the concept until recently . I'm not
11		sure if . it was the first time when . er I was told about it but em .
12		basically like the entire last year and in other situations before like
13		living in Budapest I was . pretty much how . I was communicating
14		with my friends was . there were people from all over . Central
15		Eastern Europe . and elsewhere . and that was how it is . this .
16		English . most it wasn't most people's first language . except for the
17		Americans . and the British . and nobody could understand the
18		British
19	**B**	(both laugh) nobody could understand . yeah . and what I like
20		most about the concept is . that it doesn't say this English is
21		better or this one is worse it just . it's like . that's the way it is
22		that's the way we pronounce it and we should just all make an
23		effort at understanding
24	**A**	hm
25	**B**	each other . so ... yeah being exposed to as many . accents and
26		dialects as possible as . can just enrich . your knowledge . and

27		your life
28	**A**	hm
29	**B**	I believe
30	**A**	and this. kind of makes you a better listener . too . I like learning
31		to . hear like different ways that people use to learn . it's . yeah
32		people don't listen enough . so . it's learning to listen more
33		carefully to what people are saying

Pronunciation notes

Speaker A is the only L1 user of English on the CD. In class, students might like to say which of the two speakers they find more intelligible before being given information about their respective language backgrounds.

line 10 clusters – deletion of /t/ in 'concept'
line 12 'basically' as [beɪslɪ]
line 15 /ð/ as [d̪] in 'that'
line 15 final /t/ in 'that' as a glottal stop
line 23 /ŋ/ as [ŋk] in 'understanding'

Track 2: ELF and identity

Speaker C is Hungarian (Hungarian L1) and Speaker D is Polish (Polish L1)

The speakers do not know each other, and come from quite different backgrounds in arts and sciences. Speaker C is entirely new to the concept of ELF but has been talking about it with Speaker D prior to the recording session.

1	**D**	so er what is your idea of er English as er lingua franca
2	**C**	er yes I think it's a very . er a very interesting topic it was pretty
3		new for you when I first heard this expression . but now I
4		understand that it means em . let's say a common language that .
5		many . people from absolutely different nationalities . can use for
6		communicating
7	**D**	[hm]
8	**C**	[between] them . and em . English is I think er without doubt is er
9		lingua franca number one today because . you know . besides
10		being the the language of science the language of music of I don't
11		know what this is the first people that most people, the first
12		language that most people start to [learn in er]
13	**D**	[of course]
14	**C**	in er . in school . and then . and then we were also talking about
15		the accent . that each nation have their own . accent [and]
16	**D**	[hm]
17	**C**	and is it good for us to be recognized as er Hungarian or Polish by
18		our accent or not . I think that's another interesting question what
19		do you think

20 **D** it is . well . ah . actually it's a tough one because . em . it has you
21   know it has so many connotations when you when you spe
22   because sometimes when you speak . ah yu . it also depends on on
23   your professors . on the way you [ah]
24 **C** [yes]
25 **D** you were taught on the way you learned the language . on your
26   abilities but sometimes if you if you want to ah stick to your own
27   accent . er it means that you you want to . em keep the values that
28   you have
29 **C** yes
30 **D** and not always it's er . it's perceived as something positive . em by
31   other speakers because they do not know your culture I mean you
32   know irrespectively to to some aspects they just may not may may
33   miss em . may misunderstand you . on the other hand mm I don't
34   know
35 **C** yeah but do you want to keep your identity to please others . or
36   because it's your identity [of course]
37 **D** [well I I] I'd say my identity is something that I have inside . so I
38   do not have to . reveal it while communicating . because when I
39   ask . for directions I just do not have to you know [use the . mm]
40 **C** [yeah that's for sure] . o on the other hand I think . I think I would
41   recognize a . a Polish accent . you don't have it at all . because I
42   know quite some Polish people and we always talk in English
43 **D** hm
44 **C** but many people would not I mean they hear that you have an an
45   accent that you are [probably not an English]
46 **D** [of course because it's] impossible to avoid it
47 **C** yes but they will not recognize it, ah this is a Polish guy, so they, I
     think they will . they will not you know
49 **D** hm
50 **C** identify you as ah
51 **D** [hm]
52 **C** [the Polish] guy . who has these I don't know these specialties
53   because he's from Pol Poland. I think that's not true
54 **D** and what about you . is it important
55 **C** er . I think I would be very pleased if somebody took me as an
56   English just because I would be proud of my English [knowledge]
57 **D** [of course] hm
58 **C** on the other hand I'm also proud of being Hungarian . and you
59   know if you really start to talk to somebody . the second question
60   will be . so where are you from
61 **D** of course
62 **C** and then you will say that I'm from Hungary and I'm fine with
63   that

Pronunciation notes
lines 6, 17, 41, 50, 59 word stress in 'communicating', 'recognized',
'accent', 'identify', 'somebody'
line 33   Speaker D deliberately stresses the prefix in 'misunderstand'.

Track 3: Accent and identity

Speaker E is Russian (Russian L1) and Speaker F is Argentinean (Spanish L1)

The speakers do not know each other, but have been in conversation for over twenty minutes when they start talking about how they would feel if people confused them with native speakers because of their accents in English.

1	E	if if er the people confused me with a British person . I would like
2		it mm . because also when when I studied English in the high
3		school . we had teachers from New Zealand . and they they they
4		tried to show us a really British accent
5	F	yes
6	E	so I I I would like this idea people . thinking I am British
7	F	yes
8	E	I would like
9	F	yeah I would feel more confident with my English if they thought
10		I . I were . I was American or English
11	E	yeah mm . maybe ah I I don't practise now enough . but maybe
12		after s studying in Netherlands . after this year I studied there .
13		some people maybe confused me
14	F	yeah
15	E	with English maybe . just . when I was very fresh in the morning
16		speaking eh . very quiet and relaxed
17	F	[mm]
18	E	[and] I don't know
19	F	yeah I think that . eh . in some way I would feel the same as I feel
20		now . no I would feel myself . no I I because if I speak for
21		example in I I know that I am Argentinean
22	E	[yes]
23	F	[although] they think that I . if you think I am English . I I would
24		still know that I am not English [no]
25	E	[yes of] course not just like nice thing they're telling about your
26		English . er it . it's nice

At this point Speaker F indicates that she hasn't fully understood the idea of being mistaken for a native speaker because of her accent. After clarification they return to the topic.

27	E	I I I I will feel good . I've I've it's like a thing er . people when
28		the people ask me . why do I have accent speaking in Spanish

29 **F** yeah
30 **E** after already twelve years living n in Spain . but . I tell them I like
31   my accent I don't want to I never
32 **F** [change it]
33 **E** [tried] to . to to make it disappear I never . tried to speak perfect
34   er like . accent from Madrid or something like that
35 **F** yeah
36 **E** I I th I think . yes really . in the accent there is a part of the identity
37   of the person
38 **F** yes
39 **E** also it's not er . er so about Russian accent . or . er even . different
40   Russian person has er his different voice his different . way of . er
41   giving the direction the way of . er conversation
42 **F** yeah
43 **E** also it's erm it's something really of the identity of the person
44 **F** yes it's your own [nationality I is is it . you your accent is is you]
45 **E** [yes . yes . yes it's nice yes I think it's nice] yes yes
46 **F** so why why we are going [to]
47 **E** [no] I don't want to lose it
48 **F** yeah neither me . I don't want to lose it

Pronunciation notes
general devoicing of /d/ in 'and'
line 3 devoicing of final /d/ in 'Zealand' line 15
line 3 /ð/ as [d̪] in 'the' and 'they'
line 3 clusters – vowel insertion in 'had teachers'
line 11, 34 clusters – /t/ elision in 'don't practise'
line 28 /h/ as [x]

Track 4: English in Malaysia

Speaker A is Malay (English L1) and Speaker B is German (German L1)

The speakers know each other a little. They have been in conversation for some time when Speaker B asks Speaker A about the fact that she should speak English as her first language when she is from Malaysia.

1 **B** so you're from Malaysia that's so interesting . em . but I was quite
2   surprised . when I heard you speaking English the first time it was
3   like wow
4 **A** [right]
5 **B** [she] speaks great and then . you said . you'll it's your first
6   language . h how come . I I don
7 **A** hm
8 **B** I didn't know that before

9   **A** ah yeah . most people tend to be surprised cos it's . yeah not what
10   you would expect well em . I speak English as my first language
11   because my parents were educated . in the States but also we were
12   colonized by the British . so erm when my parents were growing
13   up so from like . the fifties like the seventies our education system
14   . was . in English and then after that they switched it over to
15   Malay . which is the current . national language . but em .
16   Malaysia's such a multilingual country and so many different
17   languages are spoken . erm English is used quite a lot and
18   especially in urban areas there's a lot of people who speak
19   . English as their first . language . em . yeah and lots of people are
20   bilingual trilingual . know several . different Chinese dialects . er
21   unfortunately I don't really speak Chinese that much .
22   **B** so when you said trilingual you were referring to [Chinese and th]
23   **A** [I'm referring to other people that are not . me]
24   **B** [but . and] like . as a third language it would be Malay English and
25   **A** [erm]
26   **B** [which] which would be the third . most commonly
27   **A** well . I it t totally depends on the person . like . erm . like I have
28   friends who grew up speaking Chinese Cantonese . or Chinese
29   Mandarin Cantonese . Hokkein . Hock Chew. like several dialects
30   and then they're equally . or almost equally as fluent in like
31   English . Malay . and then Indians will often speak Tamil like . er
32   Malayam . and then also . Malay . and English . so they kind of .
33   yeah depends on the area depends on your family . where you're
43   raised but it could be any combination of like . all those languages
44   **B** and English is an . compulsory subject in school
45   **A** yeah . it it is compulsory . em . from yeah right from the beginning
46   so standard one . first grade . em everybody learns English . and
47   they've also switched back to teaching science and math in
48   English
49   **B** hm
50   **A** em . but everything else is in Malay

Pronunciation notes
lines 5, 6 clusters – elision of /t/ in 'first language'
line 8 clusters – elision of /t/ in 'didn't know'
line 14 /ð/ as [d̪] in 'that' and 'they'
line 18 /ð/ as [z̪] in 'there'
line 19 deletion of final /t/ in 'first'
line 20, 29 clusters – elision of /t/ in 'dialects'
line 30 /ð/ as [d̪] in 'they're'

Track 5: Learning English in China

Speaker G is Chinese (Chinese L1) and Speaker H is German (German L1)

The speakers do not know each other but have opted to talk about learning English. The German speaker initiates the conversation by asking about the status of English in China.

1	H	do you have more than one official language in your country
2	G	in China we only have our . official language . it's Chinese
3	H	OK . and is English important for an individual in your country or
4	G	English for . [er] people of this world is very important
5	H	[yes]
6	G	[not] only for China for . Ame France for Germany it's also
7		important but in China we study more . much more . than the
8		students the European students . we study every day . two or three
9		hours . so . it's very . if I were a . high school student . I would
10		study . much more . than the . students of . Europe of high school
11	H	and em . some people say that the only way to learn a language is
12		to go . and live in the country where it is spoken so do you agree
13		or do you think you can learn it
14	G	I don agree . I don agree . look I am er before I wen . came to
15		. Spain . I ... never go I had never had been to a country tha . that
16		speak . English . but my oral English . i I think is . mm .
17		satisfactory . so . I don't agree . er that if you want to study
18		English you should go to America you should go to . [brei] Britain
19		. no it's no [tsus]
20	H	but do you watch a lot of . English movies or do you read a [lot]
21	G	[yes] . I love the Prison Break
22	H	(laughs)
23	G	I love the American series of films like Prison Break . the . some
24		other films and . I also like er . some . horro horrible films as like
25		Saw [so Saw]
26	H	[so horror] movies
27	G	a horrible movies because . it's . very . attractive
28	H	and is it difficult for you to understand or . do you . use subtitles in
29		the movies
30	G	erm . mostly I . we wa with . we watch the subtitles
31	H	mm
32	G	subtitles . and also . mm we . capture a little . of the sound .
33	H	[yeah]
34	G	[of the voice] of the mm actors . so we are practising ... the
35		comprehension
36	H	yeah
37	G	of reading . and . in the same time . we practise a little . of the

38   listening
39 **H** yeah that's good . sometimes it's quite difficult to to understand
40   the different accents but . you get used to it .
41 **G** [yeah]
42 **H** [I mean some] . whatever British accents or
43 **G** in [China]
44 **H** [no matter]. where they're from could be . difficult .
45 **G** mm
46 **H** but
47 **G** British English . for us is *novo
48 **H** (laughs)
49 **G** so a few people a few students . like to . study a British . accent .
50   because they think ah British people mm . *novo s*novo. but for
51   most of us . we prefer American English because . American is
52   the first . coun . is the ... the country that ... is a potential (laughs)
53   country . you know what . the first one . the number one . in this
54   world . so we . prefer . to . speak American English to study
55   American English . because . in the future in the work . it . is more
56   useful than British English

Pronunciation notes
consistent /l/ for dental fricative (Speaker G)
line 4 unintelligible – possibly 'all'
line 7, 10 good nuclear stress placement in 'MUCH more'
line 9 good nuclear stress placement 'if I were you'
line 12 good nuclear stress placement in 'and LIVE in the country'
line 14 deletion of final 't' in 'don't agree'
line 14 deletion of final 't'
line 16 deletion of /l/ in 'oral'
line 18 unintelligible – possibly 'great'
line 19 unintelligible – possibly 'true'
line 24, 27 /h/ as [x]
line 34 /ð/ as [d̥] in 'the'
line 47, 56 deletion of /ʃ/ in 'British'
line 44 good nuclear stress placement in 'COULD be'
line 47, 56 deletion of /l/ in 'English'

Track 6: Problems with listening

Speaker I is from the United Arab Emirates (Arabic L1) and Speaker J is from Taiwan (Taiwanese L1)

The speakers know each other because they are both doing postgraduate studies in the UK. Because of their different L1s, English is their lingua franca. Here they talk about the problems they have with listening in English.

1	**I**	what do you think the most difficult aspects in speaking in English
2		. to me actually I suffered from listening when I listen to
3		somebody
4	**J**	mm
5	**I**	I feel like I'm working very hard . to . to understand the person in
6		front of me and it doesn't matter who that person is whether I'm
7		meeting that person face to face or . whether I'm listening from a
8		recorder . or whatever so I've got quite a problem in listening
9		and I believe I have to improve it and what do you think what
10		about you
11	**J**	I have the same problem with you . the [same as as the]
12	**I**	[what is it]
13	**J**	same as you yeah listening my listening is not very good so
14		sometimes when I listen to others oh I can't catch the total
15		meaning and sometimes I will misunderstand their meaning
16	**I**	you [misunderstand]
17	**J**	[yeah] and em [by the]
18	**I**	[pl] please [tell me]
19	**J**	[sorry] by the way . em because my vocabulary is not very . a lot
20	**I**	[you]
21	**J**	[I I didn't] know lots of *vocabularies so it's a *upscare for me
22	**I**	[it's]
23	**J**	[for me] *upscare
24	**I**	*upscare
25	**J**	yeah *upscare for me to . to listen to oth others to catch the
26		meaning
27	**I**	so it's difficult for you
28	**J**	[yes]
29	**I**	[you] mean right so you believe that this is a problem because of .
30		the vocabulary
31	**J**	mm
32	**I**	I see
33	**J**	yes
34	**I**	right . apart for me I believe that I miss the . good skill .
35	**J**	mm
36	**I**	the skill of being a good listener because er . er it's not only
37		vocabulary it is
38	**J**	[mm]
39	**I**	[just] being able . to catch . the meaning of what people say
40	**J**	[mm]
41	**I**	[or] concentrate with somebody's speech spe spe specially if the

42		speech is quite long if the speech is for more than fifteen minutes
43		or for more than twenty minutes
44	**J**	yes
45	**I**	so I have to train myself to be a good listener
46	**J**	yes . I must . improve it
47	**I**	you too [OK]
48	**J**	[yes] me too

Pronunciation notes

frequent /ŋ/ as [ŋk] or [ŋg]

line 2 clusters – vowel insertion in 'suffered from'

line 8 word stress in 'recorder'

line 14 clusters – elision of /t/ in 'can't catch'

line 19, 21 /b/ as [w] plus deletion of /l/, so that 'vocabulary' sounds like
        [voˈkæwerɪ]

line 41 clusters – vowel insertion in 'somebody's speech'

line 42 clusters – vowel insertion in 'is quite'

Track 7: Speaking with NSs and NNSs

Speaker K is Japanese (Japanese L1)

The speaker uses English, her third language, in international conferences
and seminars. Here she discusses her experiences using English both with
native speakers from Britain and the USA, and with other non-native
speakers throughout Europe.

1	**K**	we . yes when I speak with the native speaker in English . mm . I
2		prefer to . to listen the British than American in general in general
3		term . mm . because American accent . is very … very … hm hm .
4		how do I say . er .[z z] the sounds is not so clear . for for me . mm
5		. it's dark dark sound ah for me . so for me I'm . it's more di er
6		more difficult to . to catch the American pronunciation . but the
7		between among the American people I … I understand better the
8		people from the co east coast than the south part of the United
9		State . er I have very difficulty to understand what they say em em
10		American south part . mm . Texas maybe or in this in this part of
11		in the all people . and also when I . listen . mm . BBC . er . er
12		television . when they sm speak very formally with with
13		*reselected term (laughs) I I cannot I cannot follow them (laughs)
14		they are very formal very orthodox (laughs) it's I I find it difficult
15		to to follow them (laughs) . and when I speak with nn er foreigner
16		. em foreigner fo em . they are not native speaker . em they speak
17		Eng er English . em . it is easy for me . mm . to speak with the …
18		the … central north part of Europe Europe eh . they speak English

19   very orthodox and their pronunciation is very clear normally . but
20   w ff when the Spanish people (laughs) speak English (laughs) . oh
21   (laughs) it's . nn . m . many time I I don't understand what they
22   are . they are . mm they want to say they want to transmit to me .
23   mm … but in . when the Greek people speak in English . yes . it's
24   it's clear for me it's very clear . but mm maybe Italian English it's
25   not so clear . er z maybe the the pronunciation is not so good
26   normally no in in in [pari] when they speak English . I think

Pronunciation notes

consistent /ð/ as [z]
consistent /l/ as [r]
line 1, 11, 15 /w/ as [hw] in 'when'
line 3, 13 /ɜː/ as [ɑː] in 'term'
lines 14, 18, 19 /θ/ as [s] in 'orthodox', 'north', 'orthodox'

Track 8: Language – teaching English in Spain

Speaker L is Moroccan (Arabic L1)

Speaker L teaches English at a Spanish university. Here he describes how he learned English in Morocco both at school and though songs. He also talks of the ambiguous feelings he had towards English and the cultures of the UK and USA.

1   **L**   my experience with . English . is er was through . formal
2   instruction . cos English the English language was simply part of
3   the . curriculum . but later as I used to … like listening to English
4   songs . the pressure … was to understand the lyrics . so I was
5   motivated to go a little bit further . in my . language proficiency .
6   and that motivated me to study language . more seriously … but
7   honestly the target language community was not really appealing .
8   so we can talk of a clash . there between . my two conflicting
9   tendencies . one rejecting the lang target-language culture and the
10   other is . enjoying . the music of the target-language coun culture .
11   or that the music . really came from . two language . communities
12   two speech communities one . is the … English one the UK one
13   and the other the USA

Track 9: Cultural stereotypes 1

*Speaker M is Romanian (Romanian L1) and Speaker C is Hungarian
(Hungarian L1)*

The speakers do not know each other, but have just discovered that they do
share one thing in common, the city of Budapest, the capital of Hungary.
This prompts them to talk about how other Europeans perceive Romanians
and Hungarians.

1	**M**	OK so em . since I I found that you're from Hungary . so I'm
2		studying in Budapest . eh I would like to discuss some things
3		about . OK culture (laughs) … er so this this question of [vɒʔ]
4		people from other countries er what they think about your culture
5		so what do they usually think when they found out you are from er
6		from Hungary
7	**C**	usually they have no idea at all you know (laughs) they have some
8		idea Europeans know that Hungary's in Europe. that's
9	**M**	[OK]
10	**C**	[something]. maybe they know they also know that it's in eastern
11		Europe. but that's more or less it
12	**M**	but it's very blurred. everything gets
13	**C**	[eh yes, yes]
14	**M**	[blurred. I think] but [in the]
15	**C**	[actually]
16	**M**	in the case of Spain I mean er did you have the same problem I
17		mean people not knowing
18	**C**	they don they really don't know. it was the only person my doctor
19		who told me he's a very sympathetic guy
20	**M**	(laughs)
21	**C**	and he told me . well actually people here think . all the people are
22		gypsies in Hungary. that was (laughs) [that was]
23	**M**	[no] but it but no but th this is th this is a Romanian stereotype
24		you [cannot]
25	**C**	[I know]
26	**M**	[you cannot]
27	**C**	[I know]
28	**M**	steal our stereotype (laughs)
29	**C**	I'm sorry
30	**M**	no
31	**C**	and so they just you know they just expand it in the old [area].
32	**M**	[OK]
33	**C**	in the east you know there is Russia and then the gypsies and
34	**M**	OK so we're Romanian Hungarians like the [same]
35	**C**	[like the same]

36 **M** we are from the same [country]
37 **C** [yes yes]
38 **M** oh it's good to know. we are like sisters now
39 **C** we are we are . on the other hand countries that are neighbouring
40   to your er (.) to your country
41 **M** [yes]
42 **C** [they al], always have an opinion . I mean usually it's negative
43   isn't it
44 **M** of course. I mean one is . thinking about . the context of Romania
45   with Hungary [especially]
46 **C** [yes exactly]
47 **M** [yes] all the the the divergences we have among like . in terms of
48   the the historical background and our our the cultural … sharings
49   we have and the same time the the the conflict that we we still
50   have with Transylvania and eh it's very interesting

Pronunciation notes

line 3 unintelligible but probably 'what'

Speaker M initially pronounces 'th' as [θ] or [ð] (lines 1–5). As she becomes more involved in the topic and relaxes, dental [t] and [d̪] become more prevalent (line 23 onwards). In general she does not use weak forms. Speaker C regularly pronounces /ð/ as [d̪], especially in the word 'that'.

Track 10: Cultural stereotypes 2

Speaker N is Brazilian (Portuguese L1) and Speaker O is Portuguese (Portuguese L1)

The speakers know each other quite well, and to an extent have a shared cultural background. They talk about the stereotypes people have of their respective cultures.

1   **N** something . let's say interesting
2   **O** yes
3   **N** because we come from different cultures but at . at the same time .
4   we have . too much in common
5   **O** yes we have a lot in common
6   **N** do you think so . a lot
7   **O** [yes]
8   **N** [I] don't know
9   **O** I think . at least em . we know a lot about each other well about
10   each other culture I think at least . in Portugal we do know a lot
11   about . Brazil . and Brazilian people . because we everybody's got
12   . a family member . that is Brazilian or at least most of the families

13   have
14   **N**   yes this we have in common
15   **O**   (laughs)
16   **N**   everybody has got a a family member who is Portuguese (laughs)
17   it's . it's really em . amazing and at the same time er . we have er
18   maybe a . a stereotype [of]
19   **O**   [really]
20   **N**   Portuguese people yeah
21   **O**   what do you think about us
22   **N**   well let's . think about the bakery that every Portuguese . er is
23   called Manuel . and have a bakery
24   **O**   just like my uncle yes (laugh)
25   **N**   (laugh) and what about the er you in Portugal . what is the
26   stereotype jus just like everybody abroad that we have we all
27   know how to dance Samba
28   **O**   [(laughs)]
29   **N**   [and ka is k] we have carnival
30   **O**   [well]
31   **N**   [all] year all the year
32   **O**   yes because we've got some . 'scolas de Samba' . in Portugal
33   Brazilian people that
34   **N**   [really I didn't know that]
35   **O**   [when carnival] yes in carnival they dance . Samba as well yes . er
36   in Portugal . and there are lots of people in Portugal who . likes to
37   dance Samba . I don't know if we can but at least we try (laughs)
38   **N**   oh it's nice
39   **O**   yes
40   **N**   and by the way I don't know how to dance Samba
41   **O**   oh [oh
42   **N**   no] it's a [it's something ev]
43   **O**   [I used to dance when] I was small (laughs)
44   **N**   it's something everybody asks me oh you're from Brazil . oh can
45   you teach me to dance Samba no I can't (laughs)
46   **O**   (laughs) sorry
47   **N**   and they got they get . astonished
48   **O**   really
49   **N**   but we are
50   **O**   yeah
51   **N**   we are not . the way think people think we are
52   **O**   yes
53   **N**   we are different we like to work we are not in carnival all the year
54   **O**   [(laughs)]
55   **N**   [. long and] things like that
56   **O**   I guess just a minority of people live in I mean . er work the whole

57		year fo just to get ready for carnival because there are some people
58		who dedicate themselves to that right [or it's it's a minority]
59	**N**	[yes yes but in Rio] they dedicate they are professionals
60	**O**	[ah OK
	N	yes it's a kind of]
62	**O**	but not the whole country (laughs)
63	**N**	it's a kind of professional between inverted commas
64	**O**	and you've got different types of carnival right in Brazil because
65		we always think of Rio de Janeiro . but . you have other kinds of
66		carnival
67	**N**	yes yes we have the north k northern carnival er which is different
68		we have er Pernambuco's carnival yes it's er completely different
69		[from Rio]
70	**O**	[which is your] favourite
71	**N**	er I think the northern one
72	**O**	really
73	**N**	I have [in]
74	**O**	[what's] difference please
75	**N**	er people go dancing on the street and . just this it's not this kind
76		of show-off . er of Rio's carnival that is . a a a bit boring I think
77		you keep hours and hours . ten hours looking at the the people
78		there and nothing else so in . in the north people enjoy . they dance
79		everybody
80	**O**	so everybody's dancing
81	**N**	yeah yeah
82	**O**	OK

Pronunciation notes

Frequent /ð/ as [d̺] or [t̺] (Speaker N)
line 65 /r/ as [h] in 'Rio'.
lines 67, 71 /θ/ as [f] in 'north', 'northern'
(Because these speakers share L1 background, this is intelligible. If they did this with speakers from other L1s, it might be problematic.)

Track 11: Misconceptions about Turkey

Speaker O is Portuguese (Portuguese L1) and Speaker P is Turkish (Turkish L1)

The speakers do not know each other, but have both recently arrived in Spain on student exchange programmes. Here Speaker O talks about the misconceptions that she finds many Europeans have about life in Turkey.

1	**P**	they don't know much about Turkey because they that think it was
2		Turkey is still . erm . a country that was . one hundred years ago
3		fifty years ago . they think that the there is no . developments or

4   there is no . nothing new . they still er wearing the . you know .
5   [fɪːzɪz]
6 O   mm
7 P   a kind of mm . a kind of thing that they put on . in the old days of .
8   the Ottoman Empire
9 O   mm
10 P   they still think that er the people wear those . kinds of things for
11   example I I saw a film . on TV . and er it was . in Turkey . it was .
12   taken in Turkey and . the people around were wearing those .
13   [fɪːzɪz] . so I think they still think in that way
15 O   [who]
16 P   [that's] there's no development that people still wear . I don't
17   know [the]
18 O   [who] produced the film I mean was it made . was it a Turkish
19   movie or was it a
20 P   it was . from a European country
21 O   [a European country]
22 P   [I don't remember the] name exactly . it was . produced . in . a
23   European country I think … because a Turkish film wouldn't take
24   such things because there's nothing like that
25 O   yeah
26 P   and here they generally ask me . why don't you . erm . put on your
27   [vi] veil . er that's really interesting actually in Turkey it's
28   forbidden to . even to wear a scarf . it is forbidden . and it it's
29   really interesting that the people . suppose you to . wear such
30   things . for example I . sometimes I put on this hat (laughs)
31 O   yeah
32 P   and they s one of them . one of my friends er . made a joke that er
33   you have to . hide your hair . be careful (both laugh) it was really .
34   interesting why don't you er put on your veil . so I I hear such
35   things .
36 O   oh
37 P   I think they . are prejudices

Pronunciation notes
frequent /ð/ as [d̪] (Speaker P)
line 5 unintelligible – probably 'fezzes' (Until 1925, the fez was the traditional headwear for men in Turkey.)
line 7 /ŋ/ as [ŋk] in 'thing'
line 11 /l/ as [ʊ] in 'film'
line 34 /v/ as [w] in 'veil'

Track 12: Culture 1 – Easter in Greece

Speaker Q is Greek (Greek L1)

The speaker is a very proficient ELF user. Here he talks about how Easter is celebrated in Greece.

1   **Q**   one quite important celebration is er Easter time . er in Greece.
2   and er that's because erm . er families and friends are coming
3   together . and they go to celebrate er outside the big cities . in the
4   country . erm by mm … er preparing a typical let's say a typical
5   Greek dish . which is a lamb. [hm] er so they c they cook the
6   whole lamb [hm] in the countryside . and they then gather all
7   together in order to to eat and drink . and er most of the of the
8   times er they have dances I mean . they put some music they they
9   dancing traditional Greek dances er . while they're eating and they .
10   and they drinking. and this er this celebration may be . f it's mm .
11   a whole day or maybe two days. it depends

Pronunciation notes
line 5, 6 /m/ as [mp] in 'lamb'

Track 13: Culture 2 – Hanukkah

Speaker C is Hungarian (Hungarian L1), Speaker M is Romanian (Romanian L1), and Speaker D is Polish (Polish L1)

All three speakers are very proficient ELF users. Speakers C and D have known each other for a short while, but neither knows Speaker M. All three are studying in Spain. Speaker M remarks on the Spanish custom of the Three Kings at Christmas, and this prompts Speaker D to describe the Jewish festivity, Hanukkah.

1   **C**   so you know I was very surprised when I got to Spain
2   **D**   [mm]
3   **C**   [to] find out that here . it's the erm . the kings the three kings that
4   brings the [presents]
5   **D**   [mm]
6   **C**   on the sixth of [January]
7   **M**   yeah] it's true [it it was a start for]
8   **D**   [say it's marvellous]
9   **M**   for me to we don't we don't have it in the in the ox in the Orthodox
10   er celebrations
11   **C**   you know we are Catholics as that the Spanish people, but we
12   don't have it either [so]
13   **M**   [yeah it's true]

14   **D**   [and] you're you're Catholic
15   **C**   yes, yes
16   **D**   so it's amazing because like .
17   **M**   the [cultural . yes]
18   **O**   [you're Orthodox] you're [Catholic]
19   **C**   [yeah you are as well]
20   **D**   [I'm Jewish]
21   **C**   ah you're Jewish ah that's fine
22   **D**   [so]
23   **C**   [OK]
23   **M**   [so] you you don't have the three kings
24   **D**   [no]
25   **M**   [I don't] I don't
26   **C**   [(laughs)]
27   **M**   [have the three kings] . it's not right [it's not fair]
28   **D**   [no we don't have] it
29   **C**   but are . are there are there er I don't know . Christmas presents
30   [and everything]
31   **D**   [yeah] mm . there is er Hanukkah which er every year it er you know
32   the the . the date differs . because it's not solar calendar but lunar
33   calendar
34   **C**   [aha]
35   **D**   and yeah you you do have presents
36   **C**   and how do you celebrate
37   **D**   em you've got eh well . this this special kind of dinner or supper .
38   and erm you are well the the the whole family . comes . and er and
39   you eat
40   **C**   [yeah that's important]
41   **D**   [and you talk] . and then you
42   exchange gifts [mm]
43   **C**   [OK]
44   **M**   it sounds like a Christmas [no offence]
45   **C**   [yeah (laughs)]
46   **D**   [no] because at the end of the day that's almost the same . mm
47   **M**   yeah
48   **D**   it's just that you do you you should . repeat it for eight nights .
49   in a row
50   **M**   eight nights
51   **C**   mm
52   **M**   meals and presents for eight nights
53   **D**   well . not
54   **M**   [wow I wu I would like that]
55   **D**   [you know the commemoration] for eight nights because because

56   it has nothing to do with birth
57 **C** [so what do you celebrate exactly]
58 **D** [of . Christ] . well it's er Hanukkah it's the festivity of lights …
59   because it commemorates the em the event that em happened so
60   many years ago when Greeks destroyed the temple . and em in
61   Jerusalem
62 **C** hm
63 **D** and em … when er when the temple was er . taken over . by Jews .
64   ah there was this er this mm some scarce amount of er of . er oil .
65   ah to light er menora . and er it was supposed to to to be enough
66   just for one night but what do you know it was enough for [eight
67   nights . em yeah]
68 **C** [eights nights OK (laughs)]
69 **D** and now it's it's the commemoration of this event . mm
70 **C** that's great.

Pronunciation notes
frequent /ð/ as [d̪] (Speakers C and M)
line 3 /θ/ as [f] in 'three'
line 6 word stress in 'January'
line 11 /ð/ as [z] in 'that'
line 52 clusters – deletion of /t/ in 'nights'
line 64 vowel quality – 'scarce' as [skɑːs]

Track 14: Culture 3 – Chinese and Spanish cultures

Speaker G is Chinese (Mandarin L1) and Speaker R is Spanish (Spanish L1)

Neither is a proficient user of ELF, but R in particular, as a lecturer in law, regularly users English in ELF settings such as conferences and seminars. Speaker G teaches Chinese in Spain. The speakers do not know each other and decide to compare customs in the two countries.

1   **G** what do you like about a culture . your Spanish culture
2   **R** I think that er Spanish people is er . friendly … er we are . em like
3   er people er that . likes … contact with other people . so we like er
4   . going out and er . visiting our friends and I think we er . happy
5   people [and I like
6   **G** why] more *passionable
7   **R** perhaps yes
8   **G** yes in our . in our country China we think that the Spanish people
9   have . er is more *passionable is more … have more hospitality .
10   and they like to . erm . have *muse with a friends . and they go .
11   out . a lot of times . [yes]

12 **R** [mm]
13 **G** that's my opinion . well we . em . our opinion about the Spanish
14   people
15 **R** yeah I like it when people go er goes in the street and they look
16   each other . they er don . they don avoid er watching . them and
17   it's a thing I like in in Spain that we are erm . like interacting more
18   with each other . than . in other . countries
19 **G** I found that yes . the *physc contact
20 **R** [mm]
21 **G** [er] between the peoples . is much more than the *physc contact .
22   em between the American people the British people because they
23   think that . er if you just mm to know each other for the first time
24   or for the . second time . you are not . friends you are not intimate
25   friends . you can't touch your hair your body . so easily . but in ch
26   in Spain you can . touch . er the . em the bo the the beard . the .
27   body . as you want . you fr . you are giving information that you
28   want to make friends with him
29 **R** mm and what about in China [is not like here. do you think it's
30   very different]
31 **G** [in China em between the] . between the men . yes . much . much
32   erm many physic contact we're . just like here . but the . the
33   contact . between . the men and women . is ... permitted . you can't
34   er b you can't kiss like er if you want [to]
35 **R** yu you mean is not permitted . [is pro prohibited]
36 **G** [it's not permitted] it's prohib [prohibited]
37 **R** [aha] . I see so so perhaps you've got . er separate . lives or
38   separate worlds . women and and men
39 **G** yes because the physica contact with the women or between the
40   women and men . in our . traditional opinions is . is bad ... [o sea]
41   only between er boyfriend and girlfriend . they can kiss . in the
42   face and kiss . like the like the Spanish way but . er . the normal
43   way to . say hello to one . to one women . is . just . shake your
44   hands and say hello
45 **R** mm
46 **G** the
47 **R** [no kisses]
48 **G** [the first contact] no it's [horrible it's horrible]
49 **R** [and you like it] ah no . you don't like it
50 **G** ah . I . as a man I like it . to . er ju like kiss the face
51 **R** [mm]
52 **G** [to] the er Spanish er friend
53 **R** mm
54 **G** and er the . American mm some European friends but in China we
55   I can't . kiss in the face . to a Chinese girl . now

56 **R** and well you don er you don like this aspect from your cul . er
57   from your culture . eh what thing do you like . from Chinese that .
58   you don't find it here in . in Europe . [in Spain]
59 **G** [mm] I find . I like the ... the people is more . mm ... [o sea] ... the
60   people ... is more ... *mazy to talk about other topics . you can talk
61   about . er your [femɪniːz] . your theories . your ... mm private life .
62   but h here in Spain Europe . you can't talk . the topics . the very
63   pri [praɪtɪv] . topics . just like how much do you learn . do you
         earn .
64   how . er is you girlfriend how is your boyfriend . these topics
65   we're talking much

Pronunciation notes
frequent /ð/ as [l] (Speaker G)
frequent /ð/ as [d̪] (Speaker R)
line 3 trilled /r/ in 'other'
line 9 deletion of /h/ in 'hospitality'
line 24 /m/ as [ŋ] in 'time'
line 26 vowel quality – 'beard' as [beːd]
line 38 clusters – deletion of /d/ in 'worlds'
line 53 /t/ as [v] in 'private'
lines 56, 57 trilled /r/ in 'your'
line 61 'families' as ['fæmniːz]
line 61 unintelligible – probably 'families', with /l/ pronounced as [n]
line 63 unintelligible – probably 'private'

Track 15: Culture 4 – East and West Germany

Speaker A is Malaysian (English L1) and Speaker B is German (German L1)

The speakers know each other, although not very well. In a meeting prior to the recording session Speaker B had mentioned that although she was born in East Germany just before the reunification, she was raised in West Germany. Speaker A explores this topic here.

1 **A** you're from East Germany right and then you've moved . like
2   back and forth
3 **B** [that's . right]
4 **A** [and how do you feel about] that and like what has that experience
5   . been like
6 **B** yeah that's right I was . born in East Germany and then . I went to
7   school . like . from first grade . until graduation I went to school in
8   . West Germany
9 **A** hm
10 **B** em . and then for studying I went back to the east . mostly because

11   the tuition fees are . way lower
12   **A** OK
13   **B** and . lately . em after the unification . the government has .
14   supported the east quite well . so the universities are new and they
15   have lots of new equipment . and have a good reputation so for
16   these both . reasons . and . well . all the time . in school . I was
17   considered . somebody from the east
18   **A** right
19   **B** and there are still . quite some . well it's not discrimin well yeah
20   **A** [prejudice]
21   **B** [quite some] prejudice
22   **A** OK
23   **B** yeah . they make fun of you and . it's because people speak
24   differently I well I speak the German from West Germany mostly
25   **A** hm
26   **B** yeah and then going back to the east to study of course I was
27   considered somebody from West [Germany]
28   **A** [West Germany]
29   **B** yeah
30   **A** [right]
31   **B** [so]
32   **A** but when you first moved when you were much younger did you
33   sound a lot more like you were from the east
34   **B** [no]
35   **A** [like] was there a difference
36   **B** maybe but you know being like five years old you .
37   **A** [right]
38   **B** [you're] so open to all kinds of pronunciations
39   **A** so [it was]
40   **B** [and] . besides children . five six years old don . don't know the
41   difference it started .
42   **A** OK
43   **B** more like in third grade . the discrimination . I would say . they
44   [can]
45   **A** [OK] . OK so was it just because they knew you were from East
46   Germany
47   **B** [yeah]
48   **A** [not] because of
49   **B** just because they learned in school at . the age of yeah like I think
50   like in third fourth grade you start learning geography and these
51   things and then you [can]
52   **A** [OK]
53   **B** and history and then you learn . that it was divided and there are
54   people from the east and from the west and they're different and

55		that's when it all started like mm . first and second grade . the
56		same with all the immigrants . we had .
57	**A**	[hm]
58	**B**	[from] Russia . from Turkey . there are lots of . immigrants from
59		Turkey [in Germany]
60	**A**	[hm hm]
61	**B**	Polish . there was no discrimination at all even though they sp .
62		probably spoke worse English in . first grade than in third ev .
63		worse German in [first]
64	**A**	hm
65	**B**	than third grade but . it just . yeah w . when you start learning
66		about these concepts you start . discriminating that's . what I .
67		believe

Pronunciation notes

line 23 devoicing of final /d/ in 'and'

line 49 /l/ as [ʊ] in 'school'

line 63 deliberate nuclear stress placement on 'German' to correct having
said 'English' in the previous line.

Track 16: Work culture studies 1 – Moving for work

Speaker E is Russian (Russian L1) and Speaker F is Argentinean (Spanish L1)

The speakers do not know each other, but both left their respective countries of birth and now live in Spain. Speaker E is a professional musician and Speaker E owns and runs a private English language school. They had been in conversation for some time when Speaker F asked Speaker E why he had left Russia.

1	**F**	and tell me why did you . decide . to . to leave your country
2	**E**	mm . it was er . it's a . mm normal story my mother she she's
3		also professional musician . she . erm . found . a very good job in
4		. em Tenerife Symphony Orchestra as a principal viola player
5	**F**	hm
6	**E**	and erm . she left her her Moscow orchestra . and she came to
7		work here . erm . first of all f only for one year . and after she
8		moved to [mu] to . Madrid . and me I came to visit her . em . and
9		she ask me . would I try to change er to live some for a while with
10		her for a while maybe I like living in Spain because she got a very
11		good job . and erm yeah first of all I came to try to live with my
12		mother here
13	**F**	is it normal in your country to leave the country and go . and try to
14		find a job in another country or [not]

15   E   [if] specially . it's normal for people who . mm for specialists who
16   don't have . en enough . *enoughly good conditions *laboral
17   conditions in in . in Russia because . we have great *scientifics
18   musicians erm . all kind of er professions so . some of them
19   they're . they're fine to work in Russia you get very good salary .
20   others they're not so good so you need to find other country where
22   . er they find really . mm appropriate your . quality and you get .
23   *enoughly good salary for for your level like a professional
24   F   yeah
25   E   so . in my case . was . a bit . from part of my mother she was . er
           looking for better er salary for her level
27   F   hm
28   E   and me I was finishing my studies and . I found very good high
29   quality teacher here in Madrid
30   F   yeah

Pronunciation notes
line 9 clusters – elision of /t/ in 'asked'
lines 9, 10 vowel length – vowel too long in 'live', 'living'
line 13 /ð/ as [z] in 'the'
line 28 devoicing of final /d/ in 'and', 'found'

Track 17: Work culture studies 2 – Doctoral research

Speaker Q is Greek (Greek L1) and Speaker U is a native speaker (English L1)
Speaker Q talks about his research work for his doctoral thesis.

1   Q   I'm working basically on er on er on er mineralogy and
2   geochemistry . er so for example we're working with em
3   thermodynamic properties of minerals . and er the way minerals
4   crystallize and grow . er in the in the presence of er . metal cations
5   . of heavy metal cations . er yeah one one of the most important er
6   things that it has to do with this er with this study . is for example
7   erm . the elimination of er heavy metals . from water environments
8   . for example from lakes or from rivers . that are contaminated
9   with metals . er derived from er from er industry and other and
10   other human activities . so we can eliminate the concentration of
11   er of metal in er in water by throwing a natural mineral . in there
12   for example calcite aragonite or other minerals . for example if w
13   if er if we use a calcium carbonate . which is calcite . er when it
14   dissolves it produces calcium and carbonate ions which are not er
15   U   [contaminating]
16   Q   [contaminant] . so it can absorb the the dissolved metal from water

17   . but to a er and er and er the metal stays in the structure of the
18   mineral

Pronunciation notes
line 1 simplification of 'basically' to [beɪslɪ]
line 2 /ð/ as [d̪] in 'thermodynamic'
lines 4, 5 vowel length – shortened diphthongs in 'cations', which is pro-
      nounced ['kætiənz] as opposed to ['kataɪənz].
line 6 /ŋ/ as [ŋk] in 'things'
line 12 word stress in 'calcite' and 'aragonite'. Despite the correct lexical
      stress, the listener (a qualified chemist) was only later able to
      recover the meaning.

Track 18: Work culture studies 3 – Gender Studies

Speaker M is Romanian (Romanian L1), Speaker C is Hungarian (Hungarian L1), and Speaker S is Polish (Polish L1)

Speakers M and S know each other but do not know Speaker C. While the three were waiting to go into the recording studio they began to find out about each other. Speaker C is from a sciences background and was surprised to discover that the other two speakers work in Gender Studies.

1   M   I see you're a you're a *bittle *lit surprised by finding out us
2   studying Gender Studies
3   C   I never met anybody . studying gender studies before and I meet .
4   [f]ree of you .
5   M   [in one room] [laughs]
6   C   [doing the same yes] so . yes . I'm surprised
7   M   so . it was surprising the way that you had a you had a kind of
8   image or you you have a like you don't have any clue what . this is
9   [about]
10 C   [no clue] whatever . no I mean I ne I didn't even hear about it
11   before . I don't know. I don't what it means actually . you could
12   maybe tell me what . what does it mean
13 M   hm . OK . so it's it's it's very interesting mainly we are . we are er .
14   I . I wo I would like to call it feminist studies because . I'm more
15   of . I . I'm not for the neutralizing . concept of genders I'm more
16   for the feminist . so it's mainly . er looking at er the power
17   relations nowadays and try to explain how they work and how and
18   the new inequalities created between men and women . and have
19   these different approaches like . sociological anthropological like
20   look
21 S   cultural

22 **M** also cultural perspectives on on . mainly the relationship between
23   men and women
24 **C** OK that is a research
25 **M** [yeah]
26 **C** [but] what are the objectives let's say so . OK . you you put light on
27   all the all the relations between men and women but then . what
28   next
29 **S** well the the the goal are . really down to earth I mean material in a
30   sense . and on the other hand . within the symbolical sphere as
31   well . because er it overlaps the symbolical [sfiel] . sphere and em
32   . and the reality . if within the symbolical sphere we will change
33   some . em . aspects some concepts some issues some ways of
34   perceiving women in a society . perceiving women as a .
35   stereotypically . as a one that should stay at home . and … not
36   work . ah care for her children . ah … within the language the
37   same situation I mean there are no names for . ah . female
38   professors female doctors
39 **C** [OK]
40 **S** [er] if we will change the symbolical erm sphere if we will change
41   the image of women in television in media . then . I guess that . it
42   will go with the culture and it will . somehow reflect on the reality
43 **C** this [was]
44 **M** [so]
45 **C** this was my question . what are the means of changing things and
46   then . it would be . the media . right
47 **S** it's about change
48 **M** [yes]
49 **S** [feminism is about] change
50 **M** the idea is is I . is from as I said is to unmask what's what is now
51   this . the gender equality discourse it it it is not so pervasive in
52   especially in the European Union . and now . for example we had
53   this . last night we had a huge fight with with with a male friend
54   of us like … it's so general . like men believe like . but you
55   women you are liberated why why are you still have to fight for
56   you know like everything is done for you you you have so so
57   many rights . why do do you still consider yourself like oppressed
58   . so thi thi this [is interesting]
59 **C** [does your friend] study gender studies
60 **S** no [no]
61 **M** [no] he's not he's studying history . he's the [yes]
62 **C** [well] maybe that . that's why

Pronunciation notes
line 15 /ŋ/ as [ŋk] in 'neutralizing'
lines 17–19 /ð/ as [d̪] in 'they', 'the', 'these'
line 30 devoicing of /d/ in 'hand'

Track 19: Work culture studies 4 – Technology and stress

Speaker N is Brazilian (Portuguese L1) and Speaker P is Turkish (Turkish L1)

The speakers do not know each other, but after initially negotiating a topic to talk about, the Brazilian speaker initiates a conversation about the impact of modern technology on our lives.

```
 1  N  do you think modern technology reduces or increases st eh stress
 2  P  I think in a way it reduces because em . most of the times you
 3     don't have to . make . too much effort to . do what you want the
 4     technology can help you to make it easier . but in a way eh
 5     technology for example the computer is . or . I don't know ... er
 6     computers could be a good example to . show that the people .
 7     become more individual . to . they make everything on themselves
 8     . not perhaps everything but . they don't need any t . anyone .
 9     else to carry out their businesses . they're
10  N  [yeah]
11  P  [enough] for themselves . so erm you become more individual ...
12     and em I don't know you become a I think a little . alone
13  N  but you're . mm I don't know . you're stressed . because I have a
14     friend that take a look a her email . every . twenty minutes . and
15     you are . dependent on their email all the time . I don't know . it's
16     a f . on the on one hand it's a good idea to have a . your email .
17     your life . is . easier with it but not to be . dependent on it . don't
18     you think so
19  P  I don't know because em . yeah you can have an email but er
20     when you need someone ... em . an email is not that er . I don't
21     know (laughs)
22  N  but we have our lives depending on email . all the time . we send
23     our faculty works by email . we receive email by the teachers . and
24     er our friends we are . just all the time waiting for a message from
25     them . er or a ... we have the email or we have the text messages
26     on the mobile phone . we are we can't live without a mobile phone
27     any [more]
28  P  [so] you mean they are good for us
29  N  I think they are stressful . stressful
30  P  [am]
```

31 N [yeah] because I've realized that er … every day when I forget my
32   mobile at home I come back . because I can't live without it [so]
33 P [yeah] that's . that's true but . er in a way … er it's a way of life
34   that is easier and … for instance whenever you n … mm you need
35   su … you need to . call someone it's mo more eas . easier . it's
36   easier (laughs)
37 N it's it's it's easier yeah I know but er . we are too dependent on
38   that . we . we have friends on the Internet … [er don't we . so]
39 P [that's that's what yeah that's what] I'm talking about that's the …
40   er actually you're . you have a lot of friends . more than that you
41   could have without the Internet . but er . now . er it is not that .
42   sincere I think . it's very superficial
43 N do you think so? [I have good friends]
44 P [yeah because]
45 N on the [Internet]
46 P [not but] er not all of them can be … that close to you
47 N yes yes no nobody em knows . er who are you are . you are talking
       to . but maybe you know you learn about other cultures
49 P yeah [that's true]
50 N [it facilitate] . mm in this sense I . I think it's a good thing
51   [technology]
52 P [yeah it's it] has . it has good sides as well as . for me . er
53   becoming em . more … er . far away from the . society
54 N hm
55 P more depending on the devices of technology . in that sense I think
       it's . it's a disadvantage of the technology
57 N yes . like everything we have advantages and disadvantages
58 P [yes]
59 N [we have] to to find the perfect equilibrium . I don't know

Pronunciation notes
frequent /ð/ as [d̪]
line 7, 8 [ŋ] as [ŋ͡k] in 'everything'
lines 7, 11 /v/ as [w] in 'individual'
line 22, 23 word stress in 'email'
line 26 /ð/ as [t] in 'without'
line 29 clusters – vowel insertion before /str/ in 'stressful'
line 42 'superficial' as [[spəfɪʃəl] due to vowel reduction weakening the <u>
       so much that it disappears. This might be problematic for ELF, but
       here the two speakers understand each other.
line 50 /θ/ as [f] in 'think' and 'thing'
line 53 [ŋ] as [ŋk] in 'becoming'

Track 20: Mobile phones in Japan

Speaker K is Japanese (Japanese L1)

Although the speaker has lived in Spain for over 30 years and lectures in Art History, she is still very much in touch with life in Japan, and with Japanese technological prowess. Hear she talks about mobile phones.

1	**K**	the mobile telephone . is as we know is a the best best seller of
2		the the recent mo recent time no but there are two questions
3		one question the the kind of mobile telephone then that they use
4		in Japan . in Japan they develop they have developed the er the
5		very complete system of mobile mobile telephone it is very high .
6		high system but they developed it . for the Japanese market . only
7		for the Japanese market . so the mobile telephone that they use in
8		Japan . er you they cannot use it . if they if they are outside of the
9		the country (laughs) it's very erm crazy for European people but
10		one of one of the cause is because Japan is . island like England s .
11		ano another cause . is mm the . the Japanese population is very
12		[gu] very bigs . so erm . if you er inventing something . for only
13		Japanese people . yu mm you have very good mm co mm
14		commercial activity because er (laughs) the demand is very very
15		big (laughs) because of the population the mobile telephone is one
16		of that kind of developing commercial de developing em so em
17		when they deci decided to develop the mobile system they didn't
18		want erm ur erm study the commercial possibilities outside of
19		Japan

Pronunciation notes
consistent /ð/ as [z]
lines 4, 13 /h/ as [x] in 'have'
line 5 /l/ as [ɹ] in 'mobile'
line 9 'people' as ['piːpɜ˞]
lines 11, 15 /l/ as [ɹ] in 'population'
line 12 /v/ as [b] in 'inventing'
line 12 /θ/ as [s] in 'something'

NOTE: The elicitation paragraph and Transcripts 21–30 are in Appendix 1.

APPENDIX 1: THE ELICITATION PARAGRAPH

Tracks 21 – 30

The speakers were given the standard text a few minutes before entering the recording studio in an attempt to avoid 'over-preparation'. They were allowed to repeat their recording if they were not happy with their first attempt. No speaker made more than three attempts. Most made two and then chose the one they thought to be the best.

The text covers a wide range of sounds and sound combinations of English. Details of the consonants and consonant clusters are given in Appendices 2 and 3 respectively.

1	Hi Zoe. Thanks for your message and the invitation. A fancy dress
2	party. What made you think of that. It sounds amazing!
3	I wish I could join you, but I have to stay here and work. I've got a
4	small problem – my course project has to be in next Tuesday.
5	Truly depressing!
6	It shouldn't take too long – most of it's done. But I've still got to
7	include the visuals. At least I'm getting better at Freehand and
8	Illustrator. If you ever want me to do any of your things, say so. I
9	don't charge much!
10	Keep the CDs, by the way. They're just copies. I'm glad you liked
11	them. I'll send you the scripts by email.
12	OK. Take some pictures of the party and put them on your blog.
13	See you soon I hope.

Track 21 (Arabic L1) pronunciation notes
lines 2, 5, 6 /ŋ/ as [ŋk] in 'amazing', depressing', 'long'
line 7 /ʒ/ as [dʒ] in 'visuals'
line 10 clusters – vowel insertion in 'I'm glad'
lines 10–11 clusters – elision /t/, /d/ in 'liked them', 'scripts'
line 12 trilled /r/ in 'your'

Track 22 (Chinese L1) pronunciation notes
consistent /ð/ as [l]
line 1 /z/ as [dʒ] in 'Zoe'
line 2 clusters – vowel insertion in 'what made'

line 2 clusters – elision of /d/ in 'sounds'
lines 3, 6, 11 avoidance of contraction (to avoid cluster?)
lines 4, 6, 7, 12 deletion of /l/ in 'small', 'still', 'visuals', 'blog'
line 6 clusters – vowel insertion in 'take too'
line 10 vowels in 'CDs' short, so sounds like 'cities'

Track 23 (German L1) pronunciation notes
line 4 deletion of /l/ in 'small'
line 7 deletion of /l/ in 'visuals' (['vɪʒɜːz])
lines 9, 10, 11 clusters – elision of /t/, /d/ in 'don't charge', 'just copies', 'liked them', 'scripts'

Track 24 (Greek L1) pronunciation notes
line 6 /ŋ/ as [ŋk] in 'long'
lines 7, 8 <r> pronounced in 'better' and 'Illustrator'
lines 8–11 clusters – elision of /t/, /d/ in 'want me', 'don't charge', 'just copies', 'liked them'

Track 25 (Japanese L1) pronunciation notes
consistent /ð/ as [z]
line 1 <r> in 'dress' as a trill
lines 2, 5, 6 /ŋ/ as [ŋk] in 'amazing', 'depressing', 'long'
line 3 /ɜː/ in 'work' sounds like [ɔː]
line 4 /l/ as [r] in 'problem'
lines 4, 10, 11 clusters – elision of /t/, /d/ in 'project has', 'just copies', 'scripts'
line 5 /l/ in 'truly' as [r]
line 7 clusters – deletion of /d/ in 'include the'
line 7 clusters – deletion of /l/ in 'visuals'

Track 26 (Malay L1) pronunciation notes
general use of glottal stops for final /t/, /d/
line 1 /θ/ as [t̪] in 'thanks'
lines 2, 9–11 clusters – elision of /t/, /d/ in 'sounds', 'just copies', 'liked them', 'scripts'
line 4 clusters – deletion /r/ in 'problem'
line 7 'visuals' as ['vɪʃʌlts]

Track 27 (Polish L1) pronunciation notes
lines 2, 5, 6 /ŋ/ as [ŋk] in 'amazing', 'depressing', 'long'
line 9–11 clusters – elision of /t/, /d/ in 'don't charge', 'just copies', 'liked them', 'scripts'

Track 28 (Portuguese L1) pronunciation notes
consistent /ð/ as [d̪]
line 1 'fancy' as [fæns]
lines 6, 8 /ŋ/ as [ŋk] in 'long' and 'things'

lines 9–11 clusters – elision of /t/, /d/ in 'don't charge', 'just copies', 'liked them', 'scripts'

Track 29 (Russian L1) pronunciation notes

lines 3, 7 /h/ as [x] in 'have' and 'Freehand'

lines 4, 8, 10–11 clusters – elision of /t/, /d/ in 'project has', 'want me', 'just copies', 'liked them'

line 10 vowels in 'CDs' short, so sounds like 'cities'

Track 30 (Spanish L1) pronunciation notes

frequent /ð/ as [d̪]

lines 2, 5, 6 /ŋ/ as [ŋk] in 'amazing', 'depressing', 'long'

lines 8–11 clusters – elision of /t/, /d/ in 'want me', 'just copies', 'scripts'

APPENDIX 2: CONSONANTS IN THE ELICITATION PARAGRAPH

Sound	Word-initial	Medial	Final
Plosives			
/p/	party, pictures, put	copies	keep, hope
/b/	but, be, better, by		
/t/	to, take, too	invitation, party, getting, better, Illustrator	what, that, it, but, got, at, want
/d/	depressing, done, do, don't	CDs	made, could, include, glad
/k/	could, course, keep, copies	OK	take, work
/g/	got, getting		blog
Affricates			
/tʃ/	charge	pictures	much
/dʒ/	join, just	project	message, charge
Fricatives			
/f/	for, fancy		of, if
/v/	visuals	ever	have, I've
/θ/	thanks, think, things,		
/ð/	the, that, they're, them		
/s/	sounds, say, so, saying, CDs, see, soon	message, fancy, depressing	dress, course
/z/	Zoe	amazing	as, copies, CDs
/ʃ/	shouldn't	invitation	wish
/ʒ/	visuals		
/h/	hi, have, here, has, hope	Freehand	
Nasals and other consonants			
/m/	message, my, most, me, much	amazing, I'm, email	problem, them, some
/n/	next	fancy, any	join, in, done, soon
/ŋ/			amazing, depressing, long, getting
/l/	long, liked	Illustrator	small, I'll, email
/r/ *	really	* party	* for, your, here, better, ever, they're
/j/	your, you		
/w/	what, wish, work		

* rhotic accents only

APPENDIX 3: CLUSTERS IN THE ELICITATION PARAGRAPH

Cluster	Examples
Word-initial	**2-consonant** glad, blog problem, project, truly, dress, Freehand stay, still small
	3-consonant scripts
Medial	invitation, fancy, depressing include, pictures Illustrator
Word-final	**2-consonant** and, Freehand, send project, liked most, least, just pics visuals
	3-consonant next sounds, thanks, scripts shouldn't
Across word boundaries	**2-consonant** keep the what made, it sounds, it shouldn't, at least, put them could join, include the, glad you take some charge much of that, of your, of the, I've got, have to, I've still still got, I'll send, I'm getting, some pics, I'm glad on your, getting better
	3-consonant small problem course project project has shouldn't take it's done at Freehand liked them send you

GLOSSARY

accent: A variety of a language that is the result of differences in pronunciation between a speaker or group of speakers. Accents can be regional, or social. ELF sees L2 accents of English as equivalent to regional L1 accents.

accommodation: The ability to adjust your speech and other aspects of spoken communication so that they become more (or less) like that of your interlocutors. Adjustments in your pronunciation are known as phonological accommodation.

acoustic signal: The sounds and patterns of sounds that the listener has to decode in order to understand a message.

affricate: A consonant sound that is a combination of a plosive and a fricative. There are two affricates in English – /tʃ/ as in 'church', and /dʒ/ as in 'judge'.

allophone: A variation in the pronunciation of a sound that does not change the meaning of the word the sound is part of. The /r/ in 'red' is pronounced differently in Scotland and England, for example.

alveolar: Sounds such as /t/, /d/, /n/ that are made by the tongue touching the alveolar ridge. The alveolar ridge is the hard protuberance in the roof of the mouth immediately behind the top teeth.

aspiration: A small puff of air that immediately follows the consonants /p/, /t/, /k/ when they are at the beginning of a stressed syllable in English. The word 'pipe', for example, could be transcribed as [phaɪp] to show that the first /p/ is aspirated.

articulators: The movable parts of the mouth that are used to make different sounds: the sounds of English are made using the lips, the teeth, the tongue, and the jaw.

assimilation: When two consonants come together the articulation of the first one often changes to make it easier to pronounce the following sounds, e.g. the /d/ of 'red' in 'red pen' assimilates to /b/ in preparation for the /p/ of pen.

bottom-up processing: A strategy used when reading or listening that involves determining the meaning of each individual word in a text in order to reach an understanding of the text as a whole.

coalescence: A feature of rapid, colloquial native-speaker speech, involving the blending of sounds, e.g. the /t/ and /j/ in 'didn't you' (['dɪdnt jə]) blend in to /tʃ/ producing ['dɪdntʃə].

contrastive analysis (CA): The technique of comparing two language systems, especially their respective grammars, vocabularies, and pronunciations. Errors that learners made in their use of the target language were once thought to be the result of differences between the learner's first language and their target language.

contrastive stress: See unmarked stress.

dental: A consonant sound made by contact between the teeth and the tongue or lips. In English the sounds /θ/ and /ð/ are dental fricatives and are made by contact between the tongue and the top teeth. The sounds /f/ and /v/ are made through contact between the top teeth and the bottom lip and are described as being labiodental.

devoicing: The loss of voicing that occurs with certain consonants at the end of words in languages such as Polish or Russian.

dialect: A regional variety of a language that differs from other varieties in terms of grammar, vocabulary, and pronunciation. Cockney and Yorkshire are examples of dialects from the UK.

EFL: English as a Foreign Language – English taught to non-native speakers so that they can communicate principally with the language's native speakers.

ELF: English as a Lingua Franca – English taught to non-native speakers so that they can communicate principally with each other, usually in the absence of native speakers.

ENL: English as a Native Language. English used by its native speakers for communication with other native speakers.

ESL: English as a Second Language. English used in countries such as India, Singapore, Nigeria, or Kenya, where English has official status but co-exists alongside other official languages. Usually in such countries English is not a speaker's first language.

elision: A process typical of rapid, native-speaker pronunciation in which a sound is deleted to facilitate the pronunciation of a word or phrase, e.g. the /t/ in 'postman'.

fricative: A consonant sound that is made by bringing two parts of the mouth very close together and then allowing the air to escape between them, producing a hissing sound. In English /f/, /v/, /θ/, /ð/, /s/, /z/, /ʃ/, /ʒ/, /h/ are all fricatives. /t/ and /d/ are both made with the tongue and the top teeth and are called dental fricatives.

fortis: The consonants of English can de divided into two groups – fortis and lenis. These are more commonly referred to as 'voiceless' and 'voiced', respectively. The word 'fortis' comes from the Latin for 'strong', and in speech the fortis consonants such as /p/, /t/, /k/ are articulated with significant effort and energy. The lenis consonants such as /b/, /d/, /g/ are articulated in a relatively relaxed way.

general American (GA): The standard US accent.

glottal stop: A consonant sound that is made by completely closing the vocal chords and then suddenly opening them to release air from the lungs.

lax: Vowels can be classed as tense or lax depending on how much tension there is in the face muscles when pronouncing them. Lax vowels such as /ɪ/ or /ʊ/ are made with relatively little effort. Tense vowels such as /iː/ or /ɔː/ involve significant effort.

lenis: See 'fortis'.

lingua franca: A language that is used for communication between speakers who do not have a common first language.

multilingual: This describes someone who can speak or use many languages. (See 'plurilingual'.)

negotiation of meaning: The process used by the interlocutors in spoken interaction to ensure that they are understanding each other.

nuclear stress: In a short spoken phrase, one word will be stressed more than the others. This word is the nuclear stress of the phrase. In English, changing nuclear stress in a phrase changes its meaning.

palatalization: The effect of adding a [j] sound to the consonant immediately before a vowel. This is a feature of Russian English and means that 'her' [hɜː] can sound like 'here' [hje].

phonemes: The individual vowel or consonant sounds that make up a particular language. The change of only one phoneme makes a completely different word.

pidgin: A pidgin is a simplified language that has developed through the contact of at least three languages, usually because of trade between groups of people who do not share a common language. If a pidgin is passed on from parents to children, who then become native speakers of the language, it is then called a creole. Because of colonialization in the 18th and 19th centuries, many present-day creoles are English-, Spanish- or French-based.

pitch movement: In a piece of continuous speech the speaker's voice can change height and go up (a rise tone), or down (a fall tone), or do both (a fall–rise or a rise–fall tone). Changes in pitch are known as tones.

plosive: A consonant sound made by using the articulators to momentarily stop the air coming out of the mouth before suddenly allowing it to escape. There are six plosives in English, /p/, /b/, /t/, /d/, /k/, /g/.

post-vocalic r: An <r> in the spelling of a word that comes immediately after a vowel sound. In rhotic accents this <r> will be pronounced. See rhotic.

plurilingual: The word currently used to define an individual's language capacity, in contrast to 'multilingual', used to describe a society or context. (See 'multilingual'.)

productive competence: The ability to produce a sound, word, or other language feature. Most learners' productive competence is not as high as their receptive competence. In pronunciation, for example, they often understand sounds that they cannot themselves pronounce.

received pronunciation (RP): The standard British accent.

receptive competence: The ability to understand a sound, word, or other language feature when produced by other speakers.

rhotic: Native-speaker varieties of English that always pronounce the <r> in the spelling of a word are described as 'rhotic'. General American, Scottish English, and Irish English are rhotic. Non-rhotic varieties such as RP do not pronounce an 'r' when it comes after a vowel or before a consonant, as in words like 'her' or 'heard'.

schwa: A very weak vowel that is found only in unstressed syllables in spoken English.

sociolect: A variety of a language spoken by a particular social group of speakers. Linguists typically refer to working-class, middle-class, educated. or 'broad' varieties of a language.

stop: See plosive.

stress-timing: Languages can be classed as stress-timed or syllable-timed. Syllable-timed languages like Spanish have a more or less equal stress on each syllable. Stress-timed languages have stressed and unstressed syllables, with a more or less regular interval of time between each stressed syllable.

suprasegmental: The features of pronunciation at any level higher than that of the individual sound. Typical suprasegmental features of English are stress, rhythm, and intonation. (See Chapter 2.)

tense: See lax.

tone: See pitch movement.

top-down processing: A strategy used when reading or listening, that involves bringing our background knowledge or contextual clues into play so as to understand the text.

unmarked stress: When the nuclear stress in a spoken phrase falls on the last lexical item (noun, adjective, verb, or adverb) in the phrase, this is known as unmarked stress. If the nuclear stress is placed on an earlier lexical item in the phrase, or a non-lexical item, this is known as contrastive stress.

uvular: A sound made by the back of the tongue in the very back of the mouth.

variety: Languages change through the process of being used. These changes can occur because of geographical or social distance between groups of speakers. This gives rise to regional varieties (dialects) and social varieties (sociolects) respectively.

voiced: See voicing.

voiceless: See voicing.

voicing: The use or not of the vocal chords in making certain consonant sounds. Sounds that are made with vibration in the vocal chords are known as 'voiced'. When the vocal chords do not vibrate, a sound in known as 'voiceless'. The sounds /p/, /b/ differ only in voicing: /p/ is voiceless.

vowel reduction: In order to make stressed syllables stand out more clearly, native speakers of English 'weaken' most unstressed syllables by pronouncing the vowels in these syllables with a weak vowel. Usually this is schwa (/ə/).

weak forms: Some grammatical classes of words such as prepositions, conjunctions, pronouns, or auxiliary verbs, have two pronunciations in English, a strong form and a weak form. The weak form pronunciations of the words 'and' or 'for', for example, are /ənd/ and /fə/ respectively. The most common vowel in weak forms is schwa. The strong form pronunciations, /ænd/ and /fɔː/, use the full vowel quality.

word group: Spoken English is normally broken down into small, meaningful blocks of words.

BIBLIOGRAPHY

Abercrombie, D. 1949. 'Teaching pronunciation'. *English Language Teaching.* 3: 113–122.

Avery P. and **Erhlich.** 1997. *Teaching American English Pronunciation.* Oxford: Oxford University Press.

Bamgbose, A. 1998. 'Torn between norms: innovations in world Englishes'. *World Englishes* 17/1: 1–14.

Bradford, B. 1990. 'The essential ingredients of a pronunciation programme'. *Speak Out!* 6: 8–11.

Brazil, D. 1994. *Pronunciation for Advanced Learners of English.* Cambridge: Cambridge University Press.

Brazil, D. 1997. *The Communicative Value of Intonation in English.* Cambridge: Cambridge University Press. (Originally published in 1985 as Monograph 8 by the English Language Research Unit, University of Birmingham.)

Brown, A. 1995. 'Minimal pairs: minimal importance'. *ELT Journal* 49/2: 169–75.

Brown, G. 1995. *Speakers, Listeners and Communication.* Cambridge: Cambridge University Press.

Cambridge ESOL ICFE Teaching Resource – Focus on Assessment. [online] [Accessed 24.07.09] Available from the World Wide Web. <http://www.cambridgeesol.org/teach/icfe/speaking/index.html>

Cauldwell, R. 2006. Brazil's Yes–No questions. Posting to supras@mailbox.gsu.edu on 18.05.06.

Celce-Murcia, M., D. Brinton, and **J. M. Goodwin.** 1996. *Teaching Pronunciation: A Reference for Teachers of English as a Second or Foreign Language.* Cambridge: Cambridge University Press.

Civil Aviation Authority – ICAO Language Proficiency Requirements – UK implementation for existing air traffic controller licence-holders. [online] [Accessed 11.08.09] Available from the World Wide Web. <http://www.caa.co.uk/default.aspx?categoryid=43&pagetype=90&pageid=6822>

Cole, S. 2002. 'An investigation of the role of vowel quality in oral interactions between NNSs of English as an international language'. *Speak Out!* 29: 28–37.

Cruz-Ferreira, M. and **S. A. Abraham.** 2006. *The Language of Language: Concepts in Linguistic Analysis* (2nd edn.). Singapore: Prentice Hall.

Crystal, D. 1995. *The Cambridge Encyclopaedia of the English Language.* Cambridge: Cambridge University Press.

Crystal, D. 1997. *English as a Global Language.* Cambridge: Cambridge University Press.

Crystal, D. 2003. *English as a Global Language* (2nd edn.). Cambridge: Cambridge University Press.

da Silva Sili, R. 1999. 'A small-scale investigation into the intelligibility of the pronunciation of Brazilian intermediate students'. *Speak Out!* 23: 19–25.

Dalton-Puffer, C., G. Kaltenboeck, and **U. Smit.** 1997. 'Learner attitudes and L2 pronunciation in Austria'. *World Englishes* 16: 115–28.

Daniels, H. 1995. 'Psycholinguistic, psycho-affective and procedural factors in the acquisition of authentic L2 phonology'. *Speak Out!* 15: 3–11.

Dauer, R. 2005. 'The Lingua Franca Core: a new model for pronunciation instruction'. *TESOL Quarterly* 39/3: 543–50.

Derwing, T. M. and **M. J. Munro.** 1997. 'Accent, intelligibility, and comprehensibility: evidence from four L1s'. *Studies in Second Language Acquisition* 19: 1–16.

Derwing, T. M. and **M. J. Munro.** 2008. 'Putting accent in its place: rethinking obstacles to communication.' [online] [Accessed 03.07.09] Available from the World Wide Web <http://www.sfu.ca/~mjmunro/D&MHandout.pdf>

Deterding, D. and **A. Kirkpatrick.** 2006. 'Intelligibility and an emerging ASEAN English lingua franca'. *World Englishes* 25/3: 391–410.

Erling, E. J. 2005. 'Who is the global English speaker? A profile of students of English at the Freie Universität Berlin' in C. Gnutzmann and F. Intemann (eds.): *The Globalisation of English and the English Language Classroom.* Tübingen: Gunter Narr Verlag.

Field, J. 2003. 'The fuzzy notion of 'intelligibility': a headache for pronunciation teachers and oral testers.' IATEFL Special Interest Groups newsletter in Memory of Gill Porter Ladousse, 34–8.

Field, J. 2003. 'Intelligibility and the listener: the role of lexical stress'. *TESOL Quarterly* 39/3: 399–424.

Gatbonton, E. P., Trofimovich, and **M. Magid.** 2005. 'Learners' ethnic group loyalty and L2 pronunciation accuracy: A sociolinguistic investigation'. Special Issue: Reconceptualizing L2 Pronunciation. *TESOL Quarterly* 39(3), 489–511.

Gil, J. A. 2005. English in China: The Impact of the Global Language on China's Language Situation. PhD thesis, Griffith University, Australia. [online] [Accessed 02.07.09] Available from the World Wide Web < http://www4.gu.edu.au:8080/adt-root/public/adt-QGU20060105.113942/>

Gilbert, J. 1999. 'Six pronunciation priorities for the beginner student'. *Speak Out!* 25: 4–8.

Gilbert, J. 2001. *Clear Speech from the Start.* Cambridge: Cambridge University Press.

Gilbert, J. 2005. *Clear Speech* (3rd edn.). Cambridge: Cambridge University Press.

Giles, H. and **N. Coupland.** 1991. *Language: Contexts and Consequences.* Milton Keynes: Open University.

Gimson, A. C. 1989. *An Introduction to the Pronunciation of English* (4th edn.). London: Edward Arnold.

Graddol, D. 1997. *The Future of English.* London: The British Council.

Graddol, D. 2006. *English Next: Why Global English May Mean the End of English as a Foreign Language.* London: British Council.

Hancock, M. 2003. *English Pronunciation in Use.* Cambridge: Cambridge University Press.

Hancock, M. 2006. 'Pronunciation materials as language play'. *Speak Out!* 36: 20–5.

Hannam, S. 2006. 'Pronunciation teaching today: listening without prejudice'. *TESOL-SPAIN* Newsletter, Volume 29, Spring 2006: 3–6.

Hewings, M. 2004. *Pronunciation Practice Activities.* Cambridge: Cambridge University Press.

Jenkins, J. 1997. 'Teaching intonation for English as an international language: teachability, learnability and intelligibility'. *Speak Out!* 21: 15–25.

Jenkins, J. 2000. *The Phonology of English as a Lingua Franca.* Oxford: Oxford University Press.

Jenkins, J. 2002. 'A sociolinguistically based, empirically researched pronunciation syllabus for English as an International Language'. *Applied Linguistics* 23/1: 83–103.

Jenkins, J. 2003. 'Community, currency and the lingua franca core'. *TESOL-SPAIN* Newsletter, 27: 3–6.

Jenkins, J. 2004. 'ELF at the gate: the position of English as a lingua franca'. IATEFL 2004. Liverpool Conference Selections. Canterbury: IATEFL. (Also available at www.hltmag.co.uk/mar05/idea.htm)

Jenkins, J. 2007. *English as a Lingua Franca: Attitude and Identity.* Oxford: Oxford University Press.

Jenner, B. 1989. 'Teaching pronunciation: the common core'. *Speak Out!* 4: 2–4.

Kachru, B. B. 1985. 'Standards, codification and sociolinguistic realism: The English language in the Outer Circle' in R. Quirk and H. G. Widdowson (eds.): *English in the World: Teaching and Learning the Language and Literature.* Cambridge: Cambridge University Press.

Kachru, B. B. (ed.) 1992. *The Other Tongue: English Across Cultures* (2nd edn.). Urbana, IL: University of Illinois Press.

Kenworthy, J. 1987. *Teaching English Pronunciation.* Harlow: Longman.

Kirkpatrick, A. 2007. *World Englishes. Implications for International Communication and English Language Teaching.* Cambridge: Cambridge University Press.

Labov, W. 1966. *The Social Stratification of English in New York City.* Washington DC: Centre for Applied Linguistics.

Labov, W. 1982. 'Building on empirical foundations' in W. P. Lehmann and Y. Malkiel (eds.): *Perspectives on Historical Linguistics.* Amsterdam: John Benjamins: 17–92.

Larsen-Freeman, D. 1985. 'Input and interaction in the communicative language classroom: A comparison of teacher-fronted and group activities' in S. Gass and C. Madden (eds.): *Input in Second Language Acquisition.* Cambridge: Newbury House.

León Meis, M. 2000. 'Spanish-speaking EFL teachers: their needs, challenges and advantages when teaching English pronunciation'. *Speak Out!* 26: 20–9.

Lippi-Green, R. 1997. *English with an Accent: Language, Ideology and Discrimination in the United States.* London and New York: Routledge.

Luchini, P. L. 2005. 'Integrating a pronunciation component into a spoken English course in China: a case study'. *Speak Out!* 35: 14–31.

Lynch, T. 1996. *Communication in the Language Classroom.* Oxford: Oxford University Press.

MacKay, S. L. 2002. *Teaching English as an International Language.* Oxford: Oxford University Press.

Makarova, V. 2001. 'Global versus local in pronunciation teaching'. *Speak Out!* 28: 22–9.

Marks, J. 1999. 'Is stress-timing real?' *ELT Journal* 53/3: 191–199.

Mauranen, A. 2003. 'The corpus of English as lingua franca in academic settings'. *TESOL Quarterly* 37/3: 513–527.

Menyuk, P. 1968. 'The role of distinctive features in children's acquisition of phonology'. *Journal of Speech and Hearing Research* 11, 138–46.

Moore, R. 1999. Letters to the editor. The Guardian. June 22nd, 1999.

Morrow, K. E. 1979. 'Communicative language testing: revolution or evolution' in C. J. Brumfit, and K. Johnson (eds.) 143–58: *The Communicative Approach to Language Teaching.* Oxford: Oxford University Press.

Munro, M. 2003. 'A primer on accent discrimination in the Canadian context'. *TESL Canada Journal* 20: 38–51.

Munro, M. J. and **T. M. Derwing.** 1995. 'Foreign accent, comprehensibility and intelligibility in the speech of second language learners'. *Language Learning* 45: 73–97.

Ortiz-Lira, H. 2001. 'Postlexical accentuation and EFL'. *Speak Out!* 28: 19–21.

Osimk, R. 2009. 'Decoding sounds: an experimental approach to intelligibility in ELF'. Vienna English Working Papers 18/1, 64–89. [online] [Accessed 29.09.09] Available from the World Wide Web < http://anglistik.univie.ac.at/fileadmin/user_upload/dep_anglist/weitere_Uploads/Views/0901final.pdf>

Pakir, A. 1999. ' Connecting with English in the Context of Internationalisation'. *TESOL Quarterly* 33/1: 103–14.

Pennington, M. 1996. *Phonology in English Language Teaching. An International Approach.* London: Longman.

Pennnycook, A. 1994. *The Cultural Politics of English as an International Language.* Harlow: Pearson Education.

Porter, D. and **S. Garvin.** 1989a. 'The testing of pronunciation – some preliminary questions'. *Speak Out!* 4: 5–7.

Porter, D. and **S. Garvin.** 1989b. 'Attitudes to pronunciation in EFL'. *Speak Out!* 5: 8–14.

Rajadurai, J. 2004. 'The faces and facets of English in Malaysia'. *English Today* 20:4: 54–8.

Rajadurai, J. 2006. 'Pronunciation issues in non-native contexts: a Malaysian case study'. *Malaysian Journal of ELT Research* 2: 42–59.

Rajadurai, J. 2007. 'Intelligibility studies: a consideration of empirical and ideological issues'. *World Englishes* 26/1: 87–98.

Rimmer, W. 1997. 'Dictation for teaching and testing pronunciation'. *Speak Out!* 21: 36–8.

Roach, P. 1991. *English Phonetics and Phonology* (2nd edn.). Cambridge: Cambridge University Press.

Scales, J., A. Wennerstrom, D. Richard, and **S. Hui Wu.** 2006. 'Language learners' perceptions of accent'. *TESOL Quarterly* 40/4: 715–738.

Seidlhofer, B. 2004. 'Research perspectives in teaching English as a lingua franca'. *Annual Review of Applied Linguistics* 24: 209–39.

Seidlhofer, B. 2007. *Oxford Advanced Learners Dictionary*. Oxford: Oxford University Press.

Smith, L. E. and **C. Nelson.** 1985. 'International intelligibility of English: directions and resources'. *World Englishes* 4/3: 333–42.

Smith, L. E. 1992. 'Spread of English and issues of intelligibility' in B. B. Kachru (ed.). 1992.

Sobkowiak, W. 2005. 'Why not LFC?' in K. Dziubalska and J. Przedlacka (eds.): *English Pronunciation Models: a Changing Scene*. Frankfurt am Mein: Peter Lang.

Speak Good English Movement. [online] [Accessed 1.07.09] Available from the World Wide Web. <http://www.goodenglish.org.sg/2009/>

Stevens, S. 1989. A 'dramatic' approach to improving the intelligibility of ITAs'. *English for Specific Purposes* 8: 181–94.

Suárez, J. 2000. 'El Español en la clase de pronunciación inglesa (Spanish in the English pronunciation class)'. *Speak Out!* 26: 30–7.

Svartvik, J. and **G. Leech.** 2006. *English – One Tongue, Many Voices*. Basingstoke: Palgrave Macmillan.

Swan M. 1993. 'Integrating pronunciation into the general language class'. *Speak Out!* 11: 5–10.

Szyszka, M. 2007. 'More autonomy in English pronunciation learning'. *Speak Out!* 38: 22–4.

Timmis, I. 2002. 'Native speaker norms and international English'. *ELT Journal* 56/3: 240–9.

Trudgill, P. 1999. 'Standard English: what it isn't' in T. Bex and R. J. Watts (eds.): *Standard English: The Widening Debate*. London: Routledge 117–28.

Walker, R. 1999. 'Proclaimed and perceived wants and needs among Spanish teachers of English'. *Speak Out!* 24: 25–32.

Walker, R. 2001. 'International intelligibility'. *English Teaching Professional* 21: 10–13.

Walker, R. 2005. 'Using student-produced recordings with monolingual groups to provide effective, individualized pronunciation practice'. *TESOL Quarterly* 39/3: 535–42.

Walker, R. 2006. 'Going for a song'. *English Teaching Professional* 43: 19–21.

Walker, R. and **K. Harding.** 2006. *Tourism 1: Provision*. Oxford: Oxford University Press.

Walker, R. 2008. 'An achievable target for specific settings'. *Voices* 200: 8–9.

Waniek-Limczak, E. 1999. 'Vowel duration in interlanguage'. *Speak Out!* 23: 26–30.

Weir, C. J. 1990. *Communicative Language Testing*. Hemel Hempstead: Prentice Hall International (UK).

INDEX

AUDIO CD TRACK LIST

Track 1: Reactions to the concept of ELF

Track 2: ELF and identity

Track 3: Accent and identity

Track 4: English in Malaysia

Track 5: Learning English in China

Track 6: Problems with listening

Track 7: Speaking with NSs and NNSs

Track 8: Language – teaching English in Spain

Track 9: Cultural stereotypes 1

Track 10: Cultural stereotypes 2

Track 11: Misconceptions about Turkey

Track 12: Culture 1 – Easter in Greece

Track 13: Culture 2 – Hanukkah

Track 14: Culture 3 – Chinese and Spanish cultures

Track 15: Culture 4 – East and West Germany

Track 16: Work culture studies 1: Moving for work

Track 17: Work culture studies 2: Doctoral research

Track 18: Work culture studies 3: Gender Studies

Track 19: Work culture studies 4: Technology and stress

Track 20: Mobile phones in Japan

Tracks 21–30: Elicitation paragraph